# Military Veteran Employment

# Military Veteran Employment

## A Guide for the Data-Driven Leader

*Edited by*

NATHAN D. AINSPAN AND KRISTIN N. SABOE

# OXFORD
UNIVERSITY PRESS

Oxford University Press is a department of the University of Oxford. It furthers the University's objective of excellence in research, scholarship, and education by publishing worldwide. Oxford is a registered trade mark of Oxford University Press in the UK and certain other countries.

Published in the United States of America by Oxford University Press
198 Madison Avenue, New York, NY 10016, United States of America.

Library of Congress Cataloging-in-Publication Data
Names: Ainspan, Nathan D. (Nathan David), 1966– editor. | Saboe, Kristin N., editor.
Title: Military veteran employment : a guide for the data-driven leader /
Nathan D. Ainspan and Kristin N. Saboe.
Description: New York, NY : Oxford University Press, 2021. | Includes
bibliographical references and index. |
Identifiers: LCCN 2020058309 (print) | LCCN 2020058310 (ebook) |
ISBN 9780190642983 (hardback) | ISBN 9780190643003 (epub) |
ISBN 9780190643010 (digital-online)
Subjects: LCSH: Veterans—Employment—United States. | Veterans—Vocational
guidance—United States. | Veteran reintegration—United States.
Classification: LCC UB357 .M55 2021 (print) | LCC UB357 (ebook) |
DDC 331.5/20973—dc23
LC record available at https://lccn.loc.gov/2020058309
LC ebook record available at https://lccn.loc.gov/2020058310

DOI: 10.1093/oso/9780190642983.001.0001

1 3 5 7 9 8 6 4 2

Printed by Integrated Books International, United States of America

*Dedicated to Walter E. Penk, PhD, ABPP, my mentor, guide, source of support, and friend in all of my efforts in this area. My first meeting with him two decades ago exposed me to the research on the psychosocial benefits of veteran employment and military-to-civilian transitions. My continual interactions with him through speaking engagements and writing partnerships and his encouragements further developed my interest and expertise in the field. His mentoring, thoughtfulness, and kindness nurtured my work and helped me make veterans employment my life's passion and work and helped me accomplish everything that I have done in this field. You taught me to follow Goethe: "Be bold and mighty forces will come to your aid." I did and they did. And in the words of Sir Isaac Newton, "If I have seen further it is by standing on the shoulders of giants." Thank you for the shoulders that have allowed me to see such heights.*

*With my deep gratitude, NDA*

*Dedicated to my parents, Dr. Gerald Saboe, COL (ret.), and Mrs. Julie Saboe, who taught me the value of education, service before self, and a strong work ethic. And to my husband, Mike Webb, who always keeps me guessing, even on the days I don't want to guess. Thank you, Mike, for running with me and encouraging me to spread my wings farther each day.*

*With love, KNS*

# Contents

# Acknowledgments

We are grateful to our editors at Oxford University Press, Abby Gross, editor in chief of psychology and social work, and Katie Pratt, assistant editor, for their continual guidance, insights, support, and especially patience over the many years it took this book to come to fruition. We also want to express our thanks to the past presidents of the Society for Industrial and Organizational Psychology from 2012 to 2020 whose support of our work creating and leading the group's military and veterans activities led to much of the backbone of this book. They are Doctors Doug Reynolds, Tammy D. Allen, Jose Cortina, Steve W. J. Kozlowski, the late James Outtz, S. Morton McPhail, Fred Oswald, Talya Bauer, and Eden King.

I (Nathan) express deep gratitude to Dr. Susan Kelly, the first director of the Transition to Veterans Program Office of the Department of Defense, and to her successors, Dr. Karin Orvis and Tamre Newton, for creating my position and providing me with the opportunities to specialize and improve my impact on veterans' lives as the department's research psychologist specializing in veteran transitions. I am also deeply indebted to their guidance and support and their lessons in leadership by their examples. My thanks also to the family of the late Murray Mack of the Army's Civilian Personnel Evaluation Agency for all that he did in developing my interest and my career. My gratitude to my partners in my work and friends in my life: Dr. Walter E. Penk, my friend and mentor; and also my co-editor (and partner in so many veteran employment efforts) Dr. Kristin N. Saboe—you carried our work along, pushed me into new directions, and expanded our efforts in so many ways. And last but certainly not least, to my beautiful wife, Dr. Debbie Ann Doyle, for her constant love and support all of these years—and for tolerating my bad jokes and puns all these years.

I (Kristin) am appreciative of all the shoulders that I stand upon that have allowed my training, mentoring, and support to put my own unique twist on the spaces that I occupy. My deepest gratitude extends to two of my mentors in particular who patiently and kindly enabled me to find my professional voice. First, my coauthor, Dr. Nathan Ainspan, identified a spark in me many years ago. With each new professional step, you have been there as a mentor and friend selflessly encouraging my growth and aspirations no matter how large. My appreciation also extends to Dr. Leslie McFarling for helping me to find my voice as a scientist, strategist, and leader. I showed up wide eyed and excited to simply walk down the halls of the Pentagon as a young Army officer, and you, every single day, made sure I knew my voice was heard despite my rank, that I had a seat at the table no matter the audience, and that I knew the power that was within me. You are the definition of both allies and mentors. Thank you for your trust, your wisdom, and your belief in me. And most importantly, I appreciate my husband, Mr. Michael Webb, for his steadfast love, support, and understanding. You so effortlessly dream big with me and accept me to be me. For this, I am thankful.

# About the Editors

**Nathan D. Ainspan, PhD,** has conducted research, written, and spoken extensively about military–civilian transitions and veterans civilian employment. He is currently the senior research psychologist with the Military–Civilian Transition Office (MCTO) at the Department of Defense. His research has focused on improving civilian employment opportunities for returning service members and the psychosocial benefits that employment provides for wounded warriors and injured veterans. He has also authored and edited dozens of publications, including the books *The Handbook of Psychosocial Interventions for Veterans and Service Members: A Guide for the Non-Military Mental Health Clinician* (with Craig J. Bryan and Walter E. Penk; Oxford, 2016); *When the Warrior Returns: Making the Transition at Home* (with Walter E. Penk; Naval Institute Press, 2012); and *Returning Wars' Wounded, Injured, and Ill: A Handbook* (with Walter E. Penk; Praeger, 2008). Dr. Ainspan is a member of the American Psychological Association and a Fellow of Division 18 (Psychologists in Public Service), Division 19 (Military Psychology), and Division 14 (Society for Industrial and Organizational Psychology). He is also the recipient of the *Government Executive* Theodore Roosevelt Defender Government Leadership Award for distinguished achievement in national security, homeland security, and international affairs; the American Psychological Assocations' Meritorious Research Service Commendation; the Society for Military Psychology's Charles S. Gersoni Military Psychology Award for excellence in the advancement of the profession of military psychology, outstanding work on improving effectiveness of military psychology systems, and remarkable service on behalf of the welfare of military personnel; DoD's Spirit of Service Award for his outstanding performance and demonstrating honor, integrity, and excellence; the Psychologists in Public Service Award from the Psychologists in Public Service division for his contributions to public service of underserved populations; and the Society of Industrial and Organizational Psychology's Raymond A. Katzell Award for work that addresses social issues and to positively impact individuals, organizations, and society. Dr. Ainspan received his bachelor's degree from Wesleyan University and his master's and doctoral degrees from Cornell University's School of Labor Relations.

**Kristin N. Saboe, PhD,** is an industrial–organizational psychologist and Army veteran who has worked extensively across academic, defense, non-profit, and private sectors as a researcher, military officer, and Fortune 500 leader. Dr. Saboe is driven by a passion for promoting and advocating for high-impact innovation and evidence-driven policies and strategies. Her research and professional interests focus on performance optimization, applied organizational research and policy, leadership, and veteran and military spouse employment. As a subject matter expert, Dr. Saboe is a seasoned public speaker to academic, national news outlets, and professional audiences and has authored nearly two dozen publications in a variety of academic and nonacademic media. She has led, authored, and contributed to numerous international business and national defense strategies and policies focused on veterans' and military spouse employment, talent management, and risk-taking and well-being behaviors. Prior to holding positions as a corporate leader and strategist, Kristin served in the U.S. Army as an officer and research psychologist, where she conducted psychological and organizational research; oversaw the Army's science and research integration into programs, policies, and strategies related to risk-taking behaviors and psychological readiness; and served at the Pentagon as an advisor to top government leadership. She deployed to Afghanistan in 2013 as part of the Army surgeon general's Mental Health Advisory Team 9 (MHAT-9). Before putting on combat boots, Kristin was a university lecturer, researcher, and consultant. She is currently an adjunct professor at Georgetown University. Kristin completed both master's and doctoral degrees in industrial–organizational psychology at the University of South Florida. She graduated with bachelor degrees in philosophy and psychology with honors, summa cum laude, from Austin College in Sherman, Texas. She is a 2019 President George W. Bush Institute Veteran Leadership Program scholar, a highly selective designation for national leaders working on military issues. Dr. Saboe is the recipient of early career psychologist awards by both the Society for Military Psychology (2019) and Society for Industrial and Organizational Psychology (2020).

# Contributors

**Nathan D. Ainspan**, PhD, has conducted research, written, and spoken extensively about military transitions. He is currently the senior research psychologist with the Military–Civilian Transition Office (MCTO) at the Department of Defense. His research has focused on improving civilian employment opportunities for returning service members and the psychosocial benefits that employment provides for wounded warriors and injured veterans.

**Tammy D. Allen**, PhD, is a Distinguished University Professor at the University of South Florida within the Department of Psychology. She has conducted research on work–family issues, career development and mentoring, and occupational health for over two decades. She is a past president of both the Society for Occupational Health Psychology and the Society of Industrial and Organizational Psychology.

**Deborah A. Bradbard**, PhD, is a senior research associate at Syracuse University's Institute for Veterans and Military Families (IVMF), where she focuses on veteran and military spouse employment and military financial readiness and transition. She previously served as the director of research and policy at Blue Star Families and was one of the primary authors of the 2013 and 2014 Blue Star Families Annual Lifestyle Survey whose results have influenced policy on mental health, military spouse employment, and military child education.

**Krista Brockwood**, PhD, is a senior research associate at Oregon Health & Science University, in the Oregon Institute of Occupational Health Sciences. Dr. Brockwood oversees several large scale randomized control trials, primarily focusing on military samples, including veterans, National Guard and active duty. Dr. Brockwood is a Veteran, having served in the U. S. Army from 1988–1992 in signals intelligence as a German linguist.

**Sherri Eiler**, program manager of Military Programs at Walmart, led a synchronized enterprise-wide strategy to attract, recruit, hire, grow, develop, and retain talent from military community constituencies. Before joining Walmart in 2006, her military service in the U.S. Marine Corps and civilian career trajectory included roles at the University of Arkansas College of Education and Health Professions, which provided her with a portfolio of preparation and experience that has positioned her as a preeminent advocate for veterans and military families.

**Eric Eversole** is the president of Hiring Our Heroes, a program of the U.S. Chamber of Commerce Foundation, and vice president and senior advisor at the chamber. Hiring Our Heroes is a grassroots initiative to help veterans, transitioning service members, and military spouses find meaningful employment in communities across

America. He served in the Navy's Judge Advocacy General (JAG) Corps and continues to serve in the Navy Reserve, supporting the Navy's Appellate Review Activity and holds the rank of captain.

**Daniel Geller** is a dean's merit scholar at the University of Miami School of Law. Prior to attending law school, he studied industrial and labor relations at the New York State School of Industrial and Labor Relations at Cornell University, where he focused primarily on employment disability issues. He also worked in public sector arbitration and federal employment policy with the New York City Office of Collective Bargaining and the Equal Employment Opportunity Commission.

**Mark Goulart** retired in March 2020 after spending over three decades as a consulting executive leading professional services teams on projects that delivered performance improvement solutions to public sector and nonprofit clients. Since 2010 he has led major initiatives and collaborated with leading public, private, and nonprofit organizations to support military service members and spouses, veterans, and caregivers with a focus on improving employment, physical health, well-being, and educational opportunities. He also served as a captain in the U.S. Army.

**Peter A. Gudmundsson** is the CEO of BeHome247, a software solutions company in the property management space. From 2013 to 2017, he was the president and CEO of RecruitMilitary, the leading veteran hiring solutions company, which helps companies attract, appreciate, and retain high-quality veteran employees and students. RecruitMilitary manages the largest veteran online job board in the nation. He served as a U.S. Marine field artillery officer.

**Leslie B. Hammer**, PhD, is a Professor in the Oregon Institute of Occupational Health Sciences at Oregon Health & Science University, Co-Director of the Oregon Healthy Workforce Center, and a Professor of Psychology in the Department of Psychology at Portland State University. She conducts applied military research that focuses on training leaders how to better support Service members psychological health and well-being leading to reduce stress, improve health, readiness and resilience.

**Sarah N. Haverly**, PhD, is a researcher in the technology sector, and adjunct instructor. Her research focuses on how to support and improve the employment experiences, particularly those of workers experiencing unique challenges. Currently in the corporate workforce, she focuses bringing psychological principles to improve both policy and processes impacting the workplace experience for employees.

**Theodore L. (Ted) Hayes**, PhD, is a personnel research psychologist in Arlington, VA. His work focuses on leadership assessment, employment testing, and employee engagement surveys with a range of experience measuring and predicting individual, team, and organizational performance.

**J. Michael Haynie**, PhD, is the vice chancellor for strategic initiatives and innovation and the Barnes Professor of Entrepreneurship at Syracuse University, and a university professor, the most senior rank awarded to faculty at the university. In 2011, he founded Syracuse University's Institute for Veterans and Military Families (IVMF), the nation's first interdisciplinary institute created to inform and advance the policy, economic, and wellness concerns of America's veterans and families. Today IVMF programs serve over 25,000 veterans annually, and the institute is widely acknowledged as the nation's leading academic voice related to issues impacting veterans and military-connected families. He is a veteran of the United States Air Force.

**Ann M. Herd**, PhD, SPHR, SHRM-SCP, CPC, is an assistant professor of human resources and organization development at the University of Louisville. She served as a Special Forces family readiness group advisor and a military spouse for over 20 years. She researches, teaches, and regularly provides consulting services to industry, education, and the military in the areas of military career transitions, executive coaching, global leadership assessment and development, and strategic talent management.

**Robert Hogan**, PhD, is the founder of Hogan Assessment Systems in Tulsa, Oklahoma. He served as an officer in the U.S. Navy. His company leads the world in personality assessment and leadership development, with products and services in 56 countries and 47 languages. Hogan Assessment Systems is the industry leader serving more than half of the Fortune 500 companies.

**Michael Kirchner**, PhD, is an assistant professor of organizational leadership at Purdue University Fort Wayne, where he conducts research on veteran career transitions and military leader development. Dr. Kirchner is a U.S. Army veteran and served in Iraq from 2004 to 2005 before becoming the first director of the University of Wisconsin–Milwaukee's Military and Veterans Resource Center.

**William R. McLennan**, MM, MS, is the CEO of FASTPORT, Incorporated, a technology company dedicated to veteran and military spouse employment. His work includes expanding apprenticeships for the Department of Labor across multiple industry sectors, including cybersecurity and artificial intelligence. He served 6 years in the U.S. Marine Corps Reserve and holds multiple degrees in engineering and business administration.

**Ren Nygren**, PhD, is the chief consulting officer for APT Metrics, where he provides broad leadership for delivery of talent acquisition, executive assessment, and litigation support services. He maintains close involvement with APT's clients' most complex human resource challenges, including the completion of large-scale job analyses, enterprise-wide competency modeling, designing and implementing selection systems for high-volume hiring, and technical consulting associated with job analysis data.

**Sandra Olivarez**, HRPM, BS, in organizational management is a program manager of Military Programs at Walmart, where she manages and executes projects that support military initiatives across multiple business units, develops and creates communication strategies to ensure successful implementation of military programs across corporate business functions, and builds relationships and partnerships with key stakeholders. She supports and aligns efforts to build commitment for the company's military programs.

**Mark L. Poteet**, PhD, owns and operates Organizational Research and Solutions, a consulting practice that specializes in executive coaching, leadership assessment, competency modeling, employee development, and career development. He is a champion of helping employees and leaders grow and develop their capabilities to their fullest.

**Gary M Profit** is the President/Chief Executive Officer of Profit Leadership Consulting, LLC. He retired after more than 31 years in the Army with the rank of brigadier general. He was director of Human Capital Management Solutions; International Programs; and Department of Defense Business Transformation Agency Programs, Civilian and Homeland Security Solutions at General Dynamics Information Technology; and senior director of Military Programs at Walmart, where he led a collaborative team of military people brand and corporate and consumer reputation brand professionals focused on veterans and military families.

**Lisa Rosser**, MS, is CEO and founder of Value of a Veteran. She has 22 years of military experience (both active U.S. Army and Army Reserve, earning the rank of lieutenant colonel) and has 16 years of human resources, recruiting, diversity program, and training development experience. She has created training content specifically for recruiters, hiring managers, and supervisors and has provided assistance to over 400 corporations on improving and retaining military veterans in their companies. She also serves as an advisory board member for the Call of Duty Endowment.

**Kristin N. Saboe**, PhD, is a senior HR leader, researcher, public speaker, and Army veteran. She has written, advised, and led numerous national strategies, research and assessment programs, and policies aimed at improving the employment conditions, health, and performance of workers, including veterans and military families. Dr. Saboe served in the Army as an officer and research psychologist. She is an adjunct professor at Georgetown University and an avid community volunteer in addition to her role as an HR leader.

**Lisa Stern**, EdD, SHRM-CP, is the director of program impact and assessment for FourBlock, a nonprofit/high-touch organization that supports transitioning service members and veterans to achieve meaningful postmilitary careers by developing their professional networks. She has three decades of workforce and career development experience focused at the intersection of disability and employment.

**Judy Young**, MA, is the associate director of executive education at Cornell University's New York State School of Industrial and Labor Relations. She is responsible for the instructional design and management of continuing education and certificate programs for diversity and inclusion practitioners seeking to advance their organization's effectiveness in hiring and promoting diverse talent. Her special interest, expertise, and passion involve the successful integration of veterans and people with disabilities in the workforce.

# Introduction

*Nathan D. Ainspan and Kristin N. Saboe*

Military veterans can be an excellent talent pool for civilian organizations looking for talent that brings a competitive advantage to their organization. To maximize this talent pool, organizations need to know how to hire, develop, and retain them to gain the full benefit of veterans' skills, experience, and training. Leveraging the expertise of workplace science and experts, this book's chapters describe how to find, communicate with, recruit, develop, lead, and retain military veterans and their family members so that you and your company can succeed in these efforts. To get you started, this chapter introduces the U.S. military, describes how its members differ from the employees of other organizations, discusses how the military trains and educates its members, and then suggests how the service members' individual traits and the experiences and training they receive in uniform will create veterans who will bring benefits to your organization.

Companies that manage to hire and retain military veterans will gain a competitive advantage over other organizations that are unable to access and retain this talent. This is one area where human resource (HR) practitioners who understand the concepts and research of industrial/organizational (I/O) psychology and the science of people in work contexts will be at an advantage and will be able to bring extra value to their companies through their daily practices. Such an understanding will also arm business leaders and HR practitioners with the best practices detailed throughout this book to share with their chief executive officer, business leaders, and hiring managers. Research and experiences have shown that many of the issues impacting companies' abilities to hire and retain military veteran employees are in the areas of culture mismatches, cultural communication and understanding, person–job–organization fit, mentoring and training, translating skills on a résumé into cross-corporate competencies, and providing culturally sensitive mentoring and leadership. Business leaders and HR practitioners who are knowledgeable about workplace research, including research coming out

Nathan D. Ainspan and Kristin N. Saboe, *Introduction* In: *Military Veteran Employment.*
Edited by: Nathan D. Ainspan and Kristin N. Saboe, Oxford University Press. © Oxford University Press 2021.
DOI: 10.1093/oso/9780190642983.003.0001

of the discipline of I/O psychology, will be trained to understand both the science behind and the lived reality of these concepts. For those not familiar with I/O psychology, it is an applied science focused on the research behind evidence-driven employment best practices and the world of business and business acumen.

The U.S. military is a unique employer because of its employment conditions and experiences. The size of its workforce, the types of employees that it attracts, the culture that its members inhabit, the education and training they receive, the experiences they have, and the impact that the organization has on their lives and the lives of their family members, make the U.S. military exceptional in a number of ways. When service members leave the military and obtain employment in civilian organizations, the traits and experiences that they gained while in uniform will stay with them throughout their civilian careers. Military veterans form a distinct subpopulation of the nation's workforce that generally has distinctive traits, knowledge, skills, and abilities (KSAs), experiences, traits, and competencies that they can bring to civilian jobs. But in order for them to utilize the KSAs, traits, and competencies obtained while in uniform, employers will need to be able to understand this group, how it differs from other employee populations, and how to recruit, retain, motivate, and retain them in their organizations. While we speak specifically to U.S. members of the military, the best practices discussed are certainly presumed to apply to other military veterans throughout the world.

As discussed throughout this book's chapters, not only will your understanding of the benefits and ways that your employer hires and retains military veteran employees help your company prosper but also it will address a critical national need that benefits the national economy. Unemployed veterans in the United States qualify for unemployment insurance, including a fund created specifically for veterans called Unemployment Insurance for Ex-Servicemembers (UCX). The Department of Defense (DoD) receives bills from all of the states for the UCX that the states pay out to each unemployed veteran. The amount paid in UCX comes directly from DoD's operating expenses, so each UCX dollar paid out is one less dollar that DoD could spend on currently serving service members, their training, their families, and the equipment they utilize to fight and stay alive. The numbers are not insignificant: In 2011, DoD UCX spending peaked at nearly one billion dollars on 100,000 unemployed veterans, and since then it has decreased to just $310 million dollars spent on 20,000 veterans in 2016 (U.S. Congressional

Budget Office, 2017). As unemployment rates of veterans decrease each year, so do the additional government funds supporting veterans' unemployment.

Thus, in addition to your company gaining the benefits of this talented population, every veteran that your company successfully hires and retains results in both a reduction in loss and a combined gain for our nation's economy and its defense. It means more veterans are employed and contributing to the economy by paying taxes from their salaries while also enabling additional funds go toward the military's mission of enabling national and international security. In addition, as taxpayers, millions of our tax dollars have been spent to train and educate service members, and if they are sitting home unemployed and not using their skills, then this is an inefficient use of our tax dollars. The bottom line is, economically, everyone wins when veterans are employed.

Your company's efforts to improve the civilian employment prospects of military veterans also directly impacts the nation's ability to defend itself by helping the military continue to recruit and deploy talented service members. When the military draft was eliminated in 1973, it became an all-volunteer force (AVF). To maintain the AVF, the military must demonstrate to young people that military service can be a positive source of employment after they leave service in order to maintain the number of recruits and to continue to staff its ranks. This is because one of the factors that will impact a potential recruit's propensity to serve in the military is the belief that the military will help them in their lives and be a positive experience for their future employment. If prospective members of the military see high veteran unemployment, they may be less likely to consider joining. This, in turn, can negatively impact the military's ability to succeed in its goal of recruiting the best and brightest to serve in the military. Thus, your company's efforts and success with veteran hiring directly and positively supports the nation's ability to continue to recruit military volunteers in order to defend itself.

While the hiring and retention of military veterans into your company will provide a service to the nation and those who volunteer to serve in uniform, we would be shortsighted to assume employers are solely motivated to employ veterans or military family members for these reasons alone. We recommend that you do not approach veteran hiring as only a patriotic act to support our nation and our military (although this is a positive outcome if done correctly). Rather, we recommend that you approach veteran hiring as you would any other HR or business decision: identify your need, establish a solution, develop a plan to execute on your solution by understanding the implications of your timeline and needs, and identify the unique reason why employing veterans is attractive to your organization. Then, make the argument for developing and sustaining the programs and processes for hiring and retaining veterans based on how they will impact your company's priorities and bottom-line business needs (e.g., the return on investment of programs to employ veterans can be explained in financial terms that pit the costs of hiring and retaining veterans with the monetary benefits they provide to the company). As an example, large established companies may be attracted to hire veterans because they do well in large hierarchical organizations and respect authority. Conversely, entrepreneurial start-up companies may be attracted to veterans because many are good at adapting quickly in uncertain environments and flat organizational structures. A successful equation for any company developing and executing a veteran hiring and retention program is to (a) know your organization's values, culture, and structure; (b) understand the military's organization, values, and structures; and (c) evaluate how the combination of these two factors connect to increase the likelihood your company's efforts to hire and retain veteran talent and skill sets are successful for you, your organization, and your veteran employees.

## Introduction to the U.S. Military

The U.S. DoD is the United States' largest employer, and due to its size, scope, organizational structure, and mission, it is notably unique from many other employers. Civilian companies that understand the military, its strong culture, the people who self-select to join it, and the way that the military trains its members will have a competitive advantage over other organizations that lack this understanding. You cannot maximize the talent of employees within an organization without knowing about the organization and the talent itself.

The DoD employs 3.5 million individuals, including both members in uniform and the civilians that support them. This is more employees than the number of employees at Amazon, McDonalds, FedEx, Target, and General Electric combined (Carter, 2019). By comparison, as of 2019, Walmart had 2.3 million employees, McDonalds employed 1.9 million, and Amazon had 647,000 employees. In 2019, DoD's personnel included 1,304,418 active duty members (full-time soldiers, Marines, sailors, and airmen); 41,132 Coast Guard members who are activated into active duty status when needed; 1,039,398 Ready Reserve members (who can be immediately activated into active duty status if needed); 208,032 Retired Reserve; and 11,391 Standby Reserve (who are utilized in the event of a war or crisis) (DoD, Office of the Deputy Assistant Secretary of Defense for Military Community and Family Policy [ODASD MC&FP], 2019). Supporting these uniformed service members are 883,398 DoD civilian personnel. Of those serving on active duty, as of 2019, the Army was the largest of the military services, with 471,990 members in 2019; the Navy was second (325,395 members in 2019); followed by the Air Force (321,618 members) and then the Marine Corps (185,415 members). In 2019, of the active duty force 82 percent were enlisted members, and 18 percent were the officers (officers are comparable to middle managers through executives in a civilian organization).

The military is a highly diverse organization representing the population demographics of the overall U.S. population. Although the military is more diverse than most U.S. employers, it is less diverse in other ways because of the military's unique mission, entry criteria, recruiting policies, and self-selection that occurs for those who choose to join the military and a life of service. As an example, around 30 percent of the active duty force identify as a racial minority (a percentage that has increased steadily since 2010). Thirty-three percent of the enlisted members and 24 percent of the officers identified as racial minorities in 2019. Because the military has only recently opened up all of its occupations and roles to women, females are still a minority within the military but are growing rapidly in number. Women now comprise around 20 percent of the active duty population and are expected to become a larger percentage over time (DoD ODAS MC&FP, 2019). Geographically, the military is overrepresented by the southern states, with 46 percent of the military's new recruits coming from this region in 2019. The military is also geographically concentrated, with most of its members living on or near large military installations. These installations are often located away from major urban areas, where large areas of land can be obtained and utilized. As an example, 70 percent of active duty military personnel lived or worked in these 10 states (by order of the decreasing number of service members in the states): California, Virginia, Texas, North Carolina, Georgia, Florida, Washington, Hawaii, South Carolina, and Colorado (DoD ODAS MC&FP, 2019).

The military is also disproportionately young—54 percent of the active duty members were 25 years old, with an average age of 28.2 years old in 2018 (the average age for enlisted members was 26.9 years, and for officers it was 34.4 years old). It is not unusual for service members who had a career in the military to retire in their 40s. Service members are also economically different from the rest of the population—but not as different as some may think. The idea that the military attracts individuals from the lower socioeconomic areas is false as DoD data suggest that members come predominantly from the middle class (DoD Undersecretary of Defense for Personnel and Readiness, 2018c).

The military's population is more educated compared to the civilian population. This can be attributed to a variety of factors, such as tight selection criteria for entry into the military and a culture that prioritizes training and intensive on-the-job experiential training for internal promotions. In addition, those in the military have access to substantial educational resources, such as tuition reimbursement for coursework while in the military and the GI Bill for veterans pursuing higher education goals after they leave the military. With some variation among the military services, the minimum requirement for entry into the military is a high school diploma or a General Educational Development (GED) certificate in some exceptional cases. More specifically, 81 percent of service members entering the military have at least a high school diploma and some college experience (DoD ODAS MC&FP, 2019). In order to join the military services, each member must also meet citizenship requirements, pass a stringent physical examination, and continue to pass physical ability tests throughout their time in service.

Another way the military differentiates itself from many other employers is in its practices around employee attrition. The military, unlike most employers, supports every service member as they transition out of the military to civilian life by assisting service members in their job search and civilian job sector literacy. Given the young age at which many military service members join the military and the tenure and age restrictions placed on individuals as they progress in their military career, a career following military service is nearly guaranteed for every service member except in extenuating circumstances. This creates an unusual situation for the DoD as it bears the responsibility of preparing its uniformed employees for both entry and exit experiences by allowing and requiring its employees to look for their next postmilitary job or schooling opportunity and to speak with potential employers while "on the clock" as paid employees of the DoD.

Recognizing the critical nature of postmilitary career and education services for the recruitment and development of its current and future service members (i.e., potential recruiters believing that veterans have trouble finding employment will not sign up for service), the DoD has recently begun to put even more of a premium on the successful transition and postmilitary civilian employment of its veterans by devoting significant financial and other resources toward training and transitioning to civilian employment to include reaching out to private-sector employers to help them in their employment efforts.[1] Regardless of an individual's time in the military, often termed their length of service, the military's commitment to training and preparedness during and after their service creates a culture and experiences unlike other traditional employment experiences where most job searching is done discreetly and without one's supervisor being aware of or involved in the job search. Many employers have used this difference to their advantage and have developed recruiting strategies that reach out to service members months before they leave the military.

## Military Culture Develops Traits and Competencies

Given the variability among members of the military and their experiences in uniform with regard to the types of assignment and career paths that are followed, it is difficult to offer generalizations about service members and veterans or how their rank or tenure may or may not map onto specific civilian sector seniority levels. Generalizations are difficult regarding specific career paths and scope because each veteran is an individual with unique capabilities and career experiences gained during their time in uniform. While generalizations about veterans may be difficult to offer, conversely as a condition of choosing to self-select into the military and its culture and by practicing the behavioral norms needed to succeed and advance in this culture, some generalizing can occur. For instance, seeing the designation of "veteran" on an applicant's résumé can be a strong signifier that the individual possesses a number of known traits needed to succeed in the military. It is also likely that the longer that a job applicant spent in the military, the more likely they are to possess these traits and competencies as descriptive and stable characteristics, albeit in varying degrees dependent on their natural tendencies and tenure in the military. For example, the culture of the military focuses on integrity, honesty, accountability, leadership, and ethical behavior. While various versions of the statement "with character, nothing else matters and without character, nothing else matters" is often attributed to different notable leaders, the core sentiment is a valid representation of the core culture of the military. Because lives are on the line, military service members must be dependable and reliable (i.e., members soon learn that if they are 5 minutes early to a meeting in the military they are considered late), and members must be conscientious and pay close attention to the smallest details to ensure accuracy in their tasks.

Once accepted into the military, service members will be immersed in a culture that encourages, rewards, and promotes on certain traits. The last is not unlike other organizations that promote employees in part based on their values-based performance or "fit." Members who cannot or do not adhere to the culture, rules, and policies of the military will not be allowed to continue their service. An "up-or-out" system is in place in the military: It is expected that each service member will be promoted in rank and responsibility over time. Those who do not will be encouraged or forced to leave the service. The longer that service members remain in uniform and continue to receive promotions, the more likely it is that they will also become more attached, impacted, and aligned with the culture.

The traits that the military's culture cultivates in its members are highly desirable for civilian companies that are able to leverage these traits. Research suggests that veterans notably excel and/or develop many competencies and soft skills desired in the workplace at levels greater than that of comparable civilian populations due to their unique experiences and developmental opportunities. These competencies, skills, and attributes include enhanced leadership experiences (Korn Ferry, 2017); experience with team-based projects (Goodwin, Blacksmith, & Coats, 2018); cross-cultural and international experience and aptitude (Goldberg and Warner, 1987); resilience and effective responses to stress (Adler & Saboe, 2017; Haynie, 2016; McGeary, 2011); sought after and transferable skills (Hardison et al., 2017); comfort in ambiguous, discontinuous, or stressful environments (Hardison & Shanley, 2016); and building trusting relationships (Haynie & Dean, 2011).

In addition, the vast majority of service members will typically hold a security clearance as part of their military service. In and of itself, a security clearance is a valuable credential for many organizations conducting business with the government. It also suggests to an employer that these individuals are at a lower risk for misuse of illegal drugs, bankruptcy, or arrests since drug misuse and criminal history prevent individuals from maintaining security clearances. In addition, in the military, service members are subjected to ongoing and frequent background checks and drug tests so that a civilian employer looking at interviewing military veterans that recently left the service can generally rest assured that a service member's "clean" record of employment will allow for a smooth entry and onboarding process into a new civilian organization.

## How the Military Trains Service Members

Once slotted into their occupations, all service members receive extensive training and experiential learning in their occupations and in other skills that civilian employers can make use of after the members leave the military. One misconception of the military is that the majority of occupations in the military are related to combat and are not easily transferable to civilian occupations. But, research conducted by DoD disputes this by noting that based on the KSAs in the Occupational Information Network (O*NET OnLine), 86 percent of the more than 8,000 occupations in the military have a strong linkage or moderate overlap with civilian occupations, and only less than 10 percent of the military's occupations are combat related (U.S. Department of Defense, Under Secretary of Defense for Personnel and Readiness, 2018a).

The range and depth of task-based and leadership training offered in the military coupled with the experiences most service members will see at a young age means that most military veterans have seen and done things that will far surpass the life and work experiences of nonveterans in the same age group. The military recruits members at a young age, starts their training on their first day in boot camp, and continues to provide job skill and leadership training throughout their military careers. It is not unusual to see a 21-year-old service member leading their team through dangerous terrain, making life-or-death decisions or someone of the same age responsible for making decisions about and maintaining millions of dollars in equipment. Compare these experiences to a nonveteran of the same age who is just graduating from college and has landed their first entry-level job with an employer. The gravity and impact of these military experiences is significant, and their value increases incrementally with time. While civilian employers may not necessarily understand the significance when a veteran states that they "led a platoon into a combat zone and managed the logistics for operations," they can appreciate that this individual managed a reasonably large team in a high-stress and demanding environment that required agility and significant decision-making responsibilities and accountability.

The DoD spends a significant amount of time and money on teaching and training all of its members. As an example, the Air Force spends between

$5.6 to $10.2 million dollars to train just one individual to become a pilot (Mattock, Asch, Hosek, & Boito, 2019). While other military occupations may not require training as complicated or expensive, every member will receive extensive training both in the classroom and through their on-the-job experiences. Every occupation in all of the services has a training program and curriculums for the members of that occupation. Other courses are offered to all members to improve and develop additional skills and competencies. As service members advance in their careers, additional training is provided to help them become more effective leaders through the military academies (e.g., West Point in New York for the Army; the Naval Academy in Annapolis, MD; and the Air Force Academy in Colorado); officer and noncommissioned officer training schools run by the military services; and other military training institutions, such as the Naval Postgraduate School in California, National Defense University in Washington, D.C., and the Army War College in Pennsylvania.

In addition, the military services pay for voluntary education opportunities where service members can take classes and earn degrees during non-work hours with their military service paying for the classes. The number of service members taking classes and the number of classes offered to them entitles the DoD a spot on the list of the United States' largest postsecondary institutions. In fiscal year 2017, as an example, 255,729 service members took 726,305 classes through this voluntary education program at over 27,000 accredited intuitions (U.S. Department of Defense, Office of the Under Secretary of Defense for Personnel and Readiness, 2018b). By comparison, the University of California (2020) system educated 280,000 students on 10 campuses, and the University of Texas (2018) had 221,000 students in 14 locations.

All of this classroom and on-the-job training, leadership development, and experience with accountability means that service members both value training and are adept at learning new skills, reskilling, and pursuing growth opportunities that challenge them to perform at their best in some incredibly demanding situations.

## Nontechnical or "Soft" Skills

It has been said (jokingly) that the time spent in the military (especially during a deployment) is computed like dog years in that 1 year on duty in uniform will provide the experiences, training, and knowledge that could only be gained through many more years in the civilian world (if at all). In addition to teaching and training the technical skills of their occupation, each service member also learns and gains great experience with nontechnical skills. Nontechnical or "soft" skills (e.g., leadership, organizing teams, and communication) are in high demand in the civilian workforce. LinkedIn (2018) reported that soft skill training is the number one priority for talent management. Another study found that 67 percent of the HR managers surveyed would hire a candidate with good nontechnical or soft skills but lacking technical skills, while only 9 percent would hire a candidate with good technical skills but weak soft skills (Feller, 2016). Chapter 6 goes into further detail regarding how you can find and utilize soft skills among military veterans.

The military has a reputation for imparting soft skills through training and experiences into all its members and promoting the development of these skills through its culture. Because these skills and traits are so prevalent throughout the military experience, many service members may not realize that they possess these skills in abundance. As a result, many veterans may not think to mention them in their résumés or during interviews. This is analogous to a fish noticing the water in its tank—if everyone around you has strong leadership skills and shows up early to every meeting, you will not think that this is a unique or desirable trait. But these skills are gained in abundance, lacking in many younger civilian applicants, and are in high demand in the civilian workforce. For instance, the RAND Corporation (Hardison and Shanley, 2016) found that the military does a notably good job training the following in-demand nontechnical skills: cognitive skills, directing people and projects, professional development, and inter- and intrapersonal skills.

## Military Spouses

While we have focused on veterans in this chapter, we would be remiss not to mention the competitive advantage of hiring military spouses. Military spouses are a unique population that possesses many traits that make them attractive candidates for civilian employment. It is easier to describe the traits and backgrounds of service members compared to spouses because service members must meet criteria to be accepted into the military and then face regulated training and promotion paths (with forced exit if they fail to meet the standards). Military spouses, however, are not defined by such easily identifiable criteria. The only criteria to be a military spouse is to marry a service member. As with veterans, while it can be difficult to generalize about military spouses, some statements can be made about them as potential employees in your organization. In a national sample, a significantly higher percentage of military spouses held college and graduate degrees compared to a comparable nonmilitary employee population (e.g., same percentage by gender and age range). Specifically, research funded by the White House (Council of Economic Advisors, 2018) found that 40 percent of military spouses had a college degree, and 34 percent had some college with no degree, compared to 29 percent and 25 percent of an equivalent civilian population in the United States, respectively. Military spouses also showed dedication to the military but at a financial penalty. Each year, it is estimated that military spouses, when compared to comparable civilian populations, lose $12,374 in income and $189,614 over the course of their spouse's 20-year military career (Council of Economic Advisors, 2018). A service member's spouse typically moves when the service member moves (typically every 2 to 4 years), which means, like the service member, military spouses are used to change and adept at planning and adjusting to changing environments.

While there is much we still do not yet know about the employment trends and experiences of military spouses, reports on the state of spouses consistently cite common needs for military spouses to find their greatest employment success. Because military families tend to relocate often as they trail the service member, one of the best ways to support spouses is to provide career opportunities with growth and location flexibility (e.g., telework). Another way to support military spouses is to look past and appreciate perceived gaps in employment on their résumés. With a regular cadence of location moves due to their spouses' military service, military spouses are often not able to maintain continuous employment with an employer with each location move. The military spouse may struggle to find new employment with each move since many military installations are located in more rural and less urban environments.

Giving military spouses some grace about the continuity of their employment is important. Do not assume their employment discontinuity is due to a lack of loyalty, commitment, or determination. Instead, it is a condition of being a trailing spouse. Underemployment is a true concern with military spouses.

A study by the White House Council of Economic Advisors in 2018 estimated that over 50 percent of military spouses are underemployed. Related to the experience of underemployment, many military spouses will spend breaks in their career volunteering or serving as community leaders. Thus, be sure to consider the volunteer and community leadership experiences that military spouses list on their résumé as core experience in addition to their formal work record. By taking all of these points into consideration, you will more appropriately assess whether a military spouse may be the untapped talent you need in your organization.

## Performance of Military Veterans in the Civilian Workplace

Organizations that can successfully recruit and retain veteran employees not only will be able to draw on the skills already discussed but also will benefit from their productivity. Recent research suggests that veteran employees are more productive compared to employees without the military experience. As an example, one study (Schafer, Swick, Kidder, & Carter, 2016) found 68 percent of employers reported that their veteran employees performed better than or much better than their civilian peers, while another study (Barrera & Carter, 2017) reported that 59 percent of the civilian employers they surveyed said that veterans performed better than or much better than their nonveteran peers. Drawing from its enormous collection of individual employee data, LinkedIn (Boatwright & Roberts, 2019) compared the work histories of veterans and nonveteran employees in companies and found that veterans remained with their employers 8.3 percent longer than comparable employees, were 160 percent more likely to have a graduate degree or higher, have 2.9 times more work experience than nonveterans, and were 39 percent more likely to be promoted earlier than nonveterans. LinkedIn also noted that veteran employees were more likely to take jobs that were lower in seniority and were less likely to utilize their skill sets, but that they were quickly promoted to positions that did utilize their skills. Adding support to the idea that veteran employees have more experience than their peers and are looking for ways to utilize these experiences, LinkedIn found that veteran employees were less likely to obtain jobs despite having on average 4 years or more of experience, were 70 percent more likely to take a step back in seniority in their first job, but were 36 percent less likely to make a seniority jump compared to nonveteran employees.

## Retention of Military Veterans in the Civilian Workplace

Moving from an intense, mission-focused work environment to one without such a focused culture, veteran employees may find themselves lacking purpose and feeling underemployed and unappreciated in the civilian workforce if the employer does not properly engage them. Conversely, companies that find ways to provide a sense of purpose to the veteran employees and leverage the capabilities of veterans will be rewarded with highly motivated and committed employees. Fortunately, this is an area of expertise for I/O psychologists and HR practitioners who understand applied workplace science and research. Specifically, I/O psychology's research provides guidance to business leaders and can have a positive impact in helping our organizations recruit, maximize, and retain this talent pool. Analyses of veteran employee experiences compared to civilian employees suggest that if we apply evidence-based best practices related to person–organization fit, cultural sensitivity, and transferable skills, we can reduce underemployment by placing veteran employees in positions that maximize their KSAs in cultures that understand them. Enabling person–job fit further helps veterans maximize their experiences and training since research demonstrates that increased fit is related to reduced turnover, increased performance, and overall improved employee well-being.

As an example, initial research on veteran employees suggested that military veterans were more likely to leave new employment opportunities sooner than nonveteran employees. However, later research has provided a more nuanced understanding of veteran employee retention. Barrera and Carter (2017) found that nearly one third of veteran job seekers were underemployed, and that this number was 15.6 percent higher than for nonveteran jobs seekers. The Institute for Vetearns and Military Families and VetAdvisor (2014) found that between 44 veteran employees left their job in the first year; this is a rate significantly higher than comparable civilian populations. Later and more detailed research has clarified that veterans are not necessarily an attrition risk but rather are in search of job fit and may actually be more committed or loyal to their employer compared to nonveterans once job and company fit is found.

LinkedIn's Veterans Job Report (Boatwright & Roberts, 2019), for instance, reported high turnover among military veterans but noted that this turnover was seen only if they left their job in their first year. (LinkedIn found 50 percent of their veteran employee sample left their job within their first 19 months, which is consistent with Maury and colleagues' findings). Unlike prior research, LinkedIn found that military veterans who stayed in their jobs beyond the first year had higher retention rates than their nonmilitary counterparts. The Corporate Executive Board (2013) and the RAND Corporation (Schafer et al., 2016) found similar results: Veterans have lower turnover rates than their civilian counterparts, and this trend was greater for veterans past their first job postservice. These findings suggest that the more efforts that employers make to understand the skills, experiences, and training of military veteran employees; connect with veterans; and find ways to draw and motivate them into their organizations, the more that they will be able to contribute to an organization's mission.

## Perceptions of Military Veteran Employees: The Military–Civilian Divide

One way that we can help our organizations better utilize veteran talent is to help our organizations change the misperceptions, inaccurate ideas, or misunderstood notions about military veterans that may undermine the perceived value that veterans bring to the civilian workforce. Research suggests that more research and rigorous data-driven work is needed in this area; few companies do this well, though many claim to utilize internal data for decision-making. As more companies do this properly, they will be able to gain the competitive advantage that veterans can bring to organizations. One reason why many misperceptions and inaccurate notions exist about the military is that few civilians (including many hiring managers and organization leaders) have any personal or family connections to the military. The legacy of military service is predominantly shouldered by the same families through the generations. As a result of this concentration of military service in the same families, the vast majority of the U.S. population has little to no interaction with the military (excluding what the media and entertainment industry depicts). This creates a military–civilian divide based on misconceptions and misperceptions on both sides. This divide is particularly prominent when civilians with no exposure to the military rely on their often implicit or naïve misperceptions in their hiring and workplace interactions with veterans (Carter, Schafer, Kidder, & Fagan, 2017).

The global communications firm Edelman conducts research among military veterans, civilians, and employers. Their findings illustrate the difficulty that most companies experience when hiring and retaining military veterans along with the impact that this has on veterans in the civilian workforce. One of Edelman's (2018) series of surveys found that only 21 percent of employers said that they were actively hiring military veterans as a top priority for their company, 23 percent were trying to hire more veterans and were finding it difficult to do so, and 32 percent wanted to hire but did not think it was a top priority for their company. HR professionals in this study also had negative perceptions of how well veterans could perform in their workforces. Unfortunately, similar to civilian hiring managers, veterans also had negative misperceptions, with 60 percent of both the HR professionals and the veterans in the survey said that veterans may need additional education or training before they could be qualified for their civilian jobs. In addition, 60 percent of employers believed that veterans do not have successful careers after leaving the military, and 48 percent of the veterans agreed with this statement. These negative perceptions feed into a narrative around veterans that other research we previously referenced contradicts. The myth may be that veterans struggle in the civilian workforce, but recent research and data suggest that they thrive when given the opportunity.

Edelman's 2018 survey also identified some notable trends that may help explain the low overall perceptions veterans felt with regard to their civilian work capabilities. Among the veteran respondents,

- 41 percent said that they did not have the work experience that employers wanted;
- 40 percent did not have the education level employers desired;
- 37 percent did not have the skills or certifications;
- 30 percent did not know anyone in the field who they could ask for advice or support; and
- 27 percent said that they were not able to obtain a job interview in that field.

These results indicate current perceptions of veterans looking for civilian work but do not indicate the reality of job conditions for veterans. It is incumbent on those with an understanding of I/O psychology and HR best practices to help rightsize the transition to civilian life and civilian employment conditions for veterans and military spouses. This will enable their successful hiring and retention in the civilian workforce. Our military members are highly skilled and experienced professionals. With the right job and opportunity, veterans and military family members can excel in civilian organizations.

## Conclusion

We welcome you to read each of the chapters that follow. They are written by experts well versed on the research and practice of key concepts for enabling productive workers. While this book focuses on the research and best practices to set military veterans up for success in civilian employment, the concepts presented can also be applied more broadly to all employees. If a best practice exists for the broader population of employees, it likely works well with veterans and vice versa. For instance, a company that can appeal to veterans by demonstrating the importance and impact of the company's mission will also appeal to civilians who want to make an impact. And organizational leadership that is effective at understanding veteran culture through effective diversity and inclusion initiatives should be just as effective with other groups of civilian employees. Though cultural nuances and appreciation for people's past experiences are important, it is perhaps even more important when we speak about our veteran populations because they self-selected into this unique status and group. Veterans' life choices are significant—they were each so bold as to volunteer to serve a purpose greater than themselves. Veterans can be a true resource given their experiences and training. We hope that every employer can appreciate and maximize what has been called "the veteran advantage" in their workplace and in their communities. And, of course, as long as you are capitalizing on the veteran advantage, be sure to tap into the highly skilled and educated advantage that our military spouses also bring to bear. Employing veterans and military spouses is a noble pursuit, but it is more importantly a wise pursuit for any company looking to maintain a competitive advantage by investing in the right talent.

As the editors of this book, we wish you the best of luck and success with your veteran hiring and retention initiatives and great prosperity for your companies that follow your advice.

## Note

1. Full disclosure: The first editor of this book works for the DoD office that oversees the transition curriculum but worked on this book outside of his DoD responsibilities.

## References

Adler, A. B., & Saboe, K. N. (2017). How organizations and leaders can build resilience: Lessons from high-risk occupations. In M. F. Crane (Ed.), *Managing for resilience: A practical guide for employee wellbeing and organizational performance* (pp. 171–189). New York, NY: Routledge.

Barrera, C., & Carter, P. (2017). *Call of Duty Endowment and ZipRecruiter: Challenges on the home front: Underemployment hits veterans hard.* https://www.callofdutyendowment.org/content/dam/atvi/callofduty/code/pdf/ZipCODE_Vet_Report_FINAL.pdf

Boatwright, M., & Roberts, S. (2019). *LinkedIn veteran opportunity report: Understanding an untapped talent pool.* Sunnyvale, CA: LinkedIn. https://socialimpact.linkedin.com/content/dam/me/linkedinforgood/en-us/resources/veterans/LinkedIn-Veteran-Opportunity-Report.pdf.

Carter, A. (2019). *Inside the five-sided box. Lessons from a lifetime of leadership in the Pentagon.* New York, NY: Random House.

Carter, P., Schafer, A., Kidder, K., & Fagan, M. (2017). *Lost in translation: The civil-military divide and veteran employment.* Washington, DC: Center for New American Security. https://www.cnas.org/publications/reports/lost-in-translation

Corporate Executive Board. (2013). *The business case for hiring veterans.* Washington, DC: Author. https://www.callofdutyendowment.org/content/dam/atvi/callofduty/code/media_kit/CEB_Hiring_Veterans_Study.pdf

Council of Economic Advisors. (2018). *Military spouses in the labor market.* Washington, DC: White House. https://trumpwhitehouse.archives.gov/wp-content/uploads/2018/05/Military-Spouses-in-the-Labor-Market.pdf

Department of Defense, Undersecretary of Defense for Personnel and Readiness. (2018c). *Population representation in the military services: Fiscal 2017.*

Edelman Intelligence. (2018). *2018 veterans well-being survey.* Washington, DC: Author. https://www.edelman.com/sites/g/files/aatuss191/files/2018-10/2018-Edelman-Veterans-Well-being-Survey.pdf

Feller, M. (2016, April). HR's hard challenge: When employees lack soft skills. *HR Magazine.* https://www.shrm.org/hr-today/news/hr-magazine/0416/pages/hrs-hard-challenge-when-employees-lack-soft-skills.aspx

Goldberg, M. S., & Warner, J. T. (1987). Military experience, civilian experience, and the earnings of veterans. *Journal of Human Resources, 22*(1), 62–81. https://www.jstor.org/stable/145867

Goodwin, G. F., Blacksmith, N., & Coats, M. R. (2018). The science of teams in the military: Contributions from over 60 years of research. *American Psychologist, 73*(4), 322–333.

Hardison, C. M., Krueger, T. C., Shanley, M. G., Saavedra, A. R., Martin, J., Wong, J. P., . . . Crowley, J. C. (2017). *Methodology for translating enlisted veterans' nontechnical skills into civilian employers' terms.* Santa Monica, CA: RAND. https://www.rand.org/pubs/ research_reports/RR1919.html

Hardison, C. M., Krueger, T. C., Shanley. M. G., Saavedra, A. R., Martin, J., Wong, J. P., . . . Steinberg, P. S. (2017). *What veterans bring to civilian workplaces: A prototype toolkit for helping private-sector employers understand the nontechnical skills developed in the military.* Santa Monica, CA: RAND. https://www.rand.org/pubs/tools/TL160-1.html

Hardison, C., & Shanley, M. G. (2016). *Essential skills veterans gain during professional military training: A resource for leadership and hiring managers.* Santa Monica, CA: RAND. https://www.rand.org/pubs/tools/TL160z2-2.html

Haynie, J. M. (2016). *Revisiting the business case for hiring a veteran: A strategy for cultivating competitive advantage.* Syracuse, NY: Institute for Veterans and Military Families, Syracuse University. https://ivmf.syracuse.edu/article/ revisiting-the-business-case-for-hiring-a-veteran/

Haynie, J. M., & Dean, S. (2011). Toward a theory of discontinuous career transition: Investigating career transitions necessitated by traumatic life events. *Journal of Applied Psychology, 96*(3), 501–524.

Institute for Veterarns and Military Families and VetAdvisor. (2014). *Veteran Job retention survey.* https://ivmf.syracuse.edu/wp-content/uploads/2016/06/VeteranJobRetention SurveySummaryACC_03.16.18.pdf

Korn Ferry Institute. (2017). *Debunking myths in veteran hiring.* Korn Ferry. https://www. kornferry.com/content/dam/kornferry/docs/article-migration/VeteransMay2017.pdf

LinkedIn. (2018). *LinkedIn 2018 workplace learning report: The rise and responsibility of talent development in the new labor market.* Sunnyvale, CA: Author. https://learning. linkedin.com/content/dam/me/learning/en-us/pdfs/linkedin-learning-workplace- learning-report-2018.pdf

Mattock, M. G., Asch, B. J., Hosek, J., & Boito, M. (2019). *The relative cost-effectiveness of retaining versus accessing Air Force pilots.* Santa Monica, CA: RAND Corporation. https://www.rand.org/pubs/research_reports/RR2415.html

McGeary, D. D. (2011). Making sense of resilience. *Military Medicine, 176*(6), 603–604. https://doi.org/10.7205/milmed-d-10-00480

Schafer, A., Swick, A., Kidder, K., & Carter, P. (2016). *Onward and upward: Understanding veteran retention and performance in the workforce.* Washington, DC: Center for a New American Security. https://s3.amazonaws.com/files.cnas.org/documents/CNAS- Report-Onward%26Upward-Finalc.pdf

U.S. Congressional Budget Office. (2017). *Transitioning from the military to the civilian workforce: The role of unemployment compensation for ex-servicemembers.* Washington, DC: Author. https://www.cbo.gov/publication/52503

U.S. Department of Defense, Office of the Deputy Assistant Secretary of Defense for Military Community and Family Policy (DoD ODAS MC&FP). (2019). *Profile of the military community: 2018 demographics.* Washington, DC: Author. https://download. militaryonesource.mil/12038/MOS/Reports/2018-demographics-report.pdf

U.S. Department of Defense, Undersecretary of Defense for Personnel and Readiness. (2018a). *Defense manpower data center occupational database.* Washington, DC: Author. https://www.dmdc.osd.mil/owa/odb

U.S. Department of Defense, Office of the Under Secretary of Defense for Personnel and Readiness. (2018b). *Department of Defense report: Credentialing program utilization.* Washington, DC: Author. https://vetsedsuccess.org/wp-content/uploads/2018/10/dod-credentialing-program-utilization.pdf

U.S. Department of Defense, Undersecretary of Defense for Personnel and Readiness. (2018c). *Population representation in the military services: Fiscal 2017.* Washington, DC: Author. https://www.cna.org/pop-rep/2017/contents/contents.html

University of California. (2020). *The UC system.* https://www.universityofcalifornia.edu/uc-system

University of Texas. (2018, September). *Fast facts September 2018.* https://data.utsystem.edu

# 1

# The Recent History of Veteran
# Recruitment and Retention

*Lisa Rosser*

Some may believe that veterans are no longer experiencing significant challenges with finding civilian employment after the military given the currently low unemployment rates for veterans (e.g., from October 2015 until the Covid-19 pandemic in March 2020, the unemployment rate for veterans of the Gulf War II era—those who served in the period following the events of September 11, 2001—never exceeded 5 percent; DOL BLS, 2020). However, low unemployment now does not mean unemployment will remain low; historically, there have been periods of notably higher rates of unemployment compared to nonveterans. Despite the typically low unemployment rates for veterans, it is important to understand the conditions that lead to higher rates of unemployment that veterans experienced in order to ensure that employers continue to build talent programs focused on veteran recruiting and retention strategies so that they not only can continue to hire military veterans but to also can ensure that these strategies include the retention of veterans in their workforces through meaningful employment and career opportunities.

While those who have served in the military historically have experienced lower rates of unemployment compared to those who have not served, the period between 2009 and 2014 was a significant period of high veteran unemployment, with 2011 being particularly high. In 2011, the overall unemployment rate for veterans of the Gulf War II era was 12.1 percent (compared to about 9 percent for nonveterans); however, young male veterans aged 18–24 had an unemployment rate of 29.1 percent, compared to the 17.6 percent rate of male nonveterans of the same age (DOL BLS, 2020).

Lisa Rosser, *The Recent History of Veteran Recruitment and Retention* In: *Military Veteran Employment.*
Edited by: Nathan D. Ainspan and Kristin N. Saboe, Oxford University Press. © Oxford University Press 2021.
DOI: 10.1093/oso/9780190642983.003.0002

## The Response—Public and Private Sectors Take Action

Because of the relatively high veteran unemployment around 2011 a number of large-scale public and private efforts arose to engage and incentivize government and corporate employers to consider the benefits of hiring veteran talent, educate them on how military skills align with civilian positions, and enable employers to connect directly with transitioning military and veterans through online job portals and career fairs. These efforts included the following:

- President Barrack Obama signed Executive Order 13518, "Employment of Veterans in the Federal Executive Branch, " in November 2009 directing federal government agencies to promote and increase veteran hiring. Veterans represented 31.1 percent of the federal workforce as of fiscal year 2016, up from 25.8 percent when the executive order was enacted (Office of Personnel Management, 2017).
- The American Recovery and Reinvestment Act of 2009 added unemployed veterans as an eligible category to the Work Opportunity Tax Credit (WOTC). The Department of Labor collects data on the number of WOTC certifications issued by target groups, and these data show that the new WOTC veteran categories did incentivize employers to hire service members (United States Congressional Research Service, 2018).
- JPMorgan Chase's 100,000 Jobs Mission (now called the Veteran Jobs Mission) launched in March 2011. The Veteran Jobs Mission currently comprises over 230 private sector companies that collectively had hired over 610,000 service members by 2020 (Veteran Job Mission, 2020).
- The U.S. Chamber of Commerce Foundation's Hiring Our Heroes launched in March 2011. Hiring Our Heroes now has more than 2,000 large and small companies committed to hire 710,000 veterans, of which more than 505,000 are confirmed hires to date (Hiring Our Heroes, 2020).
- The White House's "Joining Forces" initiative launched April 2011. By the time the program was discontinued in January 2017, it reported that more than 1.2 million veterans and military spouses had been hired or trained by private sector partners (White House, 2020b).
- The "Veterans Opportunity to Work and Hire Heroes Act of 2011" (VOW Act) was passed by Congress and signed by President Obama into law November 2011 (The White House, 2020a). The VOW Act

required all separating service members to attend the previously optional Transition Assistance Program (TAP) and added another new category of eligible veterans to the WOTC employer incentive. The new TAP curriculum for the service members created by the VOW Act was improved to help make veterans better candidates for civilian jobs. And, since the act's creation, the government expanded its outreach efforts to civilian employers (United States Department of Veterans Affairs, 2020).

There is certainly overlap between the results of the Veteran Jobs Mission, Hiring Our Heroes, and Joining Forces initiatives, as many large employers participated in all three and were reporting the same hiring numbers to all three. That does not negate the fact that more veteran outreach and hiring efforts occurred during that time period compared to previous years. The reported number of veterans affected by outreach and policy efforts is notable because it enabled veterans to find employment and reducing the unemployment rates. In addition, more companies took advantage of the newly enacted hiring tax credits. More states also passed veteran hiring tax credit incentives during this time. More large companies made public commitments to hire veterans, which may have influenced small and midsize companies to do the same. More employers increasingly demanded training and guidance to assist with development of programs, so organizations like the Department of Labor and the Society for Human Resource Management (SHRM) created online toolkits of information to assist employers. And, more companies went above and beyond to develop significant and innovative employment programs for veterans. Here are three notable examples:

- In 2013, Walmart established the "Veterans Welcome Home Commitment," which guaranteed a position to every veteran honorably discharged. In the four ensuing years, Walmart hired nearly 188,000 veterans and promoted 28,000 more. Walmart then updated and achieved a hiring commitment to hire 250,000 veterans by 2020 (Wal-Mart Stores, 2020).
- Prudential partnered with Workforce Opportunity Services to create the VETalent program. VETalent partners with colleges and universities to train service members in the critical skills that are needed to succeed in a business environment and also assists with job placement at Prudential and other partner corporations (Prudential, 2020).

- Microsoft created the Microsoft Software and Systems Academy, providing an 18-week training for high-demand careers in cloud development, cloud administration, cybersecurity, database administration, or business intelligence administration. In addition to the training, Microsoft employees mentor the veterans involved, and an outside vendor provides career services (including résumé and interviewing assistance). At the end of training, most of the veterans are placed with either Microsoft or one of the partner employers (Microsoft, 2020).

## The Current Situation

While all of this represents tremendous progress, and the veteran unemployment rate continues to remain below 4 percent for most groups of veterans, this is not a time to declare veteran unemployment a nonissue. There are two factors to be addressed: (a) too few companies are making significant effort toward hiring veterans, limiting the overall number and variety of opportunities for veterans; and (b) retention remains an issue, with many veterans leaving their first civilian employers earlier than their civilian counterparts and in larger numbers compared to their civilian counterparts. Though veterans are finding work, they may not stay with the company, and this turnover can be costly to the veteran by delaying an effective transition and is costly for the company, which must replace employees on their departure. Finding a job is the first step but keeping a job and building a career after the military are equally important, if not more important, metrics of career success and a necessary second topic of discussion regarding veteran employment rates.

## Too Few Companies Carry the Veteran Recruiting Torch

Given the prevalence of highly visible and publically stated veteran hiring commitments, it is easy to believe that most large major corporations have a veteran recruiting program. "5,000 veterans hired by 2015!" "10,000 veterans hired by 2020!" "Every veteran who wants a job can have one with us!" A Futurestep (Korn Ferry, 2015) survey of global executives from more than 700 companies revealed that 80 percent of respondents said their organizations did not have a specific veteran hiring outreach program, and

81 percent replied they did not have clear messaging on the business benefit they will attain by hiring veterans. SHRM's *New Talent Landscape* survey (SHRM, 2016) reported similar results, finding that only 36 percent of the respondents would seek talent from nontraditional sources, including military veterans.

CareerBuilder (2016) conducted a survey of 2,587 hiring managers and human resources professionals and found that 3 percent reported that they would actively recruit veterans over the next 12 months, which is the same percentage reported the year before, possibly indicating flatlining interest in or oversaturation of generic messaging on how to develop a veteran recruitment program. Compare the relatively low corporate participation rate in veteran hiring efforts with the list of the 50 fastest growing industries with ample job prospects (i.e., expected to add at least 10,000 jobs and at least 15 percent growth in employment opportunities the next 5 years) compiled in 2020 by the Department of Labor's Bureau of Labor Statistics Office of Occupational Statistics and Employment Projections, and one will find a discrepancy between veteran efforts to hire and the fastest growing job sectors.

When you couple the fact that there is a significant number of companies and industries that are not actively hiring veterans with the large percentage of veterans leaving the jobs they first took after transitioning the military, typically within 12 to 24 months of hire, you have to wonder where the veterans are going to go after they exit that first job. Will they continue to cycle through the existing roster of large brand name companies well known in the veteran recruiting space, or will they be able to branch out and find great careers with companies in growing industries that currently have not prioritized recruiting veterans?

## High Veteran Turnover Rates

VetAdvisor and Syracuse University's Institute for Veterans and Military Families (VetAdvisor and IVMF, 2016) conducted a veteran retention survey in 2014 that revealed that 43 percent of respondents left their first civilian job prior to completing 12 months in the position, and 80 percent left prior to completing 24 months (VetAdvisor and IVMF, 2016). CareerBuilder (2016) surveyed currently employed veterans in 2016 and found that veterans expressed less contentment with the roles they had been hired into when compared to the previous year's surveys—57 percent of veteran respondents replied that they were satisfied with their role in 2016, whereas 65 percent reported satisfaction in 2015. The top two areas of dissatisfaction were

- Low-paying job (22 percent, up from 19 percent in 2015), and
- Underemployment—working a job that was below their skill level (22 percent, up from 20 percent in 2015).

Presumably, there may be a connection between these two areas of dissatisfaction, as someone who is employed at their proper skill level would likely be earning a higher salary and may be more engaged with the work, resulting in greater satisfaction with the job.

It is important to note that turnover among recently transitioned veteran new hires is not dramatically out of range of all employee turnover. Companies should review and improve onboarding efforts, cultural fit efforts, and career management for all employees, with the goal of reducing turnover for all employees. These efforts start with addressing the misperceptions about why people leave a job and the quality of the employee that decides to leave.

Willis Towers Watson's global workforce study (2014) of more than 32,000 employees from large and midsize companies studied those employees who were classified as "at risk" for leaving (employees seeing themselves at a different company in the next 2 years) or "leavers" (those who had already decided to leave and were actively looking for their next opportunity outside of the company). The survey results of civilian workers (not just veterans) identified four important characteristics of employees who leave or exit an organization:

- *Departing employees are not always the poor performers*: Of the employees who left their jobs, 34 percent were rated as "exceeds" or "far exceeds" performance expectations in their most recent performance review, and another 45 percent were rated as "met expectations."
- *Companies focus too much on recruiting and not enough on retention*: Nearly 1 in 10 employees will leave within the first year and 1 in almost 20 before the end of the second year. This suggests that companies expend a lot of effort to recruit a candidate to take a job, and that the vested efforts made by companies to impress during recruitment stop once the employee starts working.

- *Employees want to advance*: Of the employees, 70 percent reported they felt they needed to leave their current job in order to advance. This suggests that advancement is key to gaining an improved financial position and higher income.
- *Pay is important*: Thirty-two percent of employees reported being concerned about money. Low pay or minimal pay exacerbate concerns about finances and money.

The Call of Duty Endowment (Barrera and Carter, 2017), a 501(c)3 private foundation that funds high-performing nonprofits that prepare veterans for the job market, has reported similar turnover findings for the veteran community, with a slight turnover increase occurring in the early stages of their civilian careers and a reduced turnover percentage after several years in the civilian workplace. Here are a few reasons the Call of Duty Endowment identified about why veterans, in their own words, reported seeking job services:

- "Looking for a better paying job than $11.50 an hour. Feel like I am barely getting by."
- "I got out of the army after 3 years of serving with an Honorable Discharge. I wasn't lazy and got a job ASAP for a health company that got shut down 6 months later. Now I'm working for [National Retailer], but me and my wife are struggling to put food on the table."
- "I own a house and can't afford to move away, but I'm working a full-time job with no advancement or chance for a raise. I make $12 an hour at a local hospital that keeps cutting positions and shifts."
- "I have a BS degree Information Systems–Cyber Security with a 4.0 in the field and 3.26 GPA upon graduation. I have applied for junior positions in the cyber field for over 2 years just to get my foot in the door. No one has hired me. Please help, I have a beautiful wife and two awesome kids who depend on me."
- "I have a low-paying job but I need help getting a better paying job to help my family out. I took the first job I was given when I got out."
- "I lost my state job that I fought to get for 3 years, and now I deliver pizza. I plan to study and get COMP-TIA A+ Certified this next year since that is my military background. I just want to work in my field. I want my son to be proud of me as he grows up."

These responses from veterans seeking new employment could suggest a potential correlation between the high veteran turnover rate and the number of companies that do not make a specific effort to address veteran onboarding, corporate cultural adaption, and orientation to corporate processes and procedures. A One Futurestep (Korn Ferry, 2015) survey of global executives from more than 700 companies found that among the respondents,

- 71 percent said they do not provide veteran-specific training to hiring managers or recruiters; and
- 52 percent stated they do not have onboarding or transition support for new veteran hires.

Most companies still do not do a good job of tracking the specific veterans hired or identify the numbers and names of veterans they currently employ. This complicates a company's ability to assess its veteran turnover rate—If it does not know it hired a veteran or who the veterans are that already employed at the company, then how will it know when one leaves? How will the company benchmark veteran turnover rates compared to turnover rates for nonveterans or any other diverse demographic within the company? This also serves as an indication of a company's priorities and potential lack of awareness of the unique qualities, soft skills, and training veterans enter the civilian workforce with as a result of their military service.

The Center for a New American Security (Carter, Kidder, Schafer, & Swick, 2016) offers a pertinent suggestion: Employers should be incentivized to value and measure veteran fit and performance rather than focusing on hiring metrics alone. Improved retention, through programs such as mentorship and affinity groups, should be at least equally valued.

# References

Barrera, C., & Carter, P. (2017). *Challenges on the homefront: Underemployment hits veterans hard.* https://www.callofdutyendowment.org/content/dam/atvi/callofduty/code/pdf/ZipCODE_Vet_Report_FINAL.pdf

Bureau of Labor Statistics, U.S. Department of Labor. (2020). *Economic news release: Employment situation of veterans—2011.* Washington, DC: Author. https://www.bls.gov/news.release/vet.toc.htm

CareerBuilder. (2016). *Annual CareerBuilder survey finds that hiring veterans remains a strong focus, but veteran satisfaction takes a dip.* Chicago, IL: CareerBuilder. http://press.careerbuilder.com/press-releases?item=123266

Carter, P., Kidder, K., Schafer, A, & Swick, A. (2016). *Onward and upward: Understanding veteran retention and performance in the workforce.* Washington, DC: Center for New American Security. https://www.cnas.org/publications/reports/onward-and-upward

Department of Labor Bureau of Labor Statistics. (2020). *Employment situation of veterans summary.* Washington, DC: Burea of Labor Statistics. https://www.bls.gov/news.release/vet.nr0.htm

Hiring Our Heroes. (2020). Home page. https://www.hiringourheroes.org

Korn Ferry. (2015). *Futurestep executive survey finds lack of veteran recruiting and onboarding programs.* Los Angeles, CA: Author. https://www.kornferry.com/about-us/press/Korn%20Ferry-executive-survey-finds-lack-of-veteran-recruiting-and-onboarding-programs

Microsoft Corporation. (2020). *Software and Systems Academy.* Redmond, WA: Author. https://military.microsoft.com/programs/mssa/

Office of Personnel Management. (2017). *Employment of veterans in the federal executive branch.* https://www.fedshirevets.gov/veterans-council/veteran-employment-data/employment-of-veterans-in-the-federal-executive-branch-fy2017.pdf

Prudential. (2020). *Serving those who've served us all: Our commitment to veterans.* http://corporate.prudential.com/view/page/corp/31840

Society for Human Resource Management (SHRM). (2016). *The new talent landscape: Recruiting difficulty and skills shortage.* Washington, DC: Author. https://www.shrm.org/hr-today/trends-and-forecasting/research-and-surveys/Documents/SHRM%20New%20Talent%20Landscape%20Recruiting%20Difficulty%20Skills.pdf

United States Congressional Research Service. (2018). *The work opportunity tax credit.* Washington, DC: Author. https://fas.org/sgp/crs/misc/R43729.pdf

United States Department of Veterans Affairs. (2020). *Veterans opportunity to work.* Washington, DC: Author. https://www.benefits.va.gov/VOW

VetAdvisor and the Institute for Veterans and Military Families (IVMF). (2016). *Veteran Job Retention Survey summary.* https://ivmf.syracuse.edu/wp-content/uploads/2016/06/VeteranJobRetentionSurveySummaryACC_03.16.18.pdf

Veteran Job Mission. (2020). *About the mission.* https://www.veteranjobsmission.com/about-the-mission.

Wal-Mart Stores. (2020). *Your next opportunity ready and waiting.* Bentonville, AR: Author. https://one.walmart.com/content/people-experience/military/apply.html

White House. (2020a). *Executive Order 13518—Veterans Employment Initiative.* https://obamawhitehouse.archives.gov/the-press-office/executive-order-veterans-employment-initiative

White House. (2020b). *Support for service members, veterans and their families.* Washington, DC: Author. https://obamawhitehouse.archives.gov/joiningforces

Willis Towers Watson. (2014). *The Towers Watson 2014 global workforce and global talent management and rewards studies.* London, UK: Author. https://www.willistowerswatson.com/en-US/Insights/2014/10/global-trends-in-employee-attraction-retention-and-engagement

# 2

# Why Hire Veterans?

*J. Michael Haynie[1]*

Howard Schultz, former chief executive officer of the Starbucks Corporation, said, "Hiring people is an art, not a science, and résumés can't tell you whether someone will fit into a company's culture." Mr. Schultz is right. There is an art to hiring and managing an organization's most valued resource—human capital. When it comes to hiring military veterans as this capital, there is arguably too much art and not enough science. Efforts to leverage the knowledge, skills, abilities, and global experiences of the nation's veterans are lost in the midst of résumés that are not representative of those qualities—and obscured by civilian generalizations and clichés.

The widespread motivations for hiring veterans in the civilian workforce are often based on the generalization that all veterans have a certain level of leadership ability and are mission oriented—a term widely used in the military to describe the dedication and commitment to move the mission in a successful direction (National Center for Post-Traumatic Stress Disorder, 2012). While these characteristics are admirable, they do not do justice to the myriad skills and abilities veterans bring to the workplace.

In order for employers to get the full benefit of hiring veterans, they need to understand why it is in their best interest to employ and retain them. This chapter presents and expands on the typical understanding of what it means to hire a veteran. It defines the skills and knowledge the veteran brings to the organization along with the value associated with decisive efforts to integrate the veteran into the civilian workforce. This chapter explores and outlines the subsequent impact of these decisions on a company's organizational culture and competitive advantage in the marketplace, looks at the current trends in the marketplace for veteran talent, gives suggestions, and presents recommendations (for employers) to advance the success of veterans in the workplace.

This chapter addresses what employers, as well as the community, need to know about veterans and illustrates what they bring to the table in the civilian

J. Michael Haynie, *Why Hire Veterans?* In: *Military Veteran Employment.* Edited by: Nathan D. Ainspan and Kristin N. Saboe, Oxford University Press. © Oxford University Press 2021. DOI: 10.1093/oso/9780190642983.003.0003

marketplace. Ultimately, this chapter presents best practices for employers and builds the case for hiring veterans drawn from numerous sources, including the U.S. Department of Defense (DoD), the U.S. Department of Veterans Affairs (VA), numerous articles on veteran employment, along with several publications from the Institute for Veterans and Military Families (IVMF) and the RAND Corporation.[2]

## The Veteran Workforce Landscape

Today, more than 10 million veterans, approximately half of all U.S. veterans (20.3 million), are active participants in the civilian labor force (U.S. Department of Labor, 2017). By 2021 more than four million veterans have served the nation it was attacked on September 11, 2001 conflict are expected to join the workforce (Bradbard, Armstrong, & Maury, 2016). The unemployment gap between veterans and nonveterans has closed considerably in recent years due in part to a recovering U.S. economy and more employers making concerted efforts to hire veterans. Since 2009, over 400,000 veterans found employment in hundreds of corporate and governmental organizations due to the work of coalitions and initiatives collectively committed to hiring veterans (Veterans Job Mission, 2020). However, over the past decade, specific subgroups of U.S. veterans experienced greater unemployment than their nonveteran counterparts have, especially in the wake of the Great Recession. This gap was most acute for younger veterans separating from the military in their 20s, who saw the worst levels in 2011 (IVMF, 2015, Figure 3). Female veterans also fared worse in the job market than men (Kleykamp, 2013). Unemployment for younger post-9/11 veterans remains high compared to the national average (U.S. Department of Labor, 2017). As veteran unemployment improved over the years, these relationships have remained relatively consistent in recent years.

## Retaining Veterans in the Workforce

While the veteran unemployment rate has decreased over time, there are still many veterans entering the workforce who need meaningful jobs. Despite the high numbers of veterans obtaining jobs and the publicized commitments to hiring veterans by some employers, the question of how long veterans stay in these jobs is still a concern. In one study, Maury and Stone (2014) found that nearly half of all veterans leave their first postmilitary position within a year and between 60 and 80 percent of veterans leave their first civilian jobs before their second work anniversary. This means that only about 2 in 10 veterans will hold their first nonmilitary job for more than 2 years. Some, like their nonveteran counterparts, are leaving for better jobs. However, many veterans leave for less advantageous reasons. Many leave their first jobs because of underemployment, while others leave because they feel that the work lacks meaning or has limited professional development opportunities. Last, veterans may also leave their first jobs due to an unfamiliar work culture. Veterans entering the civilian workforce are required to make dramatic shifts in terminology, practices, habits, and expectations and may be unfamiliar with corporate language. Conversely, managers may see the new veteran hire as less competent or cooperative and may have trouble connecting with them due to a lack of training designed to help the employer build a better awareness of the military culture.

## Reasons to Hire Veterans

Veterans bring invaluable talent to the workplace. Along with having outstanding leadership and technical skills, veterans are likely to possess the following qualities (Cohany, 1992; Hardison & Shanley, 2016; Haynie, 2012, 2016):

- An accelerated learning curve
- Analytical skills
- Internal motivation and the ability to work well without close supervision
- Strong leadership skills
- An understanding of the value of teamwork
- An awareness of diversity and inclusion in action
- Strong attention to detail
- The ability to maintain efficient performance under pressure
- A solid respect for procedures
- Strong technical skills
- Integrity
- Loyalty

- An awareness of the importance of workplace health and safety
- The ability to triumph over adversity and demonstrate resilience
- Personal accountability
- Adaptability
- Perseverance, self-reliance, and a strong work ethic—which allow them to go above and beyond job requirements
- Strategies and personalities that make them values driven, objective focused, and quick learners
- The skills and ability to be high-impact decision-makers
- Flexibility and the ability to work in stressful, fast-paced, dynamic environments
- Tenacity to consistently complete the work
- Experience with culturally diverse and global working environments

Moreover, employing veterans builds goodwill with the community, customers, and employees. Simply put, employing veterans is just good business. However, reports also show many challenges accompany veterans transitioning into civilian life and the workforce. Finding employment is one of the top priorities for transitioning service members, and yet, it is often the most challenging part of their move (Zoli, Maury, & Fay, 2015). Additionally, studies continuously show that employers are not fully aware of all of the benefits hiring veterans brings and thus miss the opportunity to hire and retain them and are unaware of the unique skills and talents—from their military training—that can be leveraged into the workforce.

- *Veterans are entrepreneurial.* High-performing entrepreneurs have strong self-efficacy, have a high need for achievement, are comfortable with autonomy and uncertainty, and make effective decisions in the face of dynamic environments. Research illustrates that these same attributes are generally characteristic of military service members and veterans because these individuals self-select to join the military because they are individuals with a high need for achievement who demonstrate high levels of self-efficacy, trust, and comfort with autonomy and the dynamic decision-making processes (Baron, 2007).
- *Veterans assume high levels of trust.* The literature on organizational behavior highlights the ability to trust coworkers and superiors as a significant predictor of high-performing teams, organizational cohesion and morale, and effective governance systems (Hitt, 2000; Hitt, Keats,

& DeMarie, 1998). Research studies focused on both military personnel and veterans indicate that the military service experience engenders a strong propensity toward an inherent trust and faith in coworkers and a strong propensity toward trust in organizational leadership (Haynie & Shepherd, 2011). In turn, the academic literature broadly supports the finding that organizational performance is enhanced where trust between coworkers—and between employees and leadership—is strong (Godé-Sanchez, 2010).

- *Veterans are adept at skills transfer across contexts and tasks.* Skills transfer across context and tasks is the ability to transfer skills to a different setting or circumstance (Mangum & Ball, 1987). The RAND Corporation, in an effort to assess abilities, used a skills-matching matrix to identify civilian jobs to match with 10 military skills occupations (MOS, Military Occupational Specialty). RAND found, that overall, "soft skills" learned in the military across all MOSs (leadership, active listening, communication, attention to detail, etc.) apply to a broad range of jobs across many careers (Wenger et al., 2017). The study also found that the best-matching civilian occupations included some that made use of a soldiers' knowledge, skills, and abilities developed while in the service. Due to the veterans' robust skill set coupled with their ability (and training) to learn skills quickly, most civilian occupations (i.e., law enforcement and service, the medical field, STEM [science, technology, engineering, mathematics], or higher education) can utilize these skills even if they are not directly linked to the skills used in the military.
- *Scenario-Based Teachings and Training.* Active duty service members are trained (through scenario-based teachings) to develop skills regarding how to react in different—often difficult—situations. One example is military simulations. These simulations test one's ability to assess the various situations one may encounter during combat (Chang, 2009). The Joint Readiness Training Center, Operations Group, for example, provides relevant, rigorous, scenario-based training in a realistic environment. Additionally, the U.S. Army Combined Arms Center–Training also supports and enhances individual and collective scenario-based trainings in order to enhance readiness and build capabilities that support the U.S. Army and joint force commanders (U.S. Army Combined Arms Center, 2020). Such trainings are beneficial in the work environment because they help to strengthen and facilitate

knowledge/skills transfer between distinct and dissimilar tasks and situations.

- *Veterans have (and leverage) advanced technical training.* Military experience, on average, exposes individuals to highly advanced technology and technology training at a rate that is accelerated, relative to nonmilitary, age-group peers. This enhanced exposure to high-level technology contributes to an enhanced ability to link technology-based solutions to organizational challenges. Consequently military veterans, on average, not only have more advanced exposure to high-level technology relative to their age-group peers, but also make the most of that knowledge by effectively leveraging knowledge across other, disparate work-related tasks (U.S. Army Combined Arms Center).

- *Veterans are comfortable and capable of adapting in discontinuous environments.* The business environment is dynamic and uncertain, and research consistently highlights the organizational advantage of individuals who can respond to quick and decisive action in the face of uncertain and changing environments. Those in the military train to accurately perform in a decision-making environment that involves a sequence of interdependent decisions made—in real time—which change as a function of the decision sequence and require action in the face of ongoing uncertainty. For example, for those in service, it could be a military command-and-control series of decisions during battle. For a civilian, it may be choosing which route to take while driving a car or investing in the stock market while the prices are changing (Brehmer, 1992). These skills are further enhanced in individuals whose military experience has included service in combat environments (Haynie, 2016). Last-minute deployments and the ability to adjust to changing demands, along with promotions and changes in orders, contribute to the dynamic environment that the veteran is conditioned to handle.

- *Veterans exhibit high levels of resilience.* Military veterans tend to exhibit high levels of resilient behavior and tend to develop an enhanced ability to bounce back from failed professional or personal experiences more quickly and more completely, as compared to those who have not served (McGeary, 2011). This resilience gives veterans an edge in the civilian work environment, especially where intermediate or terminal failures are likely to be high, such as in new product development, early-stage ventures, sales, high-technology ventures, or environments where customer relationships are transaction based (Haynie, 2016).

- *Veterans exhibit advanced team-building skills.* Compared to those who have not served in the military, veterans are more proficient regarding (a) organizing and defining team goals and mission; (b) defining team member roles and responsibilities; and (c) developing a plan for action (Godé-Sanchez, 2010). Those with prior military service also show a high level of efficacy for team-related activities; that is, veterans exhibit an inherent and enduring belief that they can efficiently and effectively integrate and contribute to a new or existing team (Haynie, 2016).

- *Veterans exhibit a strong organizational commitment.* Military institutions are particularly adept at institutional socialization, and as a result, the military experience engenders a strong linkage between the individual and the organization. Organizational commitment is how strong of a feeling of responsibility a person (employee) has toward the mission of the organization. The stronger the commitment, the higher the work product and the likelihood that the employee will stay in that job. Military veterans bring this strong sense of organizational commitment and loyalty to the civilian workplace. One of the primary reasons veterans (80 percent) leave their first civilian job before their second work anniversary is because the job is not a good fit for them because either skills are not aligned or the veteran is underemployed (Maury & Stone, 2014). Another reason for leaving is due to the absence of a feeling of meaning and purpose in the work they are doing. Thus, a work environment that gives the veteran a strong sense of purpose and aligns well with their skill set is reflected in the veteran's sense of organizational commitment—and is reflected in a positive, high-level work product (Godé-Sanchez, 2010).

- *Veterans have (and leverage) cross-cultural experiences.* Multiple studies consistently highlight that people with military backgrounds (a) have more international experience, (b) speak more languages/more fluently, and (c) have a higher level of cultural sensitivity as compared to age-group peers who have not served in the military (Goldberg & Warner, 1987). The cross-cultural experiences characteristic of veterans represent a competitive advantage for any employer or organization, given the increasing globalization of the business environment.

- *Veterans have experience and skill in diverse work settings.* While the military has been publicly criticized for a lack of diversity on several important dimensions, research consistently highlights the fact that the all-volunteer military represents a heterogeneous workforce across myriad dimensions, including educational background, ethnicity, culture, values, and the goals or aspirations of organizational members. Consequently, those with military experience are (on average) highly accepting of individual differences in a work setting and thus exhibit a high level of cultural sensitivity regarding such differences in the workplace (Godé-Sanchez, 2010).

- *Tax credits for hiring veterans.* In addition to the numerous and diverse skills that veterans bring to the civilian workforce, there is an additional benefit to employers who hire them. Employers can earn up to $10,000 in federal and state tax credits. For each veteran hired, the federal government gives from $2,400 to $9,600 for the first year of employment, and in New York State alone, the state will give up to $2,100 for the second year of employment. The amount of tax credit depends on certain criteria, including the number of hours employed during the first year, disability status (particularly service-connected disabilities), unemployment status, and receipt of vocational rehabilitation services from a state-certified agency or the U.S. Department of Veteran Affairs. Additionally, the Special Employer Incentives program aids employers who hire veterans. Along with helping connect qualified veterans with a specific role at an organization, employers can be reimbursed for up to half the veteran's salary to cover certain supplies and equipment, additional instruction expenses, and any loss of production (U.S. Department of Veterans Affairs, 2020). As an example, employers in New York State can visit https://dol.ny.gov and look under Work Opportunity Tax Credit, U.S. Department of Veterans Affairs, and Workers With Disabilities Tax Credit (NY State[3]). For information about tax credits in all states, the U.S. Department of Veterans Affairs has information for employers at https://www.benefits.va.gov/vow/for-employers.asp and at (800) 827-1000.

## Hiring Veterans Contributes to the Bottom Line

Many private sector organizations have mobilized—at an unprecedented scale—to positively impact the employment situation of veterans in the United States (Phillips, 2002). To that end, high-profile business leaders support the development of veteran employment programs within their organizations and recognize that hiring veterans represents both good citizenship and good business. However, as private sector veteran hiring programs have evolved and matured over the past decade, discourse related to veterans' employment is beginning to take a subtle but important shift in tone and substance. Specifically, executive leaders and managers have increasingly focused on the ways and means best suited to quantify the value created for the organization, relative to the investment required to create a veteran employment program (Haynie, 2016). Consequently, specifying how and why veteran employment initiatives contribute to bottom line performance of the organization is (justifiably) important for many leaders—particularly as the answer informs future strategy and investment in such programs.

## Understanding the Return on Investment of Hiring Veterans

The return on investment (ROI), or the "value" of hiring veterans, is strong but not well understood by employers. An ROI measures the gain or loss generated on an investment relative to the amount of money invested. An ROI, expressed as a percentage, typically used for personal financial decisions, compares a company's profitability to the efficiency of different investments (Phillips, 2002). In business, the ROI is used to identify past and potential financial returns. The ROI of hiring veterans specifies how and why veteran employment initiatives contribute to the bottom line performance of the employer and whether it is justified. While these employment initiatives are crucial to maintaining and retaining veterans, this new emphasis on value creation and ROI related to veteran hiring programs can potentially have unintended and decidedly negative consequences for the employer and for the veteran.

Any effort to develop an approach or metric(s) to quantify the organizational ROI of a veteran hiring program represents an inherently complex endeavor. This can lead to the reduction or elimination of such initiatives (Haynie, 2016) and represents a potentially dangerous practice in assessing the ROI of a veteran hiring program for three primary reasons:

1. *Variations between and within organizations, markets, and industry sectors.* Given the exceptional variation that exists between and within organizations, markets, and industry sectors, it is simply an unrealistic expectation that one could develop an ROI model that is both robust and generalizable to all organizations and all types of veteran hiring

initiatives (Haynie, 2016). For example, hiring a veteran into an information technology career field would be different from, say, a sales or customer service position. Thus, creating an ROI that reflects both positions is unworkable.

2. *Variations in motivation.* In a related way, it is important to acknowledge that firms hold different (but equally valid) motivations for pursuing veteran employment programs (i.e., specific knowledge/skill acquisition, brand value, stakeholder alignment, culture/values alignment). Again, it is unlikely that a generalizable ROI model can appropriately capture this wide degree of intangible differences between firms (Haynie, 2016).

Before citing the third reason that we believe a generalizable metric—a mechanism and a measure that can be applied across the universe of private sector firms to quantify the organizational ROI of a firm's veteran hiring program—is a shortsighted objective, it is important to make clear what we are *not* suggesting. This does *not* suggest that individual and organization-specific efforts to understand and quantify the ROI of its veteran employment initiative are inappropriate or, for that matter, even to say that such an effort would be exceedingly difficult, assuming careful and organization-specific consideration of how best to inform such a calculation. However, it is to say to executive leaders, human resource executives, and midlevel managers that they should be highly skeptical of—and resist pressures to apply and adopt—externally prescribed "solutions" in instances where those metrics have not been crafted to fully incorporate the specific goals and expectations motivating your organization's veteran employment initiative. Otherwise, you are likely to do harm to both your veteran employment initiative, your veteran employees, and your organization's bottom line (Haynie, 2016). Therefore, the third reason ROI can be a dangerous practice is as in item 3.

3. *Variations in the veteran landscape.* The contemporary business landscape is such that organizations face both an increasingly competitive and increasingly resource-constrained business environment. Executive leaders and managers find themselves pressed to achieve unprecedented levels of resource efficiency while delivering on expectations of increasing sales and revenue growth. If the employer has failed to purposefully and strategically hire, deploy, and develop veterans as a differentiated human capital resource—to position them in their

first and best use within an organization—then any attempt to quantify the organizational "value" of a veteran hiring program will yield false results. Further, any attempt to act on those false results may have negative consequences for the employer, for the individual veteran, and for the future of veteran hiring initiatives across the private sector (Haynie, 2016).

In other words, the logic that underlies the business case for creating, sustaining, and ultimately institutionalizing veteran hiring programs across the private sector assumes a specific set of circumstances. It assumes that those hiring, managing, and developing veteran employees are doing so based on a purposeful strategy to place veterans as a human capital resource in their first and best use within the organization. Though this is the goal, it is far from the norm. For a company to value its veteran hiring program, it must first ensure that its organizational processes, practices, and veteran hiring strategy align with the objective of best leveraging its veteran talent as a differentiated human capital resource within the organization. If the veteran is not set up to achieve his or her best potential at the outset, measuring the success of those programs is unreliable and will likely yield false results. However, this does not mean that the practice of evaluating ROI is itself false or unreliable. It simply means that it should be considered after the foundation has been properly laid to leverage veterans as a resource. Therefore, developing and enacting a strategy with the goal of hiring, deploying, and developing veterans as a differentiated human capital resource represents a critical intermediate step toward eventually quantifying ROI, or "the value of a veteran," for the organization (Haynie, 2016).

## Getting a Better Return on Investment

Many employers report a limited understanding of the skills gained in the military and how these skills translate to civilian jobs. Equally alarming is that employers also report being misguided by negative military service stereotypes (Harrell & Berglass, 2012). Thankfully, there are things employers can do to help improve the ROI of hiring veterans and steps that they can take with veterans throughout the hiring process. For example, employers can understand the skills and experiences of veterans, utilize best practices for hiring veterans, and assist veterans transitioning to the civilian workforce.

Employers can also educate themselves and their organizations about the veteran community and the skills they bring, thus helping veterans make the transition into the workforce, and capitalize on the opportunity to hire a veteran (Haynie, 2012; IVMF 2013a, 2013b). The list that follows should be operational before the search.

- *Start "in the business."* Identify marketplace-connected skills and competencies (Box 2.1) that are central to a current and future competitive advantage for your organization or in your industry. When hiring veterans, it is imperative to think beyond skills and recognize market-connected competencies (i.e., those related to communication, critical thinking, influencing/persuading, leadership, cross-cultural understanding, helping, artistic and design proficiencies, decision-making, etc.). Role and task-specific skills can be taught or learned on the job, but what is most often overlooked and, ironically, what many employers today represent as the rarest, most valuable, and most differentiated attributes conferred to the individual by military service are not role-specific skills, but generalizable competencies.

Accordingly, when considering current and future competitive advantage in the context of leveraging a veteran employment program, extend your thinking to a competency-based framework. What are those

---

**Box 2.1  Recognizing Market-Connected Competencies**

Unlike other frameworks (i.e., a capability model that measures attributes and skills or its people), the competency-based model explains how an organization wants their people to interact and behave and is generally used to define an expected standard of performance. Competence starts as a person's capabilities. In a sense, competence is the proven abilities and improved capabilities. Competence can include a combination of knowledge, basic requirements (capabilities), skills, abilities, behavior, and attitude (Haynie, 2016). The goal of this model is to establish a mutual understanding of what good looks like in order to help people understand their strengths and development gaps. For example, a technical company would develop core competencies relevant to specific technical skills (i.e., delivery related, interpersonal, and strategic) (Mirabile, 1997).

marketplace-connected skills and competencies central to current and future competitive advantages? Create an inventory to answer this question.

- *Apply a resource endowment lens to human capital needs assessment.* Once you have identified the skills and competencies your organization needs, look across the organization to identify areas within the organization where existing skills and competencies are superior or lacking (Haynie, 2016). Developing a needs assessment to inform a hiring strategy for the organization's veteran employment program helps bolster areas within the organization where the existing skill- and competency-based resource endowments are superior. Such an assessment is also helpful to identify and cultivate market-connected skills and competencies within the organization while also addressing gaps in these areas.
- *Revisit how your organization recruits and hires veterans.* Define and introduce a competency-based recruiting and selection process into your veteran hiring initiative. This includes a process based on recruiting and selecting for the behavioral qualities, experiences, and attributes that may bolster and enhance the existing competency-based resource endowments of the organization—particularly where those resource endowments are rare, valuable, and differentiated in the marketplace, relative to competitors. Such an approach will empower the employer to think beyond the veteran candidate's military-learned skills (military specialty) and accordingly introduce a lens to the recruiting and selection process that is strategically linked to improving the organization's veteran hiring program (Haynie, 2016).

## Talent Deployment and Development: Helping Veterans Flourish in the Workplace

In order to develop and retain veteran talent, it is important to have not only a strong veteran hiring and accommodation strategy, but also a plan in place to best utilize veterans working in the civilian world. In the context of the organization's veteran employment program, the objective of talent deployment—to arrange or move strategically and/or appropriately—should be to think and act beyond the traditional lens of person–job fit. Employers need to make purposeful choices to employ veterans within the organization to deploy veterans to occupy work roles and situations such that the rare, valuable, and differentiating attributes of veterans as a human capital resource may contribute uniquely toward achieving the organizational objectives of the organization (Haynie, 2016).

Thus, it is critically important that managers employ veteran talent consistent with opportunity. This effort is shown to be one of the most significant missteps in how some organizations approach veteran hiring initiatives (Haynie, 2016). Employers traditionally hire with the intent and objective of introducing and leveraging military-learned skills and competencies within the organization, but deploy veteran talent to work in roles and situations where those skills and abilities are not relevant or even appropriate (Haynie & Shepherd, 2011). To avoid such mismatches, the following strategies[4] create value for the company as well as for the veteran:

- *Focus relentlessly on alignment with the marketplace.* Deploy veterans within the organization to occupy work roles and situations so that their rare, valuable, and distinctive attributes are leveraged to contribute toward the organization's larger strategic goals and objectives.
- *Communicate meaning and purpose.* Veterans typically have a strong, intrinsic need to find meaning and purpose in their work—meaning and purpose are often what attracted them to military service in the first place. Continually and consistently reinforce how and why the veteran's work/role contributes to the performance objectives of the organization. The absence of meaning and purpose in work is one of the primary reasons veterans leave their first and second postservice civilian jobs (Maury & Stone, 2014). Accordingly, it is important to understand and consider the motivations and self-interests of the veteran when making decisions about the specific work role assigned to a veteran within the organization.
- *Provide early, frequent, and informal performance feedback.* Veterans expect this type of engagement, will be receptive to it, and often flounder without it. Veterans frequently report a lack of understanding related to workplace norms and customs, organizational reporting structures, and the basis for performance evaluation (Maury & Stone, 2014; Wernerfelt, 1984).
- *Be able to say what is next.* Veterans come to the civilian world of work with a propensity for high levels of organization commitment and often a military experience characterized by frequent role transitions

according to a plan made in advance for development. These attributes, when combined, play out in a civilian work environment as the need to understand how to develop a career path, as opposed to simply a job. Share with the veteran opportunities for further development, training, and certification and what may be opportunities to expand, move, re-purpose, or refocus as needed.

- *Set challenging goals.* Veterans are task oriented and maintain a high need for achievement. It is critical to link their performance goals to organizational objectives and to engage the veteran in the goal-setting process to help cultivate organizational commitment.
- *Identify exemplars.* Veterans are products of a military culture based, in part, on a role-modeling approach to professional development. Accordingly, veterans will naturally seek and act on opportunities to model their behaviors on organizational exemplars. As a supervisor, be transparent with the veteran employee about who they are and what makes them good examples of organizational exemplars.
- *Understand that potential and readiness are not the same.* The difference between an employee's potential and readiness boils down to fit and performance. Potential is simply having or showing the capacity to be-come or develop into something in the future, and readiness is showing that you are fully trained and/or prepared to perform. Thus, in regard to veterans transitioning into the workplace, take the time to develop and mentor high-preforming veterans. You can achieve this by looking at their skills and knowledge and helping them build on those skills within the organization, thus ensuring that they have the right mix of experi-ence, skills, and personal qualities to assume additional organizational responsibilities and leadership.
- *Recruitment and retention.* The best thing for any organization is to get the right people hired and then retain them. According to the U.S. Chamber of Commerce, roughly two thirds of veterans are likely to leave their first postmilitary job within 2 years because of problems like low job satisfaction and limited opportunities for advancement (Harris, 2009; Maury & Stone, 2014). Veterans blame the quick job changes on a lack of advancement opportunity in their offices, tedious work requirements, and finding that the job is a poor match with their mil-itary skills (Harris, 2009). These results show the need for employers to focus not only on veteran recruiting but also on ways to keep them. These results also show the need for hiring managers to better match

job requirements with veterans' qualifications to ensure they are not bored or underutilized in their civilian posts. Additionally, traditional employee incentives, including a big paycheck or a hefty bonus, while beneficial in the short term, is not a good way to retain a highly engaged employee in the long term.

## Hiring and Retaining Veteran Employees With Disabilities

Accommodating the needs of veterans, or any person with a disability, helps an employer create an environment in which all employees can perform their jobs efficiently and effectively. These accommodations also create a welcoming environment and set the tone of the organization's culture, policies, and structures, which, if positive, can lead to long-lasting employment (United States Equal Employment Opportunity Commission [EEOC], 2016). For more on this subject, see Chapter 7 in this book. By establishing policies ahead of time that will accommodate veteran employees, there is the added benefit of creating loyalty among civilian employees as well (National Council on Disability, 2007). More information on accommodating veterans with disabilities in organizations is found on the Job Accommodation Network (JAN) website at https://askjan.org/.

The Job Accommodation Network, known as JAN, is a service provided by the United States Department of Labor's Office of Disability Employment Policy. JAN facilitates the employment and retention of workers with disabilities by providing employers, employment providers, and people with disabilities, their family members, and other interested parties with information on job accommodations, entrepreneurship, and related subjects. JAN's efforts are in support of the employment, including self-employment and small business ownership, of people with disabilities.

A veteran's disabilities can include a variety of physical and mental conditions. If the veteran has selected to disclose this information, employers are required to accommodate the needs of the veteran, whether physical or mental health related (Americans with Disabilities Act of 1990, 2008). Veterans need only disclose if or when they need an accommodation to perform the essential functions of the job. Applicants are never required to disclose this information on a job application or in the job interview, unless they need an accommodation to assist them in the application or interview process. If disclosed, employers need to know what those needs are and what to do. The cost of accommodating a disabled worker is often less than $500, with many accommodations costing nothing if they just involve offering flexible schedules or the creative use of existing materials (Veterans and the Americans With Disabilities Act; EEOC, 2016). Some of the common disabilities that may require additional accommodations are post-traumatic stress disorder (PTSD), traumatic brain injury (TBI), amputation, hearing loss, and vision impairment.

## Employer Policies, Accommodations, and Strategies for Employees With Disabilities

Employer policies, accommodations, and strategies for employees with disabilities are presented in the following list[5]:

- *Allow for a flexible schedule.* Allowing the employee to have a flexible schedule is a reasonable accommodation. Whether the person has PTSD or TBI, is in a wheelchair, is an amputee, or otherwise affected, these accommodations give the employee the time needed to perform daily activities (i.e., personal care like bathing, getting dressed, commuting, coping with stress, etc.). This flexible work environment includes flexible schedule, telework as an option for employees, a modified break schedule, time to call or leave for doctor appointments or counseling, work from home or a flex place, or even distance travel for access to healthcare (EEOC, 2016; Hitt et al., 1998).
- *Help to enhance concentration.* The employer can help the veteran employee with concentration by reducing distractions in the work area. Providing space enclosures, sound absorption panels, or a private office can accomplish this;, as can allowing the use of white noise or environmental sound machines, allowing employees to play soothing music with a computer or music player, providing uninterrupted work time, and suppling organizers to reduce clutter. Additionally, studies show that increased natural lighting or full-spectrum lighting may also help increase concentration, along with schedulers, organizers, and email applications (Bergland, 2013). Dividing large assignments into smaller tasks or restructuring the job to include only essential functions are also helpful concentration tools.

- *Provide opportunities to work effectively with supervisors.* The relationship between employees and their supervisors is critical to the successful engagement and job performance of all employees, and employees with disabilities are no different (Wagner & Harter, 2006). Providing such things as positive praise and reinforcement, written job instruction, a procedure to evaluate the effectiveness of the accommodation, and clear expectations along with developing strategies to deal with problems before they arise allows for open communication and establishes written long- and short-term goals.
- *Have an awareness of the benefits of technology in the workplace.* The increasing importance of computers and new information technologies provides special benefits for workers with disabilities by helping compensate for physical or sensory impairments (e.g., using screen readers and voice-recognition systems), which substantially increases their productivity. Another study found that people with spinal cord injuries were able to find work and increase their earnings with computers (National Council on Disability, 2007).
- *Have an awareness of the growing attention paid to workplace diversity.* Most large corporations today have diversity programs, and a growing number are including disability as one of the criteria for a diverse workforce (National Council on Disability, 2007). For those coworkers who have not worked with people with disabilities, allowing them to voice questions or concerns goes a long way toward creating a receptive environment (Lengnick-Hall, 2007). For example, prior to the arrival of a new employee with a disability—or shortly after arrival—Microsoft provides opportunities for future coworkers to have their questions about disabilities addressed in an open and safe environment. In an effort to accommodate the growing workforce diversity, many managers put forth efforts to implement a universal design (i.e., the design of products and environments to be usable by all people, to the greatest extent possible regardless of their age, size, ability, or disability) (Center for Universal Design, 2020). Half of surveyed U.S. managers in one study foresaw universal design implementation as a way to (a) improve worker productivity and satisfaction, (b) promote flexibility in employment, and (c) reduce legal risks and workers' compensation claims (National Council on Disability, 2007; Schur & Kruse, 2002).
- *Offer benefits that employees with disabilities may appreciate.* Studies on pay show that the feeling of financial security—having a secure job—has

much more influence on overall well-being than the actual amount of income (Richard & Wilhite, 2006). For many veterans, and particularly those with disabilities, compensation can be essential, but benefits related to their family and their well-being could be more important. For veterans with disabilities, coverage and accommodations for service-connected injuries and caring for children or relatives could be critical. While many of these issues (i.e., caregiving, services, and coverage) are similar to issues faced by nonveterans, unlike their civilian counterparts, veterans may suffer disproportionately from PTSD, TBI, depression, or other physical and emotional issues related to their time in combat (Rudstam et al., 2012).

## Laying the Groundwork for Veteran Employee Success

To ensure veteran success in the workplace, employers need to prepare beyond hiring and recruiting initiatives and should consider veteran employees in their onboarding, retention and development, and disability accommodation processes. It is important to lay an organizational foundation in order to successfully deploy, develop, and capitalize on veteran talent and then ensure veteran success (Maury, Stone, Bradbard, Armstrong, & Haynie, 2016). The more prepared an organization is for *employing* veterans—as opposed to simply hiring them—the more the organization can reap the rewards from this valuable human capital resource (Barney, 1986; Hitt et al., 1998). What follows is a list of practical steps employers can take to ensure that veterans—and in turn, all employees—succeed before, during, and after they are hired. Note that the introduction of these policies and programs to help recruit and retain veteran employees will also provide benefits and help your organization recruit and retain nonmilitary employees as well.

- *Employee assistance program to include veterans.* Many employers who have successfully hired and retained veterans have worked veteran-specific policies and resources into their human resources departments, such as employee assistance programs (Box 2.2; National Council on Disability, 2007). If you take the time to figure this out for veterans, it will benefit nonveteran employees as well (e.g., disability programs will benefit nonveteran employees with disabilities as finding a mission that you can explain to your veteran employees will provide a sense of

---

### Box 2.2 Employee Assistance Programs

---

Employee assistance programs (EAPs) are benefit programs and practices offered by employers and communities and are intended to help employees and their families deal with personal problems that might adversely affect their work performance, health, and well-being. An EAP service is often free for a limited number of sessions to the employee and their family members and is prepaid by the employer or funded by state or federal grants. The cost of an EAP for your organization depends on the size of your employee population, estimated or actual rate of utilization, and the range of services included in your program. For small business owners looking for low-cost EAP services, less traditional routes may be an alternative. EAPs may be available through long-term disability or life insurance carriers or an association or group insurance line. Another possibility is to find a carrier that includes a set number of sessions and services.

The EAP counselors typically provide assessment, support, and referrals to additional resources for various issues, such as substance abuse; emotional distress; major life events (birth, death, and accident); healthcare support; eldercare; work/family relationships; and financial/legal assistance. Confidentiality is maintained in accordance with privacy laws and ethical standards.

Studies indicated that offering EAPs may result in a positive ROI because as a preventive measure, the employer is more likely to have lower medical costs, reduced turnover and absenteeism, and higher productivity (Attridge et al., 2010).

---

mission to all and help everyone understand how to work with different cultures).

- *Ensure effective onboarding.* From the moment the employee is hired, there should be a process in place to begin acclimating the veteran employee to the company. Many employers have a buddy system, which pairs new employees with a current employee who can help them navigate the transition. It is always beneficial to identify a learning partner or buddy for the new hire so they have an available resource other than their supervisor (Peer Advisors for Veteran Education ([AVE], 2017). The learning partner serves as a guide, providing assistance and camaraderie as the new employee becomes acclimated to the organizational culture. This relationship is particularly important for veterans who are reentering civilian life in corporate America. To the extent possible, leverage existing veteran employees in a mentorship role with new veteran hires because they understand their unique socialization challenges of reentering the civilian workplace (Box 2.3).

- *Create a structure for feedback.* Members of the military were used to receiving frequent feedback; therefore, it is beneficial to create a structure in your organizations where employees are evaluated at intervals of 30, 60, 90, and 120 days. At the end of day 1, the manager should have a brief informal check-in with the new veteran employee. This simple act demonstrates they care, that they want to hear from the individual, and helps set the stage for future communications. After 1 week on the job, there should be another check-in. At the 30-day benchmark, the new hire should be fully acclimated and acquainted with their job responsibilities. Discussion should focus on the accomplishment of short-term goals and laying the groundwork for longer term objectives. It is also a good time to assess the individual's satisfaction. At the 90-day benchmark, the new hire should have a thorough understanding of objectives and be well on their way to achieving results. Providing individual feedback on an employee's contributions, strengths, and areas for improvement goes a long way in retaining them. At the 120-day benchmark, it is helpful for the manager to conduct a full review of the employee's

---

**Box 2.3  Veteran Mentor Programs**

One example of a veteran mentor program is the Military Support Programs and Networks (M-SPAN) at the University of Michigan. Through their Buddy-to-Buddy Volunteer Veteran Program along with PAVE (Peer Advisors for Veteran Education), they support, assist, and provide resources. The philosophy behind the program is simple—Military service is unlike any other human experience. Because of this uniqueness, no one knows more about the issues facing a service member—in combat or on the home front—than a fellow member (M-SPAN, 2020). By establishing a system ahead of time, an employer may have more success in ensuring the employee (veteran or civilian) is brought up to speed as quickly and smoothly as possible.

goals, progress, and accomplishments. Revisiting the feedback shared during the 90-day discussion will help the manager assess whether the employee is on track and making progress in the areas identified. Another way to get employee feedback is through stay interviews, which are interviews with current employees that allow them to discuss the company and their jobs without a job, promotion, or raise on the line. The stay interview is an opportunity to build trust with employees and a chance to assess the degree of employee satisfaction and engagement that exists in a department or company (Heathfield, 2017). The results of a stay interview provide insights about what the organization can do to improve and help retain valued employees. The stay interview can be extremely effective to ensure that the employee is acclimating to the organization and position and feels valued. Informal evaluations are also helpful in that an employee can voice his or her constructive criticism.

- *Mentor programs for skills development.* Mentoring or peer-to-peer learning is one of the oldest methods of employee development. This type of learning seeks to develop an employee's capabilities by connecting them to the wisdom and experience that already exists within an organization. Effective behavioral learning incorporates modeling, practice, review, and refinement. Mentors model behavior or offer suggestions on what to do, allow the learner to practice doing it, and then provide feedback on their efforts so that the individual can refine future attempts (Lester, Hannah, Harms, Vogelgesang, & Avolio, 2011). Mentoring veterans is discussed in detail in Chapter N.

## Awareness Is Key to Hiring Veterans

Once an organization's hiring and onboarding policies are revised to maximize hiring qualified veterans, a human resources department can begin the search for veteran talent. Having an awareness of what it takes to hire and retain veterans will ensure enhanced job matching (matching a veteran's characteristics and abilities to the required skills of the job) and, in the end, contribute to the success of the veteran in the workplace. These examples of policies, processes, and structures are important for developing and maintaining all employees, but specifically benefit veterans—with or without service-connected disabilities. The most important thing to remember is that these programs need to be established at the organization *before* the hiring process. Creating a foundation for employee accommodation and assimilation that includes resources and services for veterans as well as feedback and evaluation schedules maximizes the potential of veteran employees by meeting them where they are at when they begin their relationship with the organization (Drucker, 2002).

## Conclusion

The choices that employers make about hiring, deploying, and developing veteran talent within organizations has profound and surprisingly predictable implications for the veteran and his or her family (Haynie, 2016; Haynie & Shepherd, 2011).

In order to accommodate the veteran job market, organizations must incorporate new tactics to attract, retain, and develop veteran employees. It is important to highlight that the employers that will benefit the most from veteran talent are those that have laid a foundation for the development of veteran employees by establishing conscientious employee resource programs with specific networking, acclimation, and disability accommodation goals as well as employee development programs. Successful veteran programs not only provide a space for veterans to bond over their shared experiences, but also allow veterans to speak on issues, educate each other, and connect with their civilian peers. In addition to the programs, employers must provide development opportunities, coaching or mentoring, and positive reinforcement that focuses on the value this group of people brings to the organization (Harris, 2009). Employee-centric policies, accommodations, and strategies will benefit not only veteran employees, but also all employees in the organization, resulting in increased retention, satisfaction, and employee development across the board.

In summary, hiring and retaining veterans is a two-way street. It is the responsibility of both the managers and their new veteran team members to be aware of each other, their respective environments, and/or perspectives. In order for this to occur, both sides need to be educated. Veterans need an awareness of the civilian job environment, and managers, recruiters, and leaders need information and education about the military culture along with an understanding of the advantages veterans bring to their companies. Veterans all over the country are looking for work, and employers all over the country have the opportunity to employ and retain them, but the two will only connect if each is equipped with the appropriate knowledge, tools, and strategies.

## Notes

1. With contributions from Nicholas J. Armstrong, PhD; Linda R. Euto, PhD; Rosalinda Maury, MS; and Kicia Sears, MPA.
2. IVMF publications include *The Business Case for Hiring a Veteran: Beyond the Clichés*; *Revisiting the Business Case for Hiring a Veteran: A Strategy for Cultivating Competitive Advantage*; *Veteran Employment Leading Practices: Tools for Engaging Talent Toolkit*; and *The Guide to Leading Policies, Practices & Resources: Supporting the Employment of Veterans and Military Families*. These and other publications are found at https://www. ivmf.syracuse.edu. RAND is a nonprofit institution that works to improve policy and decision-making through research and analysis. For more information, visit https:// www.rand.org.
3. The Work Opportunity Tax Credit covers veterans with disabilities but mentions nonveterans with disabilities as a target group if they are enrolled in specific rehabilitation programs. However, many states offer state-level deductions for workers with disabilities (veteran or not). The federal tax credits are for small businesses that need to update their facilities to accommodate disabilities. We include New York State only here as the laws vary across states.
4. Unless otherwise cited, list items are as they appear in *Revisiting the Business Case for Hiring a Veteran* (Haynie, 2016).
5. Unless otherwise cited, list items as they appear in *Guide to Leading Policies, Practices, & Resources: Supporting the Employment of Veterans & Military Families* (IVMF, 2013a).

## References

Americans With Disabilities Act of 1990, 42 U.S.C. §§ 12112. (2008). https://www.ada. gov/pubs/adastatute08.htm#top

Attridge, M., Amaral, T., Bjornson, T., Goplerud, E., Herlihy, P., McPherson, T., . . . Teems, L. (2010). The business value of EAP: A conceptual model. *EASNA Research Notes*, *1*(10). http://www.easna.org/documents/EASNAResearchNotesNo10ValueModel MAY2010102209.pdf

Barney, J. B. (1986, October). Strategic factor markets: Expectations, luck and business strategy. *Management Science, 32*(10), 1231–1241.

Baron, R. A. (2007, February). Opportunity recognition as pattern recognition: How entrepreneurs "connect the dots" to identify new opportunities. *Academy of Management Perspectives*, 104–119.

Bergland, C. (2013, June 5). Exposure to natural light improves workplace performance. *Psychology Today*. https://www.psychologytoday.com/blog/the-athletes-way/201306/ exposure-natural-light-improves-workplace-performance

Bradbard, D. A., Armstrong, N. A., & Maury, R. (2016, February). *Work after service: Developing workforce readiness and veteran talent for the future* (Workforce Readiness Briefs, Paper No. 1). Syracuse, NY: Syracuse University, Institute for Veterans and Military Families.

Brehmer, B. (1992, December). Dynamic decision making: Human control of complex systems. *Acta Psychologica, 81*(3), 211–241. http://www.sciencedirect.com/science/article/pii/000169189290019A

Center for Universal Design. (2020). *About UD: Universal design principles.* Raleigh, NC: NC State University, Center for Universal Design. https://projects.ncsu.edu/ncsu/design/cud/about_ud/udprinciples.htm

Chang, H. (2009, April 13). Simulators always valuable in military training. U.S. Army, Presidio of Monterey Public Affairs. https://www.army.mil/article/19599/simulators-always-valuable-in-military-training

Cohany, S. (1992, June). The Vietnam-era cohort: Employment and earnings. *Monthly Labor Review,* 3–15. https://www.bls.gov/mlr/1992/06/art1full.pdf

Drucker, P. (2002, August). Discipline of innovation. *Harvard Business Review, 80*(8), 95–103. https://hbr.org/2002/08/the-discipline-of-innovation

Godé-Sanchez, C. (2010). Leveraging coordination in project-based activities: What can we learn from military teamwork? *Project Management Journal, 41*(3), 69–78.

Goldberg, M., & Warner, J. (1987). Military experience, civilian experience, and the earnings of veterans. *Journal of Human Resources, 22*(1), 62–81.

Harrell, M. C., & Berglass, N. (2012, June). *Employing America's veterans: Perspectives from businesses.* Center for a New American Security. https://www.cnas.org/publications/reports/employing-americas-veterans-perspectives-from-businesses

Hardison, C., & Shanley, M. (2016). *Essential skills veterans gain during professional military training: A resource for leaders and hiring managers.* RAND. https://www.rand.org/pubs/tools/TL160z2-2.html

Harris, G. A. (2009). Recruiting, retention, and race in the military. *International Journal of Public Administration, 32*(10), 803–828.

Haynie, J. M. (2012, March). *The business case for hiring a veteran: Beyond the clichés.* Syracuse, NY: Institute for Veterans and Military Families, Syracuse University. https://ivmf.syracuse.edu/article/the-business-case-for-hiring-a-veteran-beyond-the-cliches/

Haynie, J. M. (2016, April). *Revisiting the business case for hiring a veteran: A strategy for cultivating competitive advantage* (Workforce Readiness Briefs, Paper No. 2). Syracuse, NY: Institute for Veterans and Military Families, Syracuse University. Retrieved from https://ivmf.syracuse.edu/wp-content/uploads/2016/06/IVMF_WorkforceReadinessPaper2_April16_Report2.pdf

Haynie, J. M., & Shepherd, D. (2011). Toward a theory of discontinuous career transition: Investigating career transitions necessitated by traumatic life events. *Journal of Applied Psychology, 96*(3), 501–524.

Heathfield, S. (2017, April 13). *What is a stay interview with employees in the workplace?* https://www.thebalance.com/what-is-a-stay-interview-1917998

Hitt, M. A. (2000). The new frontier: Transformation of management for a new millennium. *Organization Dynamics, 28*(No. 3), 6–18.

Hitt, M. A., Keats, B. W., & DeMarie, S. (1998, November). Navigating in the new competitive landscape building strategic flexibility and competitive advantage in the 21st century. *Academy of Management Executive, 12*(4), 22–42.

Institute for Veterans and Military Families (IVMF). (2013a, August). *Guide to leading policies, practices & resources: Supporting the employment of veterans and military families*. Syracuse, NY: Institute for Veterans and Military Families, Syracuse University. https://ivmf.syracuse.edu/article/guide-to-leading-policies-practices-resources-supporting-the-employment-of-veterans-and-military-families-2/

Institute for Veterans and Military Families (IVMF). (2013b, February). *Veteran employment leading practices. Tools for engaging talent*. Syracuse, NY: Institute for Veterans and Military Families, Syracuse University. http://toolkit.vets.syr.edu/

Institute for Veteran and Military Families (IVMF). (2015, December). *The employment situation of veterans: December 2015*. Syracuse, NY: Institute for Veterans and Military Families, Syracuse University. https://ivmf.syracuse.edu/article/employment-situation-of-veterans-december-2015/

Kleykamp, M. (2013). Unemployment, earnings, and enrollment among post 9/11 veterans. *Social Science Research, 42*, 836–851.

Lengnick-Hall, M. (2007). *Hidden talent: How leading companies hire, retain, and benefit from people with disabilities*. Westport, CT: Praeger.

Lester, P., Hannah, S., Harms, P., Vogelgesang, G., & Avolio, B. (2011). *Mentoring impact on leader efficacy development: A field experiment*. University of Nebraska-Lincoln, Management Department Faculty Publications, 80. http://digitalcommons.unl.edu/managementfacpub/80

Mangum, S., & Ball, D. (1987). Military skill training: Some evidence of transferability. *Armed Forces & Society Spring, 13*, 425–441.

Maury, R., & Stone, B. (2014). *Veteran job retention survey: Summary*. Institute for Veterans and Military Families. Retrieved from https://ivmf.syracuse.edu/article/veteran-job-retention-survey/

Maury, R., Stone, B., Bradbard, D. A., Armstrong, N. A., & Haynie, J. M. (2016). *Workforce Readiness Alignment: The relationship between job preferences, retention, and earnings* (Workforce Readiness Briefs, Paper No. 3). Syracuse, NY: Institute for Veterans and Military Families, Syracuse University. https://ivmf.syracuse.edu/wp-content/uploads/2017/10/WORKFORCE-READINESS-ALIGNMENT.pdf

McGeary, D. D. (2011). Making sense of resilience. *Military Medicine, 176*(6), 603–604.

Military Support Programs and Networks (M-SPAN). (2020). *Buddy to Buddy volunteer program*. http://m-span.org/programs-for-service-members/buddy-to-buddy/

Mirabile, R. J. (1997, August). Everything you wanted to know about competency modeling. *Training & Development, 51*(8), 73–77.

National Center for Post-Traumatic Stress Disorder. (2012, April 6). *What it means to be mission-oriented*. Veterans Employment Toolkit [Handout]. https://va.gov/vetsinworkplace/docs/em_missionOriented.html

National Council on Disability. (2007). *Empowerment for Americans with disabilities: Breaking barriers to careers and full employment*. Washington, DC: National Council on Disability. https://ncd.gov/publications/2007/Oct2007

Peer Advisors for Veteran Education (PAVE). (2017). *Our program*. http://m-span.org/pave/our-program

Phillips, P. (2002). *The bottom line on ROI, basics, benefits, & barriers to measuring training and performance improvement*. Atlanta, GA: CEP Press.

Richard, B., & Wilhite, A. (2006). Military experience and training effects on civilian wages. *Applied Economics, 22*(1), 1–25.

Rudstam, H., Gower, W., & Cook, L. (2012). Beyond yellow ribbons: Are employers prepared to hire, accommodate, and retain veterans with disabilities? *Vocational Rehabilitation, 36,* 87–95.

Schur, L., & Kruse, D. (2002, Aug). *Non-standard work arrangements and disability income.* Champaign, IL: Disability Research Institute, College of Applied Life Studies, University of Illinois at Urbana-Champaign. http://dri.illinois.edu/research/p01-03c/final_technical_report_p01-03c.pdf

United States Army Combined Arms Center. (2020). Home page. http://usacac.army.mil/

United States Department of Labor, Bureau of Labor Statistics. (2017). *Employment status of persons 18 years and over by veteran status, age, and sex* (Table 48). https://www.bls.gov/cps/cpsaat48.htm

United States Department of Veterans Affairs. (2020). *Veterans Opportunity to Work: For employers.* http://www.benefits.va.gov/vow/for-employers.asp

United States Equal Employment Opportunity Commission (EEOC). (2016). *Veterans and the Americans With Disabilities Act (ADA): A guide for employers.* Washington, DC: Author. https://www.eeoc.gov/eeoc/publications/ada_veterans_employers.cfm

Veterans Job Mission. (2020). *About the mission.* https://www.veteranjobsmission.com/about-the-mission

Wagner, R., & Harter, J. (2006). *The elements of great managing.* New York, NY: Gallup Press.

Wenger, J., Pint, E., Piquado, T., Shanley, M., Beleche, T., Bradley, M., . . . Curtis, N. (2017). *Helping soldiers leverage army knowledge, skills, and abilities in civilian jobs.* Santa Monica, CA: RAND. https://www.rand.org/pubs/research_reports/RR1719.html

Wernerfelt, B. (1984, April). A resource-based view of the firm. *Strategic Management Journal, 5*(2), 171–180.

Zoli, C., Maury, R., & Fay, D. (2015, November). *Missing perspectives: Service members' transition from service to civilian life—Data-driven research to enact the promise of the post-9/11 GI Bill.* Syracuse, NY: Institute for Veterans and Military Families, Syracuse University. https://ivmf.syracuse.edu/article/missing-perspectives-servicemembers-transition-from-service-to-civilian-life/

# 3

# Messaging and Branding to Engage Veterans as Employees

*Peter A. Gudmundsson*

The two essential and mutually dependent foundations of any veteran hiring initiative are branding and engagement—in other words, making the case for why a veteran would want to work for your organization and then engaging with actual high-quality veterans to establish meaningful dialogues. The most compelling set of career opportunities for veterans is meaningless if they are not presented to qualified veteran talent. Likewise, one may encounter veterans physically in person or digitally, but if the recruiter has nothing of value to offer these veterans, such efforts are a waste of time and resources.

## Effective Messaging to Veterans: The Veteran-Friendly Employer Brand

In a seller's market for talent, the operative question is, why should a veteran job seeker accept a job with your company? The first-pass answer to that question is known as the employer's brand. Like any brand, there are components of a value proposition that must be addressed in such a way it resonates with the target audience. If the employer's brand resonates with job seekers, the task of talent acquisition and hiring managers is greatly simplified and enhanced. Perceptive employers know that military veterans often are a key piece to the puzzle of their continuing struggle to attract and retain high-quality talent. Managers understand that military-experienced personnel possess attitudes and abilities beyond those of most people who have not served. Thus, compared to nonveteran employees, veterans can add disproportionate value to any team or organization. Among these assets are mission orientation, ability to work with cross-functional teams, and dealing

Peter A. Gudmundsson, *Messaging and Branding to Engage Veterans as Employees* In: *Military Veteran Employment*. Edited by: Nathan D. Ainspan and Kristin N. Saboe, Oxford University Press. © Oxford University Press 2021. DOI: 10.1093/oso/9780190642983.003.0004 with stress and high standards of personal conduct like discipline, courtesy, and resilience (e.g., Haynie, 2016; Manner et al., 2017).

But as veteran unemployment dropped to historic lows in 2019 following nearly a decade of reductions in veteran unemployment, hiring managers found themselves competing aggressively for this superior talent pool. To compete effectively, companies now needed to ramp up their veteran hiring strategies. They also now must develop branding and outreach tactics that communicate clearly to veterans why their company's employment opportunities are worthy of consideration. At the core of this effort, companies had to understand what most veterans search for as they transition to their first or second civilian careers.

Fundamentally, veterans seek the same features in their careers as everyone else. But, two factors tend to set veterans apart. One factor is the alacrity, focus, and dedication with which they seek these benefits. The other is that, due to their military experience, veterans tend to develop certain sets of needs that they would prefer to find in their employment. One way to conceptualize—and remember—this group of needs is the alliterative list of the "four Ms": mission, momentum, money, and mentorship. Successful recruiters and hiring managers will pay careful attention to these needs as they craft their veteran hiring and retention strategies so that companies that dependably and consistently deliver on the four Ms will find themselves assembling high-quality teams from America's finest talent pool of military veterans.

## Mission

It is no surprise that a military-experienced candidate would find immense satisfaction in joining an organization whose mission resonates with his or her personal values and aspirations. While some join the military to fund higher education goals (e.g., college or other degrees), adventure, or specific experiences, virtually all enlist or earn commissions (in the case of officers) with an inspiration that is rooted in some level of idealism. In 2018, RAND Corporation, a bipartisan think tank, conducted a study with the U.S. Army Recruitment Command to investigate why enlisted soldiers join the military (Helmus et al., 2018). Enlisted soldiers in the study indicated the following top five motivators (participants could choose all that that applied to their motivation to enlist): adventure/travel (32 percent of respondents), benefits (25 percent), a call to serve (20 percent), job stability/pay (19 percent), and to leave a negative environment (17 percent). Notably, several of these motivators highlight the importance of pursuing mission, finding purpose, and seeking betterment through institutional affiliation and occupational commitment.

It follows that an organization that can make an authentic connection between its daily activities and a noble mission or higher purpose will better attract and retain veteran talent. The cause does not have to be especially dramatic or romantic. Not all companies can save an endangered species or cure a disease with their products or services. But companies that communicate with transparency and integrity in the execution of a worthy purpose will rise above others. For example, an airline might emphasize that it brings families together or a home improvement retailer that it allows consumers to realize their dreams about their dwellings.

In a report published in 2018 by BetterUp, a digital leadership development company, it was reported that 9 of 10 employees would exchange salary for purpose at work (Reece, Kellerman, & Robichaux, 2018). More specifically, the study found that, on average, the 2,285 American workers surveyed would give up 23 percent of their future earnings if it guaranteed they would always find meaning in their work. Workers who found meaning were retained in their jobs for longer and had lower turnover rates compared to employees who reported low meaning. Consumers of products, services, or employment opportunities, whether veterans or not, yearn for authenticity and purpose. Digital natives (those that have lived with advanced digital capabilities since birth) and those dating back to the millennial generation have grown up in a media-saturated world that enables a savvy perspective on perceived authenticity (Fromm & Garton, 2013). These modern workers can spot a fake from miles away when it comes to inauthentic or empty motives. They will avoid an organization that smacks of inauthenticity without compunction. Soft drink companies have been criticized for selling their products as components of a healthy lifestyle when sugary and diet sodas actually contribute to obesity. In other instances, companies have tried to associate themselves with political progressivism while engaging in employment or environmental practices that are antithetical to those ideals.

Some veterans have experienced combat, and all have endured screening and training experiences that have matured them and sensitized them to the important things in life. The upside of this orientation is their dedication and determination when bought into a cause. The downside is that an organization that just does not seem relevant will sustain little appeal for the veteran applicant or employee. Like the military, companies need to empha-size the relevance, authenticity, meaning, and importance of what they do in order to expect "buy-in" from its team members. When they are clear in the communication and exercise of those factors, powerful cohesion is the result.

## Momentum

After 3 to 20 or even more years in uniform, no veteran wants to experience a step back in his or her next job or career progression. Too often, veterans fear that they will enter the civilian world some notches below their current stations or level of authority or responsibility. Often, this is just a matter of perception, but more often it is a result of the rigidity of civilian employers' career progression ladders or inflexible culture. For instance, many military officers who are the formally titled senior managers and executives within the military, on leaving the military may assume that a parallel role in the civilian sector is one of "manager." However, this may not always be the case, particularly if the individual is moving to a role requiring a different know-ledge or skill set given a new context or role. If the latter, the former military officer may move into a nonmanagerial role while they learn their new con-text and skill set. In other cases, an officer may consider moving into an "ex-pert" role in which they are a consultant and not a manager. Both instances illustrate that military-to-civilian jobs are not one for one and thus require looking at civilian job descriptions with a fresh perspective and not through the lens of military rank and file.

Effective employers will examine their hiring practices to see that due credit is assigned for military experience, even when the nature of the work is not precisely that of the new role. The careful crafting of job descriptions should be inclusive of and accommodate military experience and educa-tion. For example, too many organizations insist on a candidate's posses-sion of a bachelor's degree when they really mean that they wish to attract "someone who finishes stuff they start and can write and communicate well." Why is it that a company will value a bachelor's degree as an essential prerequisite when a 4-year enlistment experience is a far better experience of maturation, personal growth, and education? Likewise, success in most jobs is a matter of getting a few key skills right and then combining that competency with general soft skills like getting along with people, being reliable, and displaying honesty (soft skills are discussed in greater detail in Chapter 6).

In 2016, RAND Corporation published a report (Hardison & Shanley) that included a tool for translating nontechnical skills acquired by military service members into essential skills in the civilian labor market. This report is a good reference for providing examples and specific nontechnical skills translation for bridging the military-to-civilian skill language gap when crafting a job description that will appeal to a diverse audience that includes military. Too many companies publish multipage "wish list" job descriptions not even the most promising applicant (and especially a recently transitioned veteran) can fulfill. Like any good writing, it often takes concentrated thought and careful drafting to create a job description that is accurate, helpful, and open-minded. Many military experiences help generate competencies in soft skills that supplement hard skills gained through technical training. In the armed forces, the culture prescribes that people finish what they start because they must do so. And good communication skills are essential when lives are at stake in urgent situations. These soft skills translate into potentially more effective individual and team performance and also define soft skills often necessary to progress in a career.

## Money

All employees desire and deserve to be paid fairly for their contributions and labor. The challenge with veterans comes from their lack of understanding of their market value. Indeed, the very notion of market value can seem strange to transitioning veterans who come from a world of fixed "time-and-grade" pay scales that place importance on seniority and rank above demonstrated competence, actual value created, and reliability. Education and transparency from employers, therefore, are the keys for veterans to make sense of civilian compensation arrangements. Veterans need to understand the relationships among contribution, value, and pay and benefits. Employers who effectively lift the veil of secrecy regarding compensation paths and progressions will find that veterans appreciate the direction and clarity in an area that might otherwise baffle them.

Patience is also required to inform veterans about the civilian cost of living once benefits like paid housing, healthcare, and subsistence have expired. For instance, service members typically only pay federal tax on their base pay but do not pay taxes on their meal and housing allowances or healthcare. The result is that when a paycheck in a civilian role includes all of these things together, a veteran may suddenly realize that a higher tax bracket means significantly more of their take-home pay goes to taxes compared to their time in the military. Recently transitioned veterans may also have little experience with state or city income tax rates and may, again, overestimate their take-home pay by not factoring in the costs of paying these additional taxes that they previously did not have to pay. Though most veterans are savvy when it comes to innovatively completing tasks, they may not be savvy when it comes to negotiating salary and benefits. Employers must be ethically responsible in such circumstances to assist veterans in establishing fair salaries and benefits during and after the hiring process to avoid taking advantage of veterans with notable work experience but potentially underdeveloped senses of job and skill worth.

## Mentorship

While civilians speak of management and sometimes avoid the term *leadership*, military members spend much of their service years in the study and practice of the latter art. Most adhere to a simple, but admittedly aspirational, definition of leadership. Aspirational leadership in this sense refers to an ideal widely believed in but not frequently achieved due to context or other factors in real life. In many ways, military culture dictates that to ascend the ranks within the military is to achieve greater and greater leadership experience and capabilities. Veterans tasked as leaders are trained to both accomplish their assigned mission and take care of their people. This dedication to the needs of team members can sometimes be lacking in a civilian environment solely dedicated to profit or other arbitrary operating metrics. That environment can seem coldly devoid of human purpose or connection compared to the military's emphasis on mission and purpose.

The ideal and expectation of military leadership is high. And while some commissioned and noncommissioned officers do not live up to these ideals on duty because they have been taught how to be a leader and experienced good leadership in their military roles, many veterans still expect some level of genuine leadership in their next civilian job that does live up to their ideals of leadership in others. Many perceive that this coexistence of idealism—found through mission and purpose—and cynicism, brought about by the realities of hard work and potentially time in combat, with little apparent contradiction is what defines the veteran experience.

Competitive employers will take leadership development seriously and dedicate resources to affirmative cultural development. As a rule, veterans expect leaders to "care for" their charges. This means inquiring about their welfare, showing interest in their personal lives, and standing up for them within the chain of command as necessary. There are multiple leadership styles that can be effective with veterans. Some civilians incorrectly assume that veterans need excessive structure or conversely more delegation and discretion. The truth is that situational leadership principles apply to all management scenarios whether the team is composed of veterans or not and that veterans can appreciate and thrive under less-structured or other leadership styles.

## Organizational Justifications for Hiring Veterans

With a greater sense of what veterans may seek in their careers, the veteran hiring leader must next consider what the organization hopes to accomplish from accessing the veteran talent pool. Effective and authentic branding derives from a clear understanding of the "why" that underlies the decision to hire veterans. Typically, the organizational justification for hiring veterans falls into one or more of four categories. These are (a) genuine talent acquisition, (b) idealism or service, (c) compliance, and (d) appearances. Sometimes, different managers may have varying motivations within the context of the overall organization's goals. For example, a chief executive officer may be driven by an idealistic sense of giving back, a front-line manager is seeking defined skill sets and the marketing or public relations vice president likes the "look" of being veteran friendly.

## Need for Quality Talent

Of the four underlying motivations for supporting veteran hiring, the genuine need for high-quality talent is the most enduring and sustainable. Companies that understand the skills, attitudes, and experiences that predict success in their environments often dedicate considerable resources to veteran hiring because they know it works. These are the companies that most "get it" and reap the highest rewards. This genuine economic understanding of the power of veteran hiring will permeate the employer's brand and infuse it with a sense of authenticity. A concrete example is a railroad company that knows from decades of experience that some of its best skilled tradespeople come from the military. They can prove, with data and experience, that military selection and experience screens for and teaches industrial safety mindsets, trainability, and respect for protocol.

## Idealism

Idealism or passion for national and community service can also fuel organizational demand for veteran hiring. Whether based on sense of service mutuality (of wanting to serve those who served the nation) or a well-intentioned if misinformed sense that veterans need extra help transitioning, many organizations hire veterans because it is the "right thing to do." There are practical limits to the ability of idealism to conjure resources and sustained commitment, but it does provide a strong emotional starting point for the creation of a veteran hiring initiative. The risk is that reliance on idealism as a justification for veteran hiring can slip into support for a "veterans-as-victims" orientation that is both inaccurate and harmful to veterans and organizations alike.

## Compliance

Compliance motivates organizations to hire veterans. Companies that earn federal contracts must comply with government regulations that govern the hiring of veterans (e.g., in order to earn the federal contracts, your company's workforce must be a certain percentage veterans). De facto quotas for veteran hiring focus the efforts of human resources professionals on the need to succeed or at least display documented efforts in hiring veterans. This is part of the reason why veteran hiring often falls under the diversity and inclusion efforts of a given company.

## Appearance

Finally, and most cynically, organizations try to hire veterans because they like the appearance of being veteran friendly. This does not mean that their intentions are insincere, but it can lead to decisions that serve the needs of neither the company nor veterans. An observed practice in the marketplace is that some lazy companies will post a few jobs on veteran websites or add a page to their website and think they are covered regarding being veteran friendly. It is not surprising when these organizations report disappointing returns on these marginal efforts. Especially irksome to veterans is when companies use military-themed stock photography that is inaccurate or offensive. It is all too common, for example, to see images that purport to display veteran support but actually contain actors with uniform errors, hairstyles out of regulation, or weapons that are not even part of the American arsenal. Like sensitivity to any other diversity category, it is better to be silent or inactive than to display the ignorance or carelessness of your organization. If you do want messaging that speaks specifically to veterans through imagery, lexicon, and other mechanisms, be sure it is accurate. This can be done by leveraging the expertise of veterans currently working for the organization or consulting with outside military organizations with deep knowledge of military culture and protocols (e.g., local veteran service organizations [VSOs]).

## Recruiting Veterans

### Metrics and Success

Having made the effort to understand both what veterans seek and the underlying organizational mandate for veteran hiring, companies that follow best practices will define clearly what success looks like and the metrics that will quantify that success. In military parlance, this is known as the desired end state. Company leaders should be able to finish the sentence, "After this effort, our veteran hiring program will result in $X$ number of new veteran hires per month or year with a 1-year retention rate of $Y$ percent." Company leaders should also be able to clearly state why they are hiring veterans (e.g., which skills or traits they value and want to add to their workforce). Such clarity of desired outcome will help define the resources required and fine-tune how they are allocated. If the worth of your career offerings and talent needs are clear, you are ready to test the offering with actual veterans. The next step is the communication of your organization's career value proposition to the appropriate veteran audiences in the appropriate place and time.

## Engagement

Armed with a clear sense of why your organization seeks to hire veterans and what benefits veterans might derive from your association, you are ready to test this message with current veterans or future veterans. Before devising a veteran talent engagement strategy, you first need to understand the dimensions of time and place. Regarding timing, organizations need to decide if they wish to target transitioning personnel or civilian-experienced veterans. There are benefits to either strategy but they offer distinct challenges and opportunities. Then, organizations need to determine what mix of in-person, traditional media or digital engagement is both desirable and effective.

## Pre- or Posttransition Veterans?

A key strategic decision is whether to target veterans before they transition out of uniform or after they have moved to a destination city or even held one or more civilian jobs. For those inexperienced with veteran hiring, this decision is very much like college recruiting. Some companies believe that supporting robust on-campus recruiting efforts allow them to access fresh talent and mold it to their organizational needs. Others conclude that college students rarely know where they fit in the world and prefer to pick up "second-move" employees. A college graduate with 2 years' experience will often arrive with maturity and insight that was unavailable previously. One advantage of pretransition veteran recruiting is that the audiences are aggregated to a discrete number of military bases and locations. The downside is that on separation most of these individuals will scatter across the country and return to their hometowns or other desired locations. The messages will be different whether one seeks pre- or posttransition veterans, but the media and methods are similar. When considering veteran career fairs, for example, some will seek to recruit on a military installation and others will prefer destination cities.

## Messaging Veterans

From my company's experiences working with thousands of veterans, we have seen that in general one characteristic of the American experience throughout generations is the curious coexistence of idealism and cynicism within each veteran. They will get goosebumps during the national anthem, but snicker at the poorly or inauthentically reasoned appeal to patriotism by a vendor or politician. Veterans are fiercely loyal and yet skeptical of overt claims of the same from brand or cause. Therefore, employer brands ought to go light on "eagles, flags, and liberty bells" when it comes to imagery and focus more on honest descriptions and low-key imagery. From our anecdotal experiences serving veterans, we have seen that veterans can sniff a fake and are instead attracted to plain speaking and authenticity.

Therefore, we recommend that your organizations should appeal directly to the underlying logic for why a certain company is a good fit for veterans. Again, this is the reason why veteran hiring organizations need to be clear as to their "why" when it comes to hiring veterans. We have seen that, despite the hype around these types of awards, veterans are skeptical of ill-defined "best companies for veterans" lists and similar campaigns in the media. They know that the criteria are random, and that they primarily support advertising-based business models. There is nothing wrong with partici-pating in such efforts, but a company should not expect to generate massive amounts of goodwill because it moved from number 31 to 29 on a "military-friendly" list. Such lists are seemingly popular among human resource executives because they provide a metric internal to a company, however imperfectly. When one reads the fine print on these award announcements, they recognize that selection is almost arbitrary or tied to consumer activity like the purchase of magazine advertising.

## Veteran Events

In-person encounters with veterans are a key tool for organizations that hire veterans. Career fairs, hiring conferences, and opportunity expos all allow recruiters, hiring managers, and veterans to interact and engage in a conver-sational manner. By simply talking, these parties can discover areas of mu-tual interest and fit. Remember that for most veterans, like college students, the largest challenge for job hunting is "opportunity awareness." This is to say that many veterans do not know what they want to do with their careers be-cause they do not know what is out there.

When selecting veteran career fairs, be sure that the event producer is ex-perienced and data driven. An effective veteran career fair producer should be able to present attendance statistics (e.g., number of candidates; rank, service, and Military Occupational Specialty or the job held by a military member) by candidate; names of employers who attended; and references from other employers and candidates. The event producer should also be transparent regarding their candidate aggregation strategy. How do they attract candidates to the events? What mix of media and proprietary candidate database do they use? Many veteran career fairs are promoted by well-meaning but ineffective nonprofits and government agencies that believe in the "build it and they will come" approach. Many of these events are free to employers, but one quickly learns that when calculated on a cost-per-impression or -hire basis, you get what you pay for. In recent years, virtual career fairs have emerged as a tool to transcend distance for candidate and employers. Some find these online chats to be useful to at least start a dialogue with groups of veteran candidates. Finally, sponsorship is a way to amplify one's presence at a veteran career fair. An employer seeking to make an impression might sponsor a veteran career fair in a city to raise its profile through pre- and postevent emails, signage, and event giveaways.

## Digital Advertising

Since the late 1990s, digital online advertising in the form of job postings, banner advertising, e-newsletters, and dedicated veteran hiring websites have claimed a large percentage of recruiting budgets. Many companies will post their open jobs with veteran-centric job boards both for applicant flow and Office of Federal Contract Compliance Programs compliance. "Post-and-pray" alone is a notoriously ineffective strategy by itself, but posting the job vacancy remains an important component of any veteran hiring engagement strategy. Banner ads have yielded fewer effective results in recent years, although retargeting and other sophisticated techniques can boost cost-per-hire impressions. E-newsletters allow employment advertising to arrive in a veteran's email inbox, usually in the presence of other jobs that may be of interest. Finally, "microsites" or dedicated veteran hiring portals within the employer's web presence are a great way to demonstrate in one place the employer's value proposition for veterans. Some examples of microsites include

https://jobs.carmax.com/career-development/military-commitment/
https://assets.recruitmilitary.com/Walgreens/

https://www.burgerim.com/burger-franchise/franchise-opportunities-
for-veterans/

## Targeted Email Campaigns and Databases

Some veteran employers maintain, often at great expense, proprietary databases of veteran talent. The good ones can slice that talent base and sell access via database subscriptions and target email campaign products. For example, an aerospace company may seek trained Air Force, Navy, or Army radar technicians who live within 50 miles of Chicago's O'Hare International Airport. The company might purchase an email campaign to target just those 37 relevant candidates with a very specific hiring need. Likewise, a trucking company might mine the database to find transportation-trained veterans from any service to serve as drivers or mechanics.

## Publicity and Social Media

As with any brand activity, word of mouth is an important component for employment brand advertising for veterans. It is critical that employers develop a content strategy to support their branding efforts. Social media and publicity via traditional print, online, and broadcast media provide opportunities to amplify these messages. Employers must leverage success stories that resonate with veterans. For example, a case study of how former Sergeant Smith's experience of leaving the Army, joining XYZ company, and now is employed as a territory manager can provide "I can do that too" pathways to other qualified veterans. Facebook, Twitter, LinkedIn, and even Snapchat can be powerful internet-based tools. Remember that veterans are members of the larger population like any other. They carry smartphones and their own computers. Reach them where they live, in the digital as well as physical worlds.

## Philanthropy

A final area where companies can develop their brand and engage with veterans is through philanthropy. Organizations that wish to raise their profile with veterans can do so by supporting causes that are dear to the military community. This is not always the most efficient way of engaging with veteran talent, but it can be satisfying. There are thousands of VSOs. One must be careful, however, to support credible charities because charities are not all equal in terms of effectiveness or reputation. Public support of the wrong VSOs can call into question the sincerity or insightfulness of a given patron. BBB Wise Giving Alliance (https://www.give.org), Charity Watch (https://www.charitywatch.org), and Charity Navigator (https://www. charitynavigator.org) provide useful perspectives and data on VSOs.

## Summary

For years, corporate recruiters have been predicting and discussing the presently termed "war for talent." When high rates of unemployment are a reality, employers can be more selective when hiring because there are more potential applicants. However, with low rates of unemployment, employers must sharpen their game if they wish to win. Since veteran talent is such a key component to an enlightened talent acquisition strategy, any serious veteran hiring effort will pay careful and consistent attention to the branding and engagement. The key to success is understanding the "why" a company should hire a veteran before executing the "how" by answering these questions:

- Why would veterans want to work for your organization?
- Why does your organization want to hire veterans?
- Do you want transitioning or civilian-experienced veterans?
- How will you engage with veterans so that they may experience your employer's value proposition?
- How will you retain veterans within your organization and make them your brand's champion?

Hiring veterans well is like anything else in that clarity of thought leads to clarity of action. If an organization gets these large questions right, the small executional steps will take care of themselves. All organizations need great talent, and hiring our military veterans is a great way to engage and hire the best.

# References

Fromm, J., & Garton, C. (2013). *Marketing to millennials: Reach the largest and most influential generation of consumers ever.* New York, NY: American Management Association.

Hardison, C. M., & Shanley, M. G. (2016). *Essential skills veterans gain during professional military training: A resource for veterans and transitioning service members.* Santa Monica, CA: RAND. https://www.rand.org/pubs/tools/TL160z3-1.html

Haynie, J. M. (2016). *Revisiting the business case for hiring a veteran: A strategy for cultivating competitive advantage* (Workforce Readiness Briefs, Paper No. 2). Syracuse, NY: Institute for Veterans and Military Families, Syracuse University. https://ivmf.syracuse.edu/wp-content/uploads/2018/11/Revisiting-Business-Case-for-Hiring-a-Veteran-Full-Report.pdf

Helmus, T. C., Zimmerman, S. R., Posard, M. N., Wheeler, J. L., Ogletree, C., Stroud, Q., & Harrell, M. C. (2018). *Life as a private: A study of the motivations and experiences of junior enlisted personnel in the U.S. Army.* Santa Monica, CA: RAND. https://www.rand.org/pubs/research_reports/RR2252.html

Manner, R., Harris, S., Blazek, E. S., & Kabins, A. (2017). *Debunking myths in veteran hiring.* Los Angeles, CA: Korn Ferry Institute. https://www.kornferry.com/content/dam/kornferry/docs/article-migration/VeteransMay2017.pdf

Reece, A., Kellerman, G., & Robichaux, A. (2018). *Meaning and purpose at work.* San Francisco, CA: BetterUp. https://get.betterup.co/rs/600-WTC-654/images/betterup-meaning-purpose-at-work.pdf

# 4

# Employer Misconceptions of Veterans and Veteran Misconceptions of Employers

*Eric Eversole*

In 2011, veterans' unemployment in the United States had increased to record high levels: While the total veteran unemployment rate languished at 8.3 percent, veterans of the Gulf War era age 18 to 24 years experienced an unemployment rate of 29.1 to 30.2 percent for men and 36.1 percent for women (Bureau of Labor Statistics, 2012). By comparison, the nonveteran unemployment rate in 2011 was 3.6 percent (Bureau of Labor Statistics). Young men and women returning from military service were getting stuck on the sidelines, unable to find employment and take this most important step back into the civilian world.

In response to these unemployment numbers, the U.S. Chamber of Commerce launched the Hiring Our Heroes (HOH) initiative in March 2011. It immediately sprang into action, working closely with a wide array of private and public sector partners. HOH is now a nationwide, grassroots initiative that helps veterans, transitioning service members, and military spouses find meaningful employment. Through private and public partnership, HOH developed these tools to help employers, transitioning service members, and veterans make the employment connection:

- *The Employer Roadmap* (https://www.vetemployerroadmap.org) to help civilian employers connect with and hire veterans
- *Veteran FastTrack* (https://vetfasttrack.org) to help veterans explore careers and help connect them with employers
- *The Veteran Employment Transition Roadmap* (https://vetroadmap.org), which provides resources for veterans' transition into civilian employment
- *The Resume Engine* (https://resumeengine.org), which helps veterans with drafting their civilian résumés

Eric Eversole, *Employer Misconceptions of Veterans and Veteran Misconceptions of Employers* In: *Military Veteran Employment.* Edited by: Nathan D. Ainspan and Kristin N. Saboe, Oxford University Press. © Oxford University Press 2021. DOI: 10.1093/oso/9780190642983.003.0005

- *Career Spark* (https://mycareerspark.org), which connects military spouses with employers

In 8 years, 2011–2019, HOH helped more than 31,000 veterans and military spouses find employment and organized the HOH campaign, which led to more than 2,000 companies committing to hire 710,000 veterans and military spouses. As HOH began to see the positive impact of its work, the mission shifted from one of helping unemployed veterans and military spouses to a more strategic effort of finding the best long-term employment opportunities for veterans and their families. Over the last few years, HOH has learned much about the veterans it serves, their perceptions and understanding of corporate America, and how those perceptions and understandings impact interactions as veterans and their family members search for meaningful career opportunities.

## Who Are the Veterans?

Neither of my parents went to college. Like many working-class parents, they offered their son two options to get ahead in life: go to college or join the military. My story is not uncommon for many young service members—a vast majority of whom are looking for better opportunities in life. Knowing and understanding this audience is critical to a company's successful veteran recruitment strategy.

Let's start with the basics: Though the military is ethnically diverse, it is much younger and more male than the rest of the American population given that only 14 percent of America's youth (19 percent of the men and 8 percent of the women) have any interest in serving in the military ( U.S. Department of Defense Joint Adverting Market Research and Studies, 2017). According to the Department of Defense (U.S. Department of Defense Office of the Deputy Assistant Secretary of Defense for Military Community and Family Policy, 2019) men make up about 84 percent of our armed forces across all branches—the percentage being lower in the Air Force and higher in the Marine Corps. Among active duty service members, 52 percent are 25 years or younger; the average age of active duty service members is 28.2 years old, with the average age of enlisted members at 26.9 years old, and the average officer at 34.4 years old. (To clarify, enlisted personnel make up 82 percent of those on active duty and are the rank-and-file members working in hundreds of roles. Experienced, more senior, enlisted personnel are also known as noncommissioned officers. Warrant officers are highly skilled technical and tactical experts. Commissioned officers are well-schooled managers who lead groups of troops from hundreds to thousands.) There are 31 percent of active duty members who self-identify as a member of a minority group (33 percent of the enlisted members and 24 percent of the officers). Service members are also more educated than the civilian population: 81 percent of the active duty members possess at least a high school diploma or some college experience, and 85 percent of their officers have at least a bachelor's degree or higher. Another review of the active duty population found that 98 percent of the individuals joining active duty have at least a high school education (U.S. Department of Defense Office of the Under Secretary of Defense, Personnel and Readiness [DoD P&R], 2019).

Socioeconomic status and geography also play an important role in the composition of the military (DoD P&R, 2019). Of all U.S. military recruits in 2018, the Southern states contributed a disproportionate number of members to the military, while the Northeastern states contributed fewer members: In percentages, 46 percent of the members came from the South, while it hosts 38 percent of the nation's 18- to 24-year-old citizens; the Northeast contributed 12 percent to the military force but hosts 17 percent of the nation's 18- to 24-year-old members. Table 4.1 shows the representation ratio for each state (which is calculated by dividing the state's number of new members to the military divided by the total accessions), which is then divided by the population share of the state's 18- to 24-year-old population (e.g., a ratio number

**Table 4.1** States Contributing the Most and Fewest Service Members

| Highest Percentage States | | Lowest Percentage States | |
| --- | --- | --- | --- |
| State | Ratio | State | Ratio |
| South Carolina | 1.54 | District of Columbia | 0.26 |
| Hawaii | 1.40 | North Dakota | 0.45 |
| Alabama | 1.35 | Vermont/Minnesota/ South Dakota/Iowa | 0.61 |
| Florida | 1.41 | Massachusetts | 0.57 |
| Georgia | 1.40 | Rhode Island | 0.59 |

*Source*: DoD P&R (2019).

of 1 implies that the state's share of new military members is equal to its share of the 18- to 24-year-old population, a number above 1 implies that the state is overrepresented in the military, and a number below 1 implies an under-representation of that state). The states that contribute the most and fewest members by percentage are listed in Table 4.1.

Military recruits also tend to come from working-class families and neighborhoods. The DoD found that new members to the military came from the middle range of the socioeconomic groups of the United States (DoD P&R, 2019). Looking at census-tract median household income data, new military members were underrepresented in the census tracts, with the lowest and highest median scores, while the middle three quintiles were overrepresented in the population of members joining the military. (Note that individuals from the lower socioeconomic neighborhoods may not meet the educational and other requirements of the military and would not be able to serve.)

Given their socioeconomic status, it is not surprising that most recruits join the military searching for greater economic opportunities. As Lutz (2008) noted,

> Those with lower family income are more likely to join the military than those with higher family income. Thus, the military may indeed be a career option for those for whom there are few better opportunities. For such enlistees, military service can open opportunities that would not otherwise be available. Indeed, research has found that military service often serves as a positive turning point in the career trajectories of enlistees from disadvantaged circumstances. (Lutz, 2008, p. 184)

Educational benefits and the pursuit of skill sets are two major reasons young Americans join military service. According to research conducted by the DoD, among young Americans (age 16 to 21) interested in joining the military, the reasons provided are listed in Table 4.2.

What does all of this mean? Military recruits come from a diverse set of backgrounds and regions of the country, though certain demographic trends certainly emerge. They have, at the very least, graduated from high school (or equivalent) and are motivated to find better lives through education and training. In other words, they are hard-working Americans looking for economic opportunity and pulling themselves up by the bootstraps to find that opportunity.

Table 4.2 Top Ten Reasons Service Members Join the Military

| Reason for Joining the Military | Percentage of 16- to 21-Year-Old Candidates |
| --- | --- |
| To pay for future education | 49 |
| Travel | 45 |
| Pay/money | 44 |
| To help others | 41 |
| Gain experience/work skills | 38 |
| Health and medical benefits | 32 |
| Experience adventure | 30 |
| It is my duty/obligation to my country | 28 |
| Pride/self-esteem/honor | 27 |
| Provides future job opportunities | 27 |

*Source*: JAMRS, 2017.

## Ships Passing in the Night

Motivation and skills, however, do not lead to automatic success—something most service members learn on transition out of the military. Understanding how to translate and apply military skills is particularly challenging for most veterans. This challenge is compounded by a hiring manager or recruiter's lack of familiarity with the military. The first few postmilitary job interviews can be frustrating and can become a disconnected experience for veterans, like two ships passing in the night.

According to a study sponsored by Prudential, "Nearly all [veterans] believe they have the skills needed to land their ideal job, but the majority express concerns about how to translate their skills to a business environment" (Prudential Financial, 2012, p. 3). Similarly, most veterans feel prepared for the job search, but almost half say they "need more help with multiple job search skills," such as networking. The Prudential study found that job-seeking veterans are most concerned with skills like networking, "closing" a job interview, and "selling" themselves to a potential employer. These needs reflect veterans' lack of familiarity with the job-hunting process.

Transitioning service members also may have unrealistic expectations about their first postmilitary job. A study conducted by the University of Southern California found that "almost all of the service providers interviewed described their veteran clients as lacking knowledge in the kind of jobs that would be available to them when they left the military" (Kintzle et al., 2015, p. 8). One provider explained "I think it has to do with the fact that a lot of times . . . the military [instills] a lot of confidence and so if [a newly discharged veteran] exits at an E7 or E8 [rank], . . . they come in with the expectation, 'Well, that's what I should be getting in the civilian world,' and that's the mindset that really trips them up" (Kintzle et al., p. 8). Another noted that, "People . . . were used to earning, I don't know, $80,000 a year, and then they expect they're going to earn the same [as a civilian]" (Kintzle et al., p. 8).

At the same time, most American recruiters and hiring managers lack a real familiarity with the military and how certain skills translate to their businesses. A 2016 study by HOH and Merck (HOH, 2016) found that a majority of human resources professionals and hiring managers lack familiarity with the military and its rank and structure. "On a scale of one to 10 (with 10 being extremely familiar and zero being not familiar at all), only 20% of the respondents ranked their military knowledge as an eight or higher" (p. 7). See Table 4.3 for the results of questions from that survey.

More recent research from Edelman Intelligence (2018) found these trends continue: Of the veterans surveyed, 51 percent said that they could not find a job in the field that they desired after they left the military, 58 percent were not able

Table 4.3   Human Resource Professionals' Familiarity With Military

| HR Professional Responses (%) | | *54% of HR professionals have little knowledge of rank and structure* | | | | | | | | | |
|---|---|---|---|---|---|---|---|---|---|---|---|
| | 25 | Little Familiarity (54%) | | | | | | Some (26%) | Familiar (20%) | | |
| | 20 | | | | | | | | | | |
| | 15 | | | | | | | | | | |
| | 10 | | | | | | | | | | |
| | 5 | 7% | 5% | 9% | 9% | 9% | 15% | 13% | 13% | 7% | 6% | 6% |
| | | 0 | 1 | 2 | 3 | 4 | 5 | 6 | 7 | 8 | 9 | 10 |
| | | Not at all familiar | | Knowledge of Military Service | | | | | | Extremely familiar | | |

*Source*: Hiring Our Heroes and MERCK (Hiring Our Heroes, 2016).

to find employment at the level that they expected, and 43 percent felt that their employers do not take full advantage of their skills and experiences. Among civilians surveyed by Edelman Intelligence, only 21 percent felt that they had a lot in common with nonveterans, and 67 percent said that they wished they knew more about the veteran experience. Eighty percent of veterans, service members, and civilians said that civilians often have a hard time relating to veterans and understanding their experiences (Edelman Intelligence, 2018).

## Veterans' Industry Perceptions Were Made by Television

For many returning veterans, their understandings of various industries are based on media representations and tied to their parents' and grandparents' perceptions, which are themselves based on media like sitcoms and movies from the 1970s. As an example, Edelman Intelligence (2018) found that 73 percent of veterans, 67 percent of nonveterans, and 72 percent of employers said that the media and popular culture portray veterans as being different from average citizens. The idea of driving a truck for a living, for example, brings up impressions set by movies like *Smokey and the Bandit*: a hard life away from your family with little pay. In reality, the trucking industry defies these stereotypes; the majority of trips are short range, meaning a driver could come home every night. Drivers for a private fleet (e.g., Walmart) make $73,000 a year on average (Gillespie, 2016). In addition, truck driving yields a clear pathway to other opportunities in logistics, warehouse management, and entrepreneurship.

When I ask young veterans whether they want a job in manufacturing, a vast majority of them say no, assuming that a "manufacturing job" means a "factory job." Many of them often respond with the same refrain, "My parents told me that if I didn't join the military, I would end up in the factory like them or my grandparents." However, if I ask the question a little differently, inquiring whether they would like a job working with lasers, robots, and advanced computer design, the responses are much different and more positive.

A veteran's lack of understanding is challenged both horizontally and vertically. On the vertical side, many veterans do not understand the depth and breadth of opportunities that exist in an individual business. A job at Home Depot, for example, is not limited to stocking shelves, but offers tremendous opportunities in information technology (IT), logistics, and accounting. At the same time, veterans' understanding of industries is challenged horizontally. IT and logistics jobs are not limited to companies in those industries but are available in nearly every industry in the United States.

Veterans also struggle with promotion pathways in corporate America. Unlike the military, which has a very linear promotion pathway, promotions in the civilian sector involve a variety of turns inside a company and/or moves to another company. The majority of Americans as a whole do not stay with a single company for their entire careers. Movement among companies is common among most professionals, with millennials (generation defined by birth between years 1981 and 1997) averaging four job jumps within 10 years of leaving college or graduate school (Long, 2016). Such movement is not a function of disloyalty, but of modern American business.

## Best Practices to Overcome Veteran and Employer Misconceptions

Companies that are most successful in hiring and recruiting veterans build programs that strive to achieve the following:

- *Sell your industry and opportunities.* Given their socioeconomic backgrounds, most transitioning service members may know very little about your company and industry. Much like the uniformed recruiter who recruited them into the military, civilian talent acquisition specialists and hiring managers must be willing to help young service members understand the depth and breadth of opportunities that exist in your company and how they will fit within your corporate culture and ethos. As noted, many service members join the military to fulfill a greater mission than self. Successful companies must help focus their recruits on that larger mission and the important role they will play in that mission. Furthermore, those companies that can illustrate long-term growth opportunities, not only within their particular organization, but also within the industry itself, will experience a greater return on investment through a higher rate of retention.
- *Training, training, training.* Like it or not, most recruiters and hiring managers lack any real familiarity with military culture, rank, and structure. That knowledge gap leads to missed opportunities and a host of bad results that impact the ability to hire and retain veterans. Companies with a successful veteran hiring program often include

veterans as part of the hiring process. Currently employed veterans that are part of the hiring process also ensure that recruiters and hiring managers have training on best practices to hire and retain new veteran hires. Training tools like HOH's Employer Roadmap (https://www.vetemployerroadmap.org) and PsychArmor's training portal (https://www.psycharmor.org) can yield significant results.

- *Mentoring and networking opportunities.* Veteran-friendly companies almost always have networking and mentoring opportunities. Those networking and mentoring opportunities may take the form of a veteran affinity group or an association that partners a newly onboarded veteran with a fellow veteran employee who can act as a mentor. These relations are critical in helping veterans understand the near-term and long-term opportunities in a company. They also help create an ever-important sense of community for many veteran employees. (See Chapter 9 of this book for more examples on mentoring and networking.)
- *Set expectations.* Most transitioning service members will not immediately manage hundreds or thousands of people in their first civilian job, even if they managed that many people in the military. The military would not promote a civilian executive to lieutenant colonel or commander simply because the person had 20 or more years of experience, and most companies would not immediately promote someone to a senior executive level in their company because of their military experience. It takes time for a newly transitioned service member to learn a business and how it ticks. Companies need to be honest about why a specific veteran employee needs to start at a certain level. At the same time, companies need to create realistic expectations about promotion opportunities and how individuals can succeed in their business. While it may be difficult to lay out a precise pathway, successful companies provide examples of veterans who have navigated the corporate ladder. When feasible, recruiters and hiring managers need to paint a clear picture of career advancement opportunities. Some organizations may also have the means to provide accelerated leadership classes or training opportunities for those veteran hires who may have a great deal of experience, but must simply start at ground zero to earn their stripes—something every veteran is familiar with. The bottom line is that veterans desire career growth and promotion opportunities as much as their civilian colleagues.
- *Be mindful of your nonveteran employees.* With so much attention placed on veterans and veteran causes, some nonveteran employees may feel left

out or, even worse, have the perception that veteran employees are receiving undue preferential treatment (HOH, 2016). Being mindful that such perceptions may exist is the first step in countering them. Companies need to help their nonveteran employees understand the value proposition of veterans in the workforce and why their experience adds to the richness and diversity of a company's workforce. Finding ways to celebrate their experience while not putting them on a pedestal is a key to success. The more a company can help bridge the veteran–civilian divide, the greater the retention potential of both veteran and civilian employees.

## Conclusion

Thanks to the exceptional power of public–private partnerships, the veteran unemployment crisis was largely abated by 2020. Now, it is time to turn our attention to the hard work of getting veterans into the right jobs—on the first attempt—and ensuring they are successfully retained through intentional engagement and development. Fully integrating veterans into the civilian workforce will take serious work for both employers and transitioning service members. Companies must take active steps to sell their industry to veterans, conduct comprehensive onboarding for veteran employees, foster meaningful work and connections, and take active measures to mitigate the civilian–military divide within their workplaces. For their part, veterans need to start the transition process early, work to translate their skills and experiences, and hold realistic expectations about the civilian workforce. It is going to take all of us—veterans, companies, veteran service organizations, and government entities—to tackle one of the most worthwhile challenges of the twenty-first century. As they say in the military, We can't rest: it's no man (or woman) left behind.

## References

Bureau of Labor Statistics, United States Department of Labor. (2012). *Employment situation of veterans—2011*. Washington, DC: Author. https://www.bls.gov/news.release/archives/vet_03202012.pdf

Edelman Intelligence. (2018). *2018 veterans' well-being survey*. Washington, DC: Author. https://www.edelman.com/sites/g/files/aatuss191/files/2018-10/2018-Edelman-Veterans-Well-being-Survey.pdf

Gillespie, P. (2016). Truck drivers wanted. Pay: $73,000. *CNN Money.* http://money.cnn.com/2015/10/09/news/economy/truck-driver-shortage/

Hiring Our Heroes. (2016). *Veterans in the workplace: Understanding the challenges and creating long-term opportunities for veteran employees.* Washington, DC: Author. https://www.uschamberfoundation.org/sites/default/files/Veterans%20in%20the%20Workplace_0.pdf

Kintzle, S., Keeling, M., Xintarianos, E., Taylor-Diggs, K., Munch, C. Hassan, A. M., & Castro, C. A. (2015). *Exploring the economic and employment challenges facing U.S. veterans: A qualitative study of volunteers of America service providers and veteran clients.* Los Angeles, CA: USC School of Social Work, Center for Innovation and Research on Veterans & Military Families. https://www.voa.org/pdf_files/a-study-of-volunteers-of-america-service-providers-and-veteran-clients

Long, H. (2016). The new normal: Four job changes by the time you're 32. *CNN Money.* http://money.cnn.com/2016/04/12/news/economy/millennials-change-jobs-frequently/

Lutz, A. (2008). Who joins the military? A look at race, class, and immigration status. *Journal of Political and Military Sociology, 36*(2):167–188. http://surface.syr.edu/cgi/viewcontent.cgi?article=1002&context=soc

Prudential Financial Inc. (2012). *Veterans' employment challenges: Perceptions and experiences of transitioning from military to civilian life.* Newark, NJ: Prudential Financial Inc.

U.S. Department of Defense Joint Advertising Market Research and Studies. (2017). *Youth polls.* Washington, DC: Author.

U.S. Department of Defense Office of the Deputy Assistant Secretary of Defense for Military Community and Family Policy. (2019). *Profile of the military community: 2018 demographics.* Washington, DC: Author. https://download.militaryonesource.mil/12038/MOS/Reports/2018-demographics-report.pdf

U.S. Department of Defense Office of the Under Secretary of Defense, Personnel and Readiness (DoD P&R). (2019). Population representation in the military services: Fiscal year 2018. Washington, DC: Author. https://www.cna.org/pop-rep/2018/contents/contents.html

# 5

# Understanding Veterans' Résumés and Conducting Veteran Interviews

*William R. McLennan*

For most human resource professionals and corporate hiring managers, understanding what people really do while they serve in the military is impossible. This is because less than 1 percent of our population currently serves—and less than 8 percent of working Americans have *ever* served. This lack of military experience can result in recruiters and hiring managers' frustration as they read résumés and interview recently transitioned veterans. So, how can you avoid this frustration? You can become fluent in the *military transition language*. Fluency depends on gaining a two-prong understanding of (a) how military careers (and the occupations within those careers) translate to civilian occupations and (b) how pay grades indicate employability, regardless of the service member's military occupation. In addition, knowing the training an individual receives in the military provides valuable insight into his or her knowledge, skills, and abilities beyond the service member's primary occupation. To gain this knowledge, review the applicant's Verification of Military Experience and Training (VMET, DD Form 2586), which all veterans will have. As part of this form, the Joint Services Transcript (JST) translates an individual's military experience and training into postsecondary educational credit hours accepted by the American Council on Education (ACE).

We explore how to become proficient in the military transition language through an example of one recently retired Army veteran. We then introduce you to tools and information provided by the U.S. government and veteran service organizations (VSOs) that are used by leading veteran employment practitioners and offer suggestions on how to translate the material in this soldier's résumé so you can understand what skills he can bring to your organization.

Over the past few years, military leadership has emphasized helping service members reintegrate into civilian life, which includes a focus on career

William R. McLennan, *Understanding Veterans' Résumés and Conducting Veteran Interviews* In: *Military Veteran Employment*. Edited by: Nathan D. Ainspan and Kristin N. Saboe, Oxford University Press. © Oxford University Press 2021. DOI: 10.1093/oso/9780190642983.003.0006

**Box 5.1** Factors integrated into the military résumé.

**MORRIS KAROKOFSKY**
500 Main Street
Washington, DC 20225

(703) 555 - 1212
morrisk@gmail.com
LinkedIn: morriska

Regional Deputy Director and Military Veteran with a Secret Security Clearance and 20 years of proven experience in the United States Army. Accomplished measurable results while leading teams of 100+ in a dynamic, fast-paced environment. Possess a comprehensive background in Leadership and Program Management derived from conducting domestic and global operations in the Middle East and domestically. Managed risk upon multiple lines to protect assets, property, and equipment valued over 10 million dollars while meeting the expectations of senior leadership. Possess extensive knowledge in Business Development. Recipient of multiple awards for outstanding performance and professionalism. Career supported by a Bachelor of Science in Organizational Leadership.

- Communication
- Business Development
- Collaboration
- Management
- Solution-oriented
- Program Management
- Marketing
- Operations Planning
- Microsoft Office Suite

**PROFESSIONAL EXPERIENCE**

**UNITED STATES ARMY** – Various Locations                                           2002–2016

**Regional Deputy Director, U.S. Army Soldier for Life Program; Crystal City, VA**      2013 – 2016

- Responsible for the organization of multiple industries, non-profit resources, and government organizations to participate in over 40 Hiring Fairs, Job Expos, and Transition Summits across the United States, benefitting 3,000+ service members and their families.
- Developed and implemented training to over 500 Human Resource Managers, Recruiters and other Talent Acquisition staff on how to hire, on-board, and retain veterans, increasing veteran hiring in multiple Fortune 100 – 1000 Companies.
- Trained over 300 faculty, staff, and other providers in student services in multiple institutions of higher learning in contemporary resources available for veterans of Post-9/11 conflicts.

**Senior Operations Manager / Senior Manager; Fort Knox KY/ Fort Benning, GA**      2009 – 2013

- Senior manager in an armor one station unit training (OSUT) company responsible for the annual training of 660 initial entry training (IET) soldiers.
- Responsible for the supervision, discipline, health, welfare, and professional development of 10 training managers, 30 supporting staff, and their families.
- Oversaw the training, accreditation, and command inspection programs, resulting in a consistent 100% pass rating during the duration as Senior Operations Manager.
- Program lead for the movement of a training school with resources valued at over 10 million dollars from Kentucky to Georgia four months ahead of schedule, saving the Army operating costs up to 1 million dollars.

**Manager; Friedberg and Baumholder, Germany / Hit, Sadr City, Iraq**                2003 – 2009

- Responsible for the supervision, discipline, health, welfare, and professional development of over 60 employees while operating under extreme conditions in Sadr City, Iraq.
- Managed the maintenance and accountability of over 20. Military vehicles and equipment worth in excess of 10 million dollars.

- Analyzed quantitative data from numerous sensitive intelligence sources under time-sensitive and highly stressful conditions on a daily basis to model enemy patterns of life, activity, and locations resulting in removal of 13 high-level enemy combatants from the battlefield.

**U.S. Army Recruiter; Delray Beach, FL**                                                    2002 – 2005
- Contacted, interviewed, qualified, and processed applications for applicants to enlist in the United States Army during a time of high demand and a country entering multiple wars simultaneously.
- Performed continual market, industry, economic, and competitor research and analysis resulting in the creation and continual refinement of recruiting activities and programs.
- Top producer for the 3$^{rd}$ QTR, 2003, recruiting over 55 new hires for the quarter, resulting in being awarded the 2$^{nd}$ highest U.S. Army recruiting award for excellence.


## VOLUNTEER EXPERIENCE
Advisory Board Member, Operation College Promise, Trenton, NJ – 2016


## EDUCATION
### Waldorf University
Bachelor of Applied Science, Organizational Leadership, Forest City, IA – 2016

### Department of Defense
Basic Leader Course, Fort Hood, TX – 2002
Advanced Leader Course, Fort Knox, KY – 2005
Senior Leader Course, Fort Knox, KY – 2010
U.S. Army Recruiting School, Fort Jackson, SC – 2001
Basic Instructor Course, Fort Knox, KY – 2010
Sexual Harassment / Assault Response Program Course, Fort Knox, KY – 2010
Executive Leadership Course, Fort Jackson, SC – 2012


## CERTIFICATIONS
Sexual Harassment / Assault Response Certification – 2010
Army Lean Six Sigma Black Belt Course - 2016


## SELECT AWARDS
### Bronze Star
Meritorious Service Medal (3)
Army Commendation Medal (2)
Army Achievement Medal (4)

## *VMET for an Army Officer*

placement. Since this new focus began, improved résumé quality is a major indicator of its success. Few résumés coming from transitioning service members will contain unusable descriptions of what they did and the results they drove. An excellent example is provided here in Box 5.1 of a recently transitioned Army veteran that shows chronological detail of his military experience expressed in entirely civilian terms.

This veteran highlights his leadership and management span of control and scope of responsibilities. He provides excellent examples of his personal contributions and accomplishments. He has also outlined key military training, awards, and certifications. This soldier has taken full advantage of the transition assistance provided to him, which has greatly improved his probability of being interviewed and employed.

You can also see in his résumé he does not use nomenclature like his Military Occupation Specialty (MOS) Code or does describe what military rank he has attained. This is because the U.S. Department of Defense's Transition Assistance Process (TAP)—a program that all service members are required to attend as part of their exit from the military—is structured to help veterans translate their occupations into a civilian résumé by leveraging their VMET with their JST to create their résumé (see Figure 5.1). While TAP has helped many service members to translate their service into a professional résumé, it is imperative that employers cultivate their own understanding of military occupational training, pay grades, and the JST. This knowledge is necessary since many service members will downplay their skills due to their ingrained focus on team-based accomplishments rather than their individual talents and contributions. If employers rely solely on as-written résumés, they may miss out on great candidates.

## Translating Military Occupations Into Civilian Terms

### Military Careers

The first step to effectively read veterans' résumés is to understand what type of work they did while serving in the military. A common misconception is that most veterans had military-specific jobs that do not translate well into civilian occupations. This is inaccurate. Over 85 percent of military personnel serve in occupations that also exist in the civilian workforce. For example, high-skilled jobs requiring postsecondary education (e.g., doctors and lawyers); jobs that require high levels of technical skills (e.g., truck driving, vehicle maintenance, and software programming); and jobs that are familiar to every employer (e.g., human resources, public relations, and administration) are present within the military.

The best study we have found that explains military careers at an aggregate level is the *Occupational Outlook Handbook* published biennially by the U.S. Department of Labor (DOL) (DOL Bureau of Labor Statistics, 2002). It is located at https://www.bls.gov/ooh/military/military-careers. htm. This online publication describes and categorizes occupations within the military for both officers and enlisted personnel. This handbook is an outstanding resource to help employers understand the different types of occupational groupings within our military. The DOL also publishes the number of enlisted personnel and officers employed within each occupational grouping by military service branch in handy tables. The handbook's occupational groupings for enlisted personnel are presented in Table 5.1.

The following are more detailed examples provided by the DOL that help you understand some of the jobs within the five highest occupational groups for enlisted personnel:

1. *Vehicle and machinery mechanical personnel* conduct preventive and corrective maintenance on aircraft, automotive and heavy equipment, and powerhouse station equipment. These workers specialize by the type of equipment that they maintain.
2. *Engineering, science, and technical personnel* perform a variety of tasks, such as operating technical equipment, solving problems, and collecting and interpreting information. They perform technical tasks in information technology, environmental health and safety, or intelligence.
3. *Combat specialty personnel* train and work in combat units, such as the infantry, artillery, or special forces. For example, infantry specialists conduct ground combat operations, armored vehicle specialists operate battle tanks, and seamanship specialists maintain ships. Combat specialty personnel may maneuver against enemy forces and fire artillery, guns, mortars, or missiles to neutralize them. They may also operate various types of combat vehicles, such as amphibious assault vehicles, tanks, or small boats. Members of elite Special Forces teams

**Table 5.1** Active Duty Enlisted Personnel by Broad Occupational Group and Branch of the Military and Coast Guard, June 2019

| Enlisted | Army | Air Force | Coast Guard | Marine Corps | Navy | Total Enlisted Personnel in Each Occupational Group |
|---|---|---|---|---|---|---|
| *Occupational group* | | | | | | |
| Administrative | 5,015 | 13,937 | — | 10,490 | 19,147 | 48,589 |
| Combat Specialty | 96,790 | 666 | — | 27,661 | 9,151 | 134,268 |
| Construction | 14,581 | 4,509 | — | 5,235 | 3,976 | 28,301 |
| Electronic and Electrical Equipment Repair | 26,851 | 28,806 | — | 7,415 | 45,005 | 108,077 |
| Engineering, Science, and Technical | 35,907 | 48,426 | — | 22,258 | 42,486 | 149,077 |
| Healthcare | 25,303 | 14,888 | — | — | 25,732 | 65,923 |
| Human Resource Development | 15,424 | 13,035 | — | 8,267 | 4,026 | 40,752 |
| Machine Operator and Production | 4,172 | 5,957 | — | 2,370 | 9,761 | 22,260 |
| Media and Public Affairs | 4,687 | 7,100 | — | 1,541 | 3,860 | 17,188 |
| Protective Service | 19,206 | 33,832 | — | 9,469 | 13,282 | 75,789 |
| Support Service | 9,913 | 1,420 | — | 1,661 | 8,992 | 21,986 |
| Transportation and Material Handling | 45,907 | 27,567 | — | 21,440 | 36,534 | 131,448 |
| Vehicle and Machinery Mechanic | 43,683 | 41,608 | — | 16,052 | 48,138 | 149,481 |
| Non-occupation or unspecified coded personnel | 28,161 | 21,235 | — | 31,186 | 5,384 | 85,966 |
| Total enlisted personnel for each military branch and Coast Guard | 375,600 | 262,986 | 32,436 | 165,045 | 275,474 | 1,111,541 |

*Sources:* U.S. Department of Defense, Defense Manpower Data Center; https://www.bls.gov/ooh/military/military-careers.htm.

are trained to perform specialized missions anywhere in the world on a moment's notice.

4. *Transportation and material-handling personnel* transport military personnel and cargo. Most personnel within this occupational group are classified according to the mode of transportation, such as aircraft, motor vehicle, or ship.

5. *Electronic and electrical equipment repair personnel* maintain and repair electronic equipment used by the military. Repairers specialize in an area such as aircraft electrical systems, computers, optical equipment, communications, or weapons systems. For example, weapons electronic maintenance technicians maintain and repair electronic components and systems that help locate targets and help aim and fire weapons.

Note that the top five occupations listed in the *Occupational Handbook* represent 60 percent of the total active duty enlisted force across all five military service branches. You will notice in the descriptions that less than 12 percent of enlisted roles are combat specific, with about 40 percent related to repair or material handling. The descriptions provided are also tactical and task oriented, suggesting that individual contributor and supervisory roles are the best organizational fit for a civilian counterpart opportunity. There is a high percentage of jobs specific to the movement and maintenance of equipment across all service branches. This is because most of what our military does is associated with the movement of people and equipment. If we were to classify the military into a civilian industry, we would classify them as part of the transportation and logistics or supply chain sector. That is why there is such a heavy proportion of occupations related to the operation and maintenance of equipment.

Officers represent about 18 percent of the military and are a very different employment cohort. You can see from Table 5.2 that there is a higher concentration of officers within their top five occupations at 77 percent. While combat specialty occupations rank third as with enlisted occupations and represent about the same 14 percent of the population, there is a much higher percentage of officer corps in the engineering, science and technical, and transportation occupations. You can also see executive, administration, and management represents about 14 percent of the officer corps, with healthcare professions at about 10 percent.

**Table 5.2** Active Duty Officer Personnel by Broad Occupational Group and Branch of Military and Coast Guard, June 2019

| Officer | Army | Air Force | Coast Guard | Marine Corps | Navy | Total Officer Personnel in Each Occupational Group |
|---|---|---|---|---|---|---|
| *Occupational group* | | | | | | |
| Combat specialty | 18,990 | 4,231 | — | 5,069 | 6,034 | 34,324 |
| Engineering, science, and technical | 22,498 | 14,342 | — | 3,827 | 10,230 | 50,897 |
| Executive, administrative, and managerial | 15,418 | 8,079 | — | 2,249 | 6,780 | 32,526 |
| Healthcare | 10,337 | 8,964 | — | — | 6,821 | 26,122 |
| Human resource development | 2,795 | 1,911 | — | 721 | 3,539 | 8,966 |
| Media and public affairs | 284 | 305 | — | 169 | 264 | 1,022 |
| Protective service | 2,925 | 922 | — | 328 | 1,202 | 5,377 |
| Support service | 1,624 | 759 | — | 30 | 1,008 | 3,421 |
| Transportation | 10,488 | 17,029 | — | 4,696 | 10,455 | 42,668 |
| Nonoccupation or unspecified coded personnel | 7,824 | 7,511 | — | 4,680 | 9,142 | 29,157 |
| Total officer personnel for each military branch and Coast Guard | 93,183 | 64,053 | 8,814 | 21,769 | 55,475 | 243,294 |

*Sources*: U.S. Department of Defense, Defense Manpower Data Center; https://www.bls.gov/ooh/military/military-careers.htm

The DOL also provides detailed examples that help you understand some of the jobs within the five highest occupational groups for officers:

1. *Engineering, science, and technical officers'* responsibilities depend on their area of expertise. They work in scientific and professional occupations, such as atmospheric scientists, meteorologists, physical scientists, biological scientists, social scientists, attorneys, and other types of scientists or professionals. For example, meteorologists in the military may study the weather to assist in planning flight paths for aircraft.

2. Transportation officers manage and perform activities related to the safe transport of military personnel and equipment by air and water. They operate and command an aircraft or a ship.

3. *Combat specialty officers* plan and direct military operations, oversee combat activities, and serve as combat leaders. They may be in charge of tanks and other armored assault vehicles, artillery systems, special operations, or infantry units. This group also includes naval surface warfare and submarine warfare officers, combat pilots, and aircrews.

4. *Executive, administrative, and managerial officers* manage administrative functions in the Armed Forces, such as human resources management, training, personnel, information, police, or other support services. Officers who oversee military bands are included in this category.

5. *Healthcare officers* provide medical services to military personnel in order to maintain or improve their health and physical readiness. Officers such as physicians, physician assistants, nurses, and dentists examine, diagnose, and treat patients. Other healthcare officers provide therapy, rehabilitative treatment, and additional healthcare for patients.

You can see from reading the occupation descriptions provided by the DOL that officers are the leaders, planners, and managers of larger scale operations compared to enlisted personnel. They also have far more technical and specialized advanced occupations. These specialized technical occupations typically require postsecondary education in addition to military training. Within the officer group, about 42 percent have obtained a bachelor's degree, with another 41 percent having secured an advanced degree. In contrast, only about 8 percent of the enlisted force have earned a bachelor's degree or higher; however, 92 percent have obtained their high school or equivalent diploma. Understanding these military careers is the first step to understanding the military experience and how it might apply to civilian opportunities.

## Military Occupations

From an occupational perspective, the military is much like any employer in that there are common jobs for common activities across all military service branches. Additionally, there are branch-specific jobs because of the differences in the mission and infrastructure of that service branch. For example, all of the service branches have recruiters, instructors, lawyers, and administrative personnel among other occupations. However, the Air Force and Navy have jobs that are specific to maintaining and operating complex weapons systems like ships and fixed-wing aircraft. The Army and Marine Corps are primarily ground operations, so they have entirely different jobs that are centered on the support of the Soldiers and Marines executing the ground operations. The Army and Marines also have specialized equipment to support ground operations like helicopters and assault vehicles. All service branches have maintenance technicians who excel in rapid diagnostics and repair of the equipment entrusted to them.

Combined, there are nearly 1,200 unique military occupations within the service branches (see Table 5.3). Each branch uses a unique code tied to a job title and description. The number of primary occupations by service branch can be found in the table compiled using data from each branch's military career websites. You can find the occupational descriptions of military jobs by service branch in the following list:

- Air Force: https://www.airforce.com/careers/
- Army: https://www.goarmy.com/careers-and-jobs.html

Table 5.3 Number of Occupations by Military Service

| Service Branch | Air Force | Army | Coast Guard | Marine Corps | Navy | Total |
|---|---|---|---|---|---|---|
| Totals | 123 | 520 | 20[a] | 411 | 108 | 1,182 |

[a]Coast Guard only includes major job classifications.

- Navy: https://www.navy.com/careers.html
- Marine Corps: https://www.marines.com/being-a-marine/roles-in-the-corps.html
- Coast Guard: https://www.gocoastguard.com/active-duty-careers/enlisted-opportunities/view-job-descriptions

For all service branches, the occupations are aggregated in logical groupings, typically by broad career types, and have an identifier associated with each occupation. The Army and Marine Corps call their occupation identifiers MOSs, the Air Force calls them Air Force Specialty Codes (AFSCs), and the Navy calls them Naval Enlisted Classifications (NECs). The Coast Guard does not use classification codes, but follows closely with the Navy's rating system. Examples of the military occupation codes for the service branches for military recruiters are in Table 5.4. Note that these are not the only designations for a recruiter in the services as there are additional occupation codes that represent recruiting as a primary or specialty occupation.

There are several resources available that list all of the military occupations and descriptions of the military occupation codes. We recommend you refer to the military service branch websites provided above to review each military occupation and the corresponding job description. Those links also include some very useful videos that provide additional insights into the roles and tasks of many military occupations.

Despite all of the available descriptions of military occupations, specific challenges remain with matching military job knowledge, skills, and abilities (KSAs) to a variety of civilian job counterparts. These challenges include

**Table 5.4**  Military Occupation Codes for the Recruiting Occupation

| Branch | Occupation Code | Description |
| --- | --- | --- |
| Air Force | 8R000 | Recruiter |
| Army | 79R | Recruiter |
| Marine Corps | 8911 | Recruiter |
| Navy | 9585 | Recruiter |

1. Military-specific jobs that have no civilian job counterpart (e.g., sniper)
2. Military jobs with civilian job counterparts that do not exactly match the civilian job requirements (e.g., logistician)
3. Military jobs that do not receive civilian industry-required certifications (e.g., diesel mechanic)
4. Military jobs that do not receive the same level of formal training as required by the civilian job counterpart (e.g., licensed vocational nurse)
5. Military leadership positions that are not easily understood by civilians (e.g., company commander)

Leading employers of veterans can overcome these challenges with a keen understanding of all military occupations and how each occupation can map into each available position within their organizations.

While many military occupations provide direct industry experience, it is important to recognize service members' skills that transcend career type since many veterans will want to pursue an entirely different career than their military career. It is also important to consider the many soft skills and leadership experiences veterans bring to new work settings regardless of the technical skill set needed.

## Military Skills Converters

Much work completed by DOL to assist military personnel translate their occupations directly into comparable civilian careers. DOL has created a very useful online portal called O*NET OnLine (https://www.onetonline.org/crosswalk/) that enables users to enter a military occupation and generate a list of civilian occupations that most closely match the military occupation. For example, entering a Marine Corps MOS 0341 (mortarman) in Figure 5.2 converts the military occupation to five civilian jobs that are security or

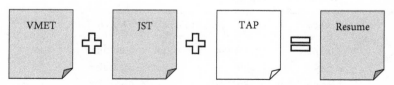

**Figure 5.2** Elements that go into a transitioning Service member's resume.
Available at O*NET Online at O*Net Online (https://www.onetonline.org/crosswalk/).

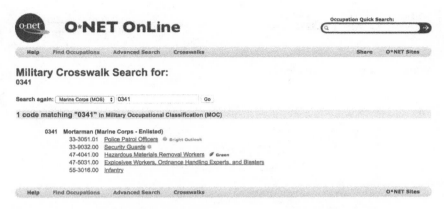

**Figure 5.3** O*NET OnLine results for Army indirect fire infantryman.
Available at O*NET Online at O*Net Online (https://www.onetonline.org/crosswalk/).

explosive ordnance related. One crosswalk is to a military infantry position, which is not useful when searching for a civilian career. These results are generated because of the specific KSAs a Marine mortarman obtains to do that job efficiently and effectively. On the surface, these are logical civilian occupation crosswalks because Marine mortarmen are familiar with explosives and the security of munitions.

Figure 5.3 is what the O*NET crosswalk generates for an Army 11C, indirect fire infantryman, which is also a mortarman.

The Army mortarman occupation is currently crosswalked into 20 possible civilian occupations, in contrast to only 3 for the Marine mortarman. The Army mortarman crosswalks only four of the five Marine mortarman civilian occupations. Are these two mortarman jobs so different that they would generate such a different number of civilian occupations? The answer is no. We chose to illustrate this example to highlight some inadequacies in the current crosswalks and make the point that they are not as reliable as they could be.

Another website to assist veterans in their transition is My Next Move for Veterans (https://www.mynextmove.org/vets/). This site enables a search by civilian keyword occupations or industry, or a veteran can input their military occupation code and search for civilian careers that best match their military job. Figure 5.4 shows the results of searching for civilian occupations that best fit an Army infantryman (11B) occupation. You can see 12 civilian careers came back as a match with *some* of their military duties. Of the 12

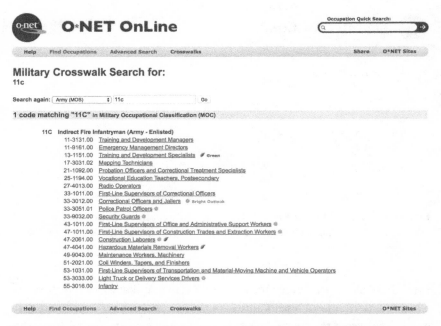

**Figure 5.4** MyNextMove for Veterans occupational converters for infantrymen.
Available at MyNextMove for Vets at (www.mynextmove.org/vets/).

civilian occupations, Figure 5.4 suggests only a construction laborer is immediately attainable without additional training. Additional information provided in the figure includes the suggested pay grade that matches the civilian occupation.

The My Next Move for Veterans portal will yield the exact same results as the O*NET OnLine portal because both portals access the same DOL database of occupations for the crosswalks. The O*NET OnLine and My Next Move for Veterans portals have been designed for individuals seeking to understand a civilian occupation. The data are organized and standardized so civilian occupations can be researched down to the task levels with useful descriptions of the KSAs required to perform on the job. There is no such database for employers to search at this level to understand what each military occupation does. However, there is an online portal, CareerOneStop (https://www.careeronestop.org), that has a crosswalk for civilian occupation to military occupation code. Here, you will see, for example, in Figure 5.5, if you input the civilian occupation of transportation manager, the database returns a list of 135 military occupations that are deemed closely qualified.

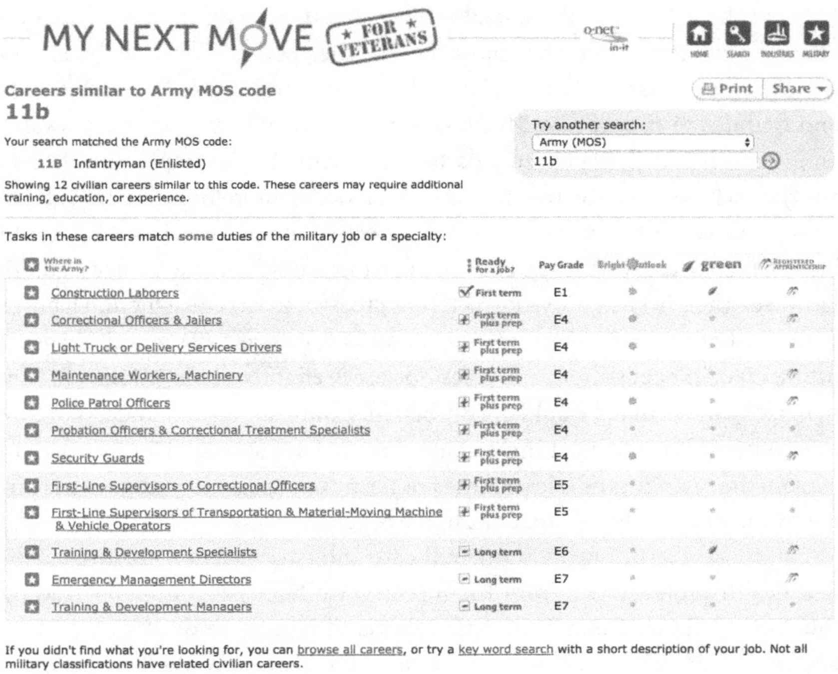

**Figure 5.5** CareerOneStop occupational translator.
Available at CareeerOneStop at (www.mynextmove.org/vets/).

You will also see under the "Branch" sidebar that every service branch has occupations that have been crosswalked into a transportation manager civilian role. This can be a useful start for employers. However, this reverse translator has the same limitations as the military-to-civilian crosswalks because it pulls from the same database. While the alleged military job matches are interesting, they do not really help a civilian recruiter understand the KSAs a veteran would have gained through their training and experiences in any of those military occupations.

There have been some excellent academic and practitioner studies that have focused on the specific training and abilities obtained in certain military occupations with a direct crosswalk to civilian jobs that best fit. The RAND Corporation published *Helping Soldiers Leverage Army Knowledge, Skills, and Abilities in Civilian Jobs* (Wenger et al., 2017; https://www.rand.org/pubs/research_reports/RR1719.html). This is an exceptional study that focused on the 10 most populous occupations in the Army and attempted to isolate the

KSAs of the soldiers in these fields and match them with the best fitting civilian occupations requiring those KSAs. The methodology, analysis, and results are informative. The RAND study then compared their research results and findings to the current My Next Move for Veterans military crosswalks and recommended improvements for the Army. For example, the RAND study concluded that the best fitting civilian occupation for an Army 11B infantryman is a fireman. Furthermore, a very poor match for an 11B would be as a construction laborer, and the worst fit would be as a security guard. However, the My Next Move for Veterans crosswalk lists construction laborer as the best fitting civilian occupation for an 11B, lists security guard as a good fitting civilian occupation, and does not list firefighter at all. Military hiring managers or recruiters would greatly benefit from reading and understanding this study, as it is the most important work we have seen to date that tries to explain the real KSAs of at least these few Army occupations—and work is underway to analyze the occupations in the other services.

For those recruiting in the healthcare industry seeking to hire qualified health professionals from the military, we highly recommend reading the 2016 National Council of State Boards of Nurses study *A Comparison of Selected Military Health Care Occupation Curricula With a Standard Licensed Practical/Vocational Nurse Curriculum* (https://www.ncsbn.org/16_NCSBNAnalyiss_MilitaryLPNVN.pdf). This study analyzes the KSAs and trainings for Army, Navy, and Air Force healthcare specialists and compares them directly to the civilian Licensed Practical Nurse/Vocational Nurse (LPN/VN) occupations. The research identifies that while the formal training within each service branch is standard, there are differences in training across the military branches. It further identifies that there can be vast differences in skill levels because of the individual's unique experiences within the military. For example, some military nurses or corpsmen might have extensive experience inserting chest tubes or performing small surgical procedures, whereas others might have more limited experience. The study concluded that the differences in training and experience levels preclude granting an LPN/VN license without additional coursework and clinical experience.

Several private enterprises have created and are marketing military crosswalks. All of the private sector crosswalks we have seen utilize the O*NET OnLine database as the baseline and attempt to modify the civilian job matches by "tailoring" them to a potential employer's open positions. Therefore, they have the same limitations of not having a deep understanding of the KSAs for the military occupations and the KSAs for the specific civilian jobs, coupled with an empirical measurement of job fit as the RAND Corporation has developed. Furthermore, a veteran's personal experiences within the same military occupation can be substantially different from another veteran's experience even though they have the same occupation.

In addition to relatively weak KSA matches related to occupational cross-walk tools, another challenge can be that military occupations do not carry the same level of licensures or certifications as a similar civilian occupation. One example is that a military truck driving license is not valid for a civilian truck driver job, and the veteran would need to obtain a state-issued commercial driver's license to secure employment. Other examples are military diesel mechanics who are not trained to Automotive Service Excellence standards and the additional training required for LPN/VN licensure mentioned above. There are numerous schools that provide the necessary training for industry licensure and credentialing to fill these jobs, and military veterans tend to excel at achieving these positions since they are already very well trained.

The Department of Defense has also developed pathways for transitioning service members to train for new career skills on or near their military installations. This is called the SkillBridge program; employers offer to train transitioning military personnel in new skills while they are in their final 90 days of active duty service. The training curriculum typically lasts between 12 and 14 weeks. You can learn more about SkillBridge at https://www.military.com/hiring-veterans/resources/using-dod-skilbridge-to-recruit-qualified-veterans.html.

One of the best examples of a SkillBridge program is the Microsoft Software and Systems Academy where a consortium of employers are involved in training and employing transitioning service members for careers in technology. You can read more about this specific program (https://military.microsoft.com/programs/mssa/).

For the U.S. Navy, Marine Corps, and Coast Guard, there are opportunities for those service members to complete formalized apprenticeships through the U.S. Military Apprenticeship Program (USMAP). The USMAP has over 100 occupations approved by the DOL for apprenticeships that vary from occupations like computer operator, retail store manager, power plant mechanic, nurse assistant, counselor, police officer, and office manager. The USMAP is an important part of the national apprenticeship landscape as the military trains about 25 percent of apprentices. You can find more about the USMAP online (https://www.dol.gov/asp/evaluation/completed-studies/The_United_Services_Military_Apprenticeship_Program_(USMAP).pdf).

Employers that establish qualified apprenticeships will have a competitive advantage in hiring veterans because veterans working through an approved apprenticeship can be eligible to receive certain GI Bill benefits. In our work at FASTPORT as a DOL-contracted industry intermediary helping educate employers and expanding the number of apprenticeships, we have seen employers attract nearly 40 percent of their apprenticeship program members are veterans, with all employers reporting much longer retention rates of those veteran apprentices compared to nonveteran apprentices. Employers wishing to initiate registered apprenticeship programs can begin the process at https://www.dol.gov/featured/apprenticeship/employers.

## Transition Assistance

In our opinion, the most important legislation signed to assist our veterans since the Servicemen's Readjustment Act was signed in 1944 (also known as the GI Bill) was the VOW (Veterans Opportunity to Work) to Hire Heroes Act signed in 2011. The enduring feature of the VOW Act was making the TAP mandatory for all service members moving on to civilian life to help them secure jobs through résumé writing workshops and career counseling. For employers seeking to hire transitioning veterans, it is important to know the TAP process and the support our veterans receive as they exit military service. Understanding this process is important because the process contains relevant details about how our military service members are being prepared to enter the civilian sector and what they are being taught to help them secure civilian employment. The guiding process to transition assistance into employment is the Departmet or Labmor's Employment Workshop. The participant guide to this class is located at (United States Department of Labor, 2019, https://www. dol.gov/sites/dolgov/files/VETS/files/DOLEW-Participant-Guide.pdf.

As a prerequisite to transition training, service members are requested to participate in a class on the Military Occupational Codes (MOC) crosswalk module designed to translate their specific military occupation and experiences into a civilian occupation they desire. The resources veterans use are their personal VMET DD Form 2586, discussed previously, and their Joint Military Transcripts (JMT).

One of the first resources a veteran is directed to use is the O*NET OnLine (https://www.onetonline.org/). O*NET OnLine is the DOL database initiative that consolidates and categorizes information about occupations across all industry sectors. It currently contains 974 occupations with 277 descriptors that tie the KSAs required for each job. The occupations are listed in the Standard Occupational Classification system by the federal statistical agencies to classify workers into occupational categories for the purpose of collecting, calculating, or disseminating data. This is the best resource for understanding occupations and the requisite KSAs. It is also the system veterans first use to help them with their MOC crosswalk.

O*NET has a crosswalk feature that enables a veteran to input their military occupation and discover which of the 974 civilian occupations best matches their military KSAs. It is a terrific resource. Let us start the process for our retired Army veteran. He was trained as an M1 Abrams tank crewmember, which the Army designates as 19K in its MOS codes. When we enter Army 19K in an O*NET search, as shown Figure 5.6 the crosswalk returns the list of civilian occupations based on the best matched KSAs.

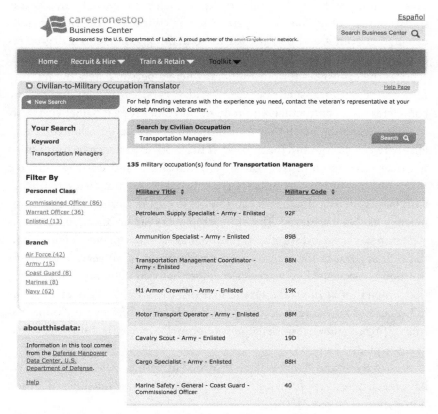

**Figure 5.6** Military crosswalk search for the tank crewmember.

There are 13 civilian occupations that match to his MOS. This a high number for a military-specific job. If we examine the type of job and level of position for our 19K M1 armor crewman you will see eight of the positions are typically entry-level individual contributor jobs, and five are supervisor/ manager positions.

We have previously discussed the limitations of the military skills converters, but it is important to understand this is the process all military personnel undertake on exiting military service and therefore is leading some veterans toward these crosswalked careers.

## Translating Educational Credentials

### Joint Services Transcript

Transitioning out of the military is a major life event—much like transitioning out of college. A person enters college for a period of time, usually between 4 and 6 years, learns something, completes a degree re-quirement, and looks for a job in their field when they transition out of school. The same goes for our military, where a person enters the military for a period of time, usually between 4 and 8 years, learns their occupation, completes their contractual requirement, and looks for a job not necessarily in their occupation when they transition out of service. Another common-ality between college and the military is that both experiences are grounded in proven classroom instruction to gain knowledge and skills specific to a major of study or job. The military typically takes instruction a step further with hands-on training over several weeks to ensure a critical level of com-petency has been achieved. Therefore, employers can be certain of the KSAs a veteran has achieved specific to the job they have performed. Like college, the military tracks the training and development of all service members through transcripts. Every service member has two documents that verify the completion of the training; the first is the VMET, and the other is the JST. A useful brochure describing the details of the JST can be found on-line (http://www.acenet.edu/news-room/Documents/Joint-Services-Transcript-Brochure.pdf).

A recently retired Army veteran provided us with his VMET and JST. We have taken an excerpt from both documents to illustrate the differences and how they are connected.

Box 5.2 is the VMET that describes the Army recruiter course our veteran had taken earlier in his military career. The VMET shows the course length at 390 hours. You will also see the course description provided by the ACE. ACE works across all military service branches to provide standardized course description and, more importantly, the recommended credits an accredited college should provide toward elective or required coursework in pursuing an associate's and bachelor's degree.

We have extracted the corresponding Army recruiter course information on this veteran's JST. Box 5.3 shows the JST contains the course, date enrolled, and location where the course was completed. It includes a brief description and identifies the same three course study areas as the VMET with the recommended semester hours determined by ACE.

---

**Box 5.2  VMET for an Army Officer**

ARMY COURSE: 501-SQI4, Army Recruiter
    LENGTH: 8 weeks (390 hours)
    VERIFICATION OF MILITARY EXPERIENCE AND TRAINING
Page 10 of 14

COURSE DESCRIPTION FROM AMERICAN
COUNCIL ON EDUCATION:
    (AR-1406-0103, Exhibit dates JAN 2001–JUL 2012)
    Upon completion of the course, the student will be able to prospect, develop sales presentations, interview prospective recruits, and make a sales presentation. Methods of instruction include lectures, role playing, and classroom discussions. Topics covered include sales prospecting, market analysis, effective communication, public speaking, interviewing skills and techniques, and time management.

CREDIT RECOMMENDATION FROM AMERICAN
COUNCIL ON EDUCATION
    (AR-1406-0103, Exhibit dates JAN 2001–JUL 2012)
    In the upper division baccalaureate degree category, 3 semester hours in selling or marketing, 3 in human resources management, and 3 in business interpersonal communication (3/02)(3/02).
    (ARMY TRAINING HISTORY COURSE: 501SQI4)

---

**Box 5.3  JST for an Army Recruiter**

---

501-SQ14 AR-1406-0103 16-OCT-2001 to 07-DEC-2001
Army Recruiter
Recruit and Retention School
Ft. Jackson, SC
Upon completion of the course, the student will be able to prospect, develop sales presentations, interview prospective recruits, and make a sales presentation.
Business Interpersonal Communication 3SH U
Human Resources Management 3SH U
Selling or Marketing 3SH U

---

The Army recruiter course is intensive and covers a broad range of topics required to succeed in this role. ACE recommends that a total of nine upper division (equivalent to junior or senior year studies) credit hours be granted to soldiers who complete this class. The recommended credit hours apply equally to selling or marketing, human resources management, and business interpersonal communications.

It is important to note ACE reports over 2,300 colleges and universities are providing postsecondary educational credit for military classroom and experiential training. This overwhelming support by so many academic institutions is why recruiters need to view military service and experience in a similar light to college recruiting. Our military is providing a high quality of academic learning and formal training. You can read more about the college credits in military classes online (http://www.acenet.edu/news-room/Pages/Transcripts-for-Military-Personnel.aspx). Employers that are successful in employing veterans understand the quality of training and utilize the VMET and JST to verify the KSAs obtained during different assignments while in the military. Some employers even request a copy of the JST in addition to the résumé as it provides the most detailed insight to a veterans overall military experience.

As you have seen from the TAP process, veterans are encouraged to utilize their VMET and JST to help them frame their résumés. Our subject veteran has done an outstanding job here as he has clearly articulated the job he performed as an Army recruiter and also provided salient measures of performance unique to his personal contributions.

One item that does not appear in this veteran's résumé is he was trained as an M1 Abrams tank crewman, or Army MOS 19K. You will find this information on his VMET and his JST. This is important because it means he accepted the Army recruiter assignment and needed to learn the new skills associated with becoming a successful recruiter. Since recruiting skills are very different from the skills required to drive and load tanks, this information would provide an employer with strong evidence of the individual's ability to learn and grow into different organizational roles. This is not an isolated example. We receive very consistent feedback from employers with veteran hiring programs that the veterans they have hired are able to quickly learn new skills and have a great willingness to adapt in new roles. This is really what military training is all about. Military training helps condition veterans to learn, grow, and accept new and larger responsibilities. Leading employers of veterans understand this and create an employment environment that helps them recruit more veterans. This environment typically starts with hiring a veteran to assist with or lead the veteran hiring initiatives.

The military provides much additional training that is relevant to civilian employment. For example, Lean Six Sigma courses are taught where veterans can receive Black Belt and Green Belt certification and project management coursework and certifications that are applicable to any industry. These are examples of additional specialized coursework our military has access to. In many cases, access to these specialized courses is the result of a rigorous selection process, like the Army or Marine Corps Drill Instructor School, where they only accept the highest performing soldiers and Marines. This is another way a recruiter can identify a veteran who has excelled during their military career.

## Military Pay Grades

Why do military pay grades matter? This is because they are commensurate with the levels of responsibility in civilian roles and can be used to identify and match crucial skills needed in supervisory, management, and leadership opportunities. Military pay grades are often used synonymously with military ranks. While they are related within each service branch, military pay grades represent major steps in the promotion progression of military service and are consistent across all service branches. Pay grades are broken into three classifications: enlisted, warrant officer, and officer pay grades. There are nine enlisted pay grades that range from lowest level E-1 to the highest level E-9, five warrant officer pay grades W-1 to W-5, and 10 officer pay grades O-1 to O-10. The Air Force has discontinued the use of warrant officer pay grades. Military rank refers to the seniority of people within the same pay grade and across pay grades. Ranks can be confusing as the same rank nomenclature can have a different pay grade in a different military branch. For example, the rank of captain in the Navy is an O-6 pay grade whereas the rank of captain in the Army is an O-3 pay grade. The captain in the Navy therefore is a higher rank than that of the subordinated Army captain. You can find a good description and tables of pay grades and military ranks for enlisted and officer in the index of this book and online (https://www.defense.gov/About/Insignias/). While all officers are senior to all enlisted personnel, it is important to note that an O-1 is a very junior officer, while an E-8 is a very senior enlisted pay grade. The E-8 will typically have many more years of experience in the military and within their occupation than junior officers will have. Therefore, a senior noncommissioned officer (NCO) might be a much better fit for certain management positions.

The appendix of this book has a list of the military pay grades and comparable civilian equivalents.

Pay grades are often overlooked when considering military talent as most employers focus on the military occupation that best matches their open positions. The most successful employers understand what the training and responsibilities are across pay grades and seek to match supervisory, management, and leadership level openings to the corresponding pay grade of veteran candidates.

Let us examine our veteran again. He retired from the Army with the pay grade E-8 and rank of master sergeant. This is very high up the chain of command and demonstrates he has been one of the very best soldiers at his job within the Army. You can be confident in this because the military has a rigorous meritocracy where you either are promoted to the next level of responsibility or you are asked to exit the service. There are exceptions for certain in-demand occupations, but this "up-or-out" policy is the rule. Looking at his résumé, he has noted a number of leadership courses taken from the Army as part of his military experience. These leadership courses are the equivalent of college credit of 13 semester hours of lower level college credits and 18 semester hours of upper level college credits. This is 31 total semester hours of formal classroom leadership training.

This total of training is equal to an entire year of leadership classes in a college environment. What you need to know is every E-8 in the Army is required to complete the four levels of leadership training to continue advancing. The Army and all other service branches start leadership training at the E-3 or E-4 level. You can find the Army structured leadership courses for NCOs online (https://www.goarmy.com/soldier-life/being-a-soldier/ongoing-training/leadership-training.html).

Highly successful employers have expanded their veteran hiring results with a focus on hiring by pay grade more than by hiring by military occupation. From a best practices perspective, the chart in Figure 5.7 translates military pay grade as a proxy for civilian levels of responsibility that leading employers of veterans have found to be very successful. The shaded boxes denote the best fit military pay grade to civilian job level crosswalk.

Looking at the chart, you will see the pay grades are broken into ranges beginning with E-1 to E-3 (enlisted ranks) and ending with O-7 to O-10 (officers). The pay grade ranges are ordered from lowest levels of military responsibility to highest. At the low end, E-1s are typically new recruits just entering military service, whereas E-2s and E-3s can be considered as journeymen in their specific occupations. While they have become very proficient in their primary duties, they have yet to gain any supervisory or leadership experience. Therefore, from a civilian equivalent level of responsibility, our

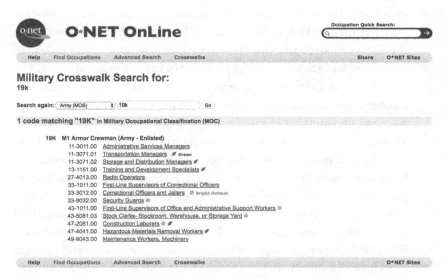

**Figure 5.7** Occupations available to an Enlisted Soldier my Armor Crewman.

leading employers target these pay grades for any entry level positions in their company, or they focus on their military occupation for an exact match, such as a truck driver or recruiter.

- *Enlisted.* E-4 to E-6 pay grades are *NCOs* and are highly sought for supervisor positions. This is because typically supervising people is their primary responsibility at this pay grade. They are truly front-line supervisors in the military, responsible for training, performance, and safety of small teams consisting typically from 3 to 20 or more individuals. NCOs also have become more experienced in their military occupation and can easily qualify as Level II, III, or IV individual contributor candidates in certain technical fields.
- Occupying the top of the enlisted pay grade range are the *senior* NCOs in pay grades E-7 to E-9. These candidates are typically exceptional leaders and managers. As you saw from our example résumé, senior NCOs receive a significant amount of leadership training. The best employers seek to hire these candidates into management roles, with many capable of succeeding at the director level.
- *Warrant officers* are a different type of candidate as they typically have highly specialized and technical occupations in the military. Army warrant officers are also combat leaders, trainers, and advisors. They are commissioned officers culled from the best senior NCO candidates in each service branch, except Air Force as they no longer use warrant officer pay grades. W-1 to W-5 veterans have deep domain expertise in their military occupation and become highly productive in a civilian equivalent job. They are also very capable of leading and managing. The most successful employers of veterans seek to hire warrant officers as directors and managers in areas requiring high levels of training, equipment maintenance, and facility management.
- Those in the *officer corps* are the leaders within the military. Nearly all have earned postsecondary degrees and are immediately thrust into leadership roles. Junior officers, O-1 to O-3, have the same relative experience as junior enlisted in that officers enter the military as an O-1 and progress as they learn and excel. Junior officers are fully prepared to succeed in management and certain leadership-level positions. Successful employers target officers to manage programs and projects as well. Senior officers in pay grades O-4 to O-6 are the leaders with an

expansive span of controls and scope of responsibility. This is the most difficult cohort to place in civilian organizations because the military places its midgrade officers in very large and complex leadership roles. With the exception of specialists like doctors, lawyers, and engineers, this cohort of veterans typically seek large functional or general management leadership roles. The biggest skill gap is that the military does not operate with profit and loss objectives, which makes it difficult to hire midlevel officers into profit and loss responsibility. This skill gap significantly narrows the number of opportunities available for this veteran cohort.

- *General officers* occupy the O-7 to O-10 pay grades. These are the people who help set strategy, shape policy, and ensure the long-term readiness of our military. They lead very large organizations with huge budgets under intense scrutiny. This talented cohort could be high contributors on a board of directors, with many capable of running a business, large functional organization, nonprofit organization, or large-scale projects.

Another reason to examine and utilize pay grades as an effective candidate capability filter is pragmatism. There are nearly 1,200 military occupations but only 23 pay grades. If you are trying to hire veterans and focus only on their occupation, it will be much harder and more expensive to recruit veterans by their military job versus their pay grade. You can gain a terrific understanding of the demographics of the military by studying the most recent Department of Defense's demographics profile online (https://download. militaryonesource.mil/12038/MOS/Reports/2019-demographics-report. pdf).

Nearly half of the population densities for nearly half of all military personnel represents individuals in the E-4 to E-6 pay grade cohort. If you want to have a successful veteran employment program, it is essential you understand the KSAs obtained within these pay grades and target this cohort accordingly. An additional advantage of recruiting the E-4 to E-6 pay grade population is that the E-1 to E-3 cohort represents 24 percent of the remaining military population and reports directly to the E-4 to E-6 cohort. Therefore, targeting the NCOs provides the largest potential referral network for an employer to quickly build a successful veteran hiring program. Leading employers of veterans always report that referrals are a primary source of their veteran recruiting results.

---

**Box 5.4  Army Veteran's Military Awards**

---

SELECT AWARDS
  Bronze Star
  Meritorious Service Medical (3)
  Army Commendation Medical (2)
  Army Achievement Medical (4)

---

## Understanding Military Awards

There are mixed debates from veterans and employers whether veterans should include listing their military awards, medals, and decorations. Many veterans I have spoken with are uncomfortable with mentioning their service medals because they do not understand how their medals can apply to a civilian career. Similarly, I have heard from dozens of employers who assert no interest in learning about the medals a veteran has earned or awarded as they have no direct relevance to an open position. Leading employers with robust veteran hiring programs disagree and seek specific medals that convey much about the type of prospective employee.

Our Army veteran has provided the military awards on his résumé; these are shown in Box 5.4. What do they mean, and how should a recruiter or hiring manager use this information to help them make an informed hiring decision?

Military awards, also known as medals and/or ribbons, can be broadly classified into four broad categories in the order of precedence: personal decorations, unit awards, campaign and service medals, and service and training awards. All military service branches have their own unique medals, with many medals sharing the same name and award requirements across all branches. There is also a precedence among individual medals, with the most prestigious being the Medal of Honor. A brief overview of the categories in reverse order of precedence are as follows:

- *Service and Training Awards*: These are the lowest level of importance and typically are awarded for participation in unique service activities (e.g., being stationed overseas). From a résumé perspective, these military decorations are interesting, but they are not as applicable to civilian employment. Additional medals are awarded for professional development, like completion of the Army NCO leadership courses and becoming a Marine Corps drill instructor. These experiences are far more relevant to civilian employment and are included in the JST. Therefore, most employers do not focus on service and training medals a veteran might have been awarded, and we recommend veterans list only those professional development awards on their résumés.

- *Campaign and Service Medals*: These are awards for serving during times of conflict and for being involved in service campaigns against enemy forces. Examples include the National Defense Service Medal and the Afghanistan Campaign Medal. These two medals convey that the veteran served in time of conflict and was deployed to Afghanistan. While the KSAs a veteran has obtained in a foreign theater of operation are important and relevant to a civilian career, the fact of serving during conflict and being deployed by themselves do not convey sufficient information for an employer to gauge qualification from. Therefore, we recommend to veterans they not list these type awards on their résumés.

- *Unit Awards*: These are awarded for significant accomplishments at the unit level. The unit can be as large as an army or as small as a company or a ship. While unit awards celebrate the accomplishments of the team, they can be an indicator of individual leadership for the commanding officer of the unit receiving the award and for the quality of training and dedication of all of the members of the unit. We encourage veterans to include any unit award they may have received as they provide a terrific opportunity during an interview for the veteran to explain their role in a high-performing team.

- *Personal Decorations*: These are awarded for significant individual accomplishments of the service member. Among personal decorations are several medals that could be awarded to an individual for gallantry and heroism in combat. Most civilians understand there are medals awarded for bravery. Veterans and employers each have mixed emotions about seeing these on a résumé. Unless the heroism award is the Medal of Honor, we recommend they be left off a résumé. There are also medals that can be awarded for outstanding performance or distinguished service related to the individual in their job. These medals can help employers differentiate a veteran, much like graduating with honors or distinction in college does for civilians. Successful employers like to see these medals on the résumé and use them as discussion points in follow-on interviews.

In our experience, the military awards employers want to see on a résumé include the following personal decorations tied to professional achievement, along with a brief description of the award qualification:

- *Distinguished Service Medal* awarded for "exceptionally meritorious service to the Government of the United States in a duty of great responsibility." This award is reserved for senior officers in a position of significant scope and influence.
- *Bronze Star Medal* awarded for "either heroic achievement, heroic service, meritorious achievement, or meritorious service in a combat zone."
- *Meritorious Service Medal* awarded for "outstanding meritorious achievement or service to the United States."
- *Commendation Medal* is presented for "sustained acts of heroism or meritorious service."
- *Achievement Medal* awarded for "meritorious service or achievement in either combat or noncombat situations based on sustained performance or specific achievement of a superlative nature."
- *Good Conduct Medal* is currently awarded to any active duty enlisted member of the U.S. military who completes three consecutive years of "honorable and faithful service."
- *Military Outstanding Volunteer Service Medal* is awarded to military personnel who "perform substantial volunteer service to the local community above and beyond the duties required as a member of the United States Armed Forces. Such volunteer service must be made in a sustained and direct nature towards the civilian community, must be significant in nature to produce tangible results."

These military awards can help identify the highest performers in their respective occupations in the military. The most successful employers seek to find veterans who have distinguished themselves with these recognitions. Going back to our Army veteran, you can now appreciate why he has included his Bronze Star, Meritorious Service, Army Commendation, and Army Achievement medal awards. This provides further demonstrable evidence of the consistent high level of performance and achievement of this veteran within his occupation and reinforces why he has achieved such a high pay grade during his Army career.

## Interviewing Veterans

Most veterans have little understanding of the interview process and how companies are organized. The TAP process recognizes this and provides very good instruction to help veterans. For example, there is a section on how military terminology translates into some civilian terms to help orient veterans and an extensive section on how to prepare for an interview. We recommend you become familiar with this training to gain valuable perspective on how veterans are likely to approach the interview process. Interviewing veterans is really no different from interviewing any potential employee for a specific position in that you are primarily seeking to understand how well trained or competent the individual is for the position and how well they will fit into your organization. If you are seeking to hire a veteran in a directly related occupation like computer programmer, cybersecurity analyst, or diesel mechanic, for example, you will need to ask some questions specific to their training and experiences. Recall the nurse example with the possibility of different levels of skill because one veteran might be assigned to a more urgent care facility than another.

Employers know that during the interview process there are certain questions that are not legal to ask candidates, such as political affiliation, marital status, and religious affiliation. Veterans are also protected by law from additional questions, including the following:

- What kind of discharge did you get from the military? (Unless the job requires a security clearance)
- Will you get deployed again?
- Have you ever killed anyone?
- Have you ever been injured or wounded in combat?
- Are you physically or mentally disabled?
- Do you suffer from post-traumatic stress or depression?

We highly recommend to employers that want to establish a meaningful veteran hiring program that they employ a veteran to run the program. More specifically, the most successful employers we work with have hired a veteran with military recruiting experience. This is because a military recruiter needs to be well versed in the military occupations of that service branch. This is a high-value recruiting role as they are able to not only translate a candidate's military experience but also serve as translator for your company in a way that a veteran candidate can more easily relate to. If there is insufficient budget to employ a dedicated military recruiter, it is strongly recommended that you include a veteran in your organization who works in a similar career field in the interview.

We have outlined the key challenges in crosswalking a military occupation to civilian counterpart previously. Because of the uniqueness of military careers, it is important to ask very detailed questions specific to the military occupation and daily responsibilities. Some helpful specific questions during the interview include, How many people do you directly supervise? What is the budget you are responsible for? How does the budgeting process work in the military? How do you ensure your team is well trained and performing at a high level? Can you describe a typical day in your role?

We also recommend during interviews to ask questions of candidates specific to their training and experiences described on the VMET and JST. Utilizing the VMET and JST is the best method to gain additional insight. This method also helps put a veteran at ease during the interview process because you are signaling your understanding and appreciation of their experience.

The VMET and JST are also key to discovering a specialized skill you are interested in that a veteran may not think applies to any civilian career. A good example of this is specialized training in nuclear, biological, and chemical (NBC) warfare. I have spoken with dozens of enlisted and officer personnel who have NBC training but have not included it in their résumés. When I ask these veterans if they would like to continue serving the public by being a supervisor or manager in a company that does environmental cleanup after a natural disaster or industrial accident, most have told me that type of career is highly appealing. They simply do not know there are industries and employers that value that specific experience. It is important for recruiters to examine these documents and ask those questions.

For candidates you are interviewing for supervisor, management, and leadership positions, it is important to ask detailed questions about their span of control and scope of responsibilities. I also recommend asking questions about major projects the candidate might have been responsible for. In the military, there are typically large-scale personnel and equipment movements, communication, and temporary installation setups. For example,

- Can you describe your leadership training and how you have applied that to managing and holding accountable your teams?
- Are you comfortable providing performance reviews, and can you explain how you have helped a subordinate improve their performance?
- Can you describe a specific project that you managed and how you controlled the deliverables within budget and the project timeline?

In all interviews, I highly recommend asking questions to understand a candidate's specific role, responsibilities, and deliverables that led to any of the key military awards they list on their résumé. If a candidate does not list any military awards, I recommend asking a general question if they have ever received individual merit or unit commendations.

Beyond asking the veteran questions about their knowledge and experiences, it is critical to also explain how career progressions and advancement works in your company. Veterans are coming out of a highly structured environment with predictable pay grade advancements everyone understands. Helping veterans understand your career advancement process will lead to more veterans accepting your offers.

## Top 10 Recommendations

As this chapter shows, there is much to learn about our military to enable confidence in reading résumés to develop an effective military hiring program. To recap all we have covered, here is a list of the top 10 recommendations all recruiting and hiring managers should follow in order to implement and maintain a successful military hiring program:

1. Hire a veteran to lead your veteran recruiting efforts and shortcut the learning process.
2. Know the demographics of the military to improve your targeting and hiring results.
3. Learn about the TAP process to understand how transitioning service members are being trained to write résumés and prepare for interviews.

4. Study the military occupations that are closely related to your career opportunities.
5. Understand military pay grades and hire into supervisor, management, and leadership positions to increase your military hiring readiness.
6. Utilize the VMET and JST to gain additional insights to a candidate's military training and experience.
7. Look for key military awards to learn which candidates are high performers and ask about their individual contributions that led to the awards.
8. Ask specific questions about span of control and scope of responsibilities.
9. Sell your company career paths, training, and development to increase your hiring rates of veterans.
10. Leverage your recent military hires to build a referral network.

## References

Bureau of Labor Statistics, U.S. Department of Labor. (2002). *Occupational outlook handbook: Military careers on the Internet.* Washington, DC: Author. https://www.bls.gov/ooh/military/military-careers.htm

National Council of State Boards of Nurses. (2016). *A comparison of selected military health care occupation curricula with a standard licensed practical/vocational nurse curriculum.* Chicago, IL: Author. https://www.ncsbn.org/16_NCSBNAnalyiss_MilitaryLPNVN.pdf

United States Department of Labor. (2019, November). *Department of Labor Empolyment Workshop Participant Guide.* https://www.dol.gov/sites/dolgov/files/VETS/files/DOLEW-Participant-Guide.pdf

Wenger, J. B., Pint, E. M., Piquado, T., Shanley, M. G., Beleche, T., Bradley, M. A., Welch, J., Werber, L., Yoon, C., Duckworth, E. J., et al. (2017). *Helping soldiers leverage Arym knowledge, skills, and abilities in civilian jobs.* Santa Monica, CA: The RAND Corporation. https://www.rand.org/pubs/research_reports/RR1719.html

# 6

# The Soft Skills Veterans Bring
# to the Workforce

*Theodore L. Hayes and Robert Hogan*

One of the benefits of hiring military veterans is the skill set they bring to the civilian workforce. This chapter describes the skills, particularly the non-technical skills ("soft skills"), that service members gain while in the military. To understand the unique personality factors that veterans can bring to civilian employers, we organize our discussion in terms of the five-factor model of the "Big Five" model (e.g., Garras & Wong, 2016) and describe how civilian companies can use these skills in their organizations.

Veterans represent a cost-efficient way to use the military's selection and training processes to bring these skills immediately into an existing workforce rather than paying for the cost of developing them in nonveteran employees. Although many civilian sector employers expect new employees to possess the skills needed for the jobs for which they were hired, the U.S. Department of Defense (DoD) takes a different approach: It expects to train uniformed service members on the skills and competencies necessary to complete their jobs. The majority of new recruits to the military are high school graduates. Although some will have had experience with the military in high school Junior Reserve Officer Training Corps programs, most will have had no formal military training prior to joining the military. Each service (e.g., Air Force, Army, Marines, Navy, Merchant Marine, Space Force, and Coast Guard) must train their new recruits in the many skills, tasks, and competencies needed in the military both generally and specifically for each new recruit's selected occupation. The DoD is also one of the world's largest providers of training to create competent teams of experts on a wide variety of technical skill areas and nontechnical competencies. The military's success requires all the technical proficiencies needed for a community to survive, including mechanics, engineers, lawyers, physicians, cooks, and cyber codebreakers. The military trains service members in their areas of technical

Theodore L. Hayes and Robert Hogan, *The Soft Skills Veterans Bring to the Workforce* In: *Military Veteran Employment*. Edited by: Nathan D. Ainspan and Kristin N. Saboe, Oxford University Press. © Oxford University Press 2021. DOI: 10.1093/oso/9780190642983.003.0007 proficiency as well as the nontechnical soft skills of management and leadership that are inherently required of all members.

Each service has its own dedicated training command (e.g., the Army has its Training and Doctrine Command), and each command ensures that its members are trained using the most up-to-date/state-of-the-art methods, which, themselves, are continually revised to reflect best practices. Each military training command ensures the transfer and application of new knowledge in a variety of high-demand contexts.

All service members eventually leave the military to pursue civilian careers following a 4- to 24-year (many senior military leaders serve past 24 years) careers in the military. And when they leave, they take with them all the years of training they have received. This technical and soft skill training comes free to, and can be leveraged by, any subsequent civilian employer. The remainder of this chapter outlines the technical and nontechnical skills that veterans bring to the civilian workplace and why these skill sets matters for the success of civilian organizations.

## Technical Skills and Veteran Credentials

Technical or "hard skills" represent behavior that can be evaluated relative to some agreed-on performance standard. Examples include throwing a knuckleball in baseball, a surgeon performing aortic valve replacement surgery, or executing a sniper's 2-mile kill shot. A significant amount of practice and coaching over a period of years is needed to achieve mastery of these skills (e.g., Ericsson, 2015; Ericsson, Krampe, & Tesch-Römer, 1993). There is also an agreed-on performance hierarchy through which people progress as they develop hard skills, such as the progression of medical students graduating and becoming interns, then residents, and eventually attending physicians. Maintenance of expert status depends on continued practice (one either can perform at the specified level or not) and physical or psychomotor skills that will deteriorate due to aging. Other models of expertise (e.g., Gobet, 2016; Macnamara et al., 2018; Macnamara, Hambrick, & Oswald, 2014) identify individual differences such as cognitive ability as the means by which one achieves higher performance using these skills.

Hard skills can frequently be qualified through certifications, educational degrees, and other credentials. As mentioned in previous chapters, 85 percent of the U.S. military's occupations correlate directly with a civilian sector

counterpart. Although civilian hiring managers will need to practice translating military knowledge, skills, and abilities to civilian terminology, a direct correlation already exists between occupations, training, certifications,
and professional degrees required for civilian occupations.

The military has a robust educational system that not only trains technical skills but also enables additional credentialing for its members such
that employers can understand and leverage the certifications that come with
hiring veterans. On joining the military, each member is assigned an occupation based on a robust selection and review system aimed at identifying characteristics (e.g., skills, aptitude, aspiration) of individuals that predispose
them successfully to receive training in certain jobs and occupations. Service
members receive continuous training in skills during their time in uniform
relevant to their military roles and job demands as they advance in their
careers. Many will receive skill certifications that civilian employers will recognize, such as programming certifications. In other cases, military members
will not be required to earn certificates that are required of their civilian
equivalents (e.g., military truck drivers do not have to hold the same license
that civilian truck drivers must maintain). Other types of credentials and
certificates that veterans may bring to a new employer include active security
clearances, advanced degrees (e.g., a Master's in Business Administration degree), and acquisitions and contract certifications.

## Social (Soft) Skills

Soft skills refer to how we manage ourselves and our relations with others.
They are the tools that enable people to communicate, interact, and get along
with others; learn, seek help, and have their needs met in appropriate ways;
develop healthy relationships; protect themselves; and generally be able to
interact with society harmoniously (Dowd & Tierney, 2005). Some soft skills
concern being able to work effectively with others, which we refer to as *interpersonal competence,* while others concern being able to manage one's
emotions effectively, or *intrapersonal competence.* Low intrapersonal competence can be reflected in low resilience, high anxiety, or yelling at people.
Although hierarchical organizations such as the military can allow individuals with low intrapersonal competence to succeed by hiding behind their
rank instead of using their soft skills to interact with others, the military
excels in teaching and developing many of these socially oriented soft skills

in their members. Methods also exist to measure soft skills. These methods can be high tech, such as "web scraping" (i.e., doing automated content analysis on an applicant's social media site; e.g., Meaden & Kind, 2019; Vega, Xie, Halder, & Bumgardner, 2019), or can be assessed through in-person interviews. Not all veterans will score well on these assessments, and not all civilian applicants score well either.

Employers appreciate the inter- and intrapersonal skills that veterans bring to their organization because these skills bring added value to their organizations. However, we offer a caveat about veterans and their soft skills: It is unrealistic and unfair for employers and veterans to expect that all veterans will have the social skills needed for success in any civilian environment. Soft skills vary greatly among individuals, and each veteran will have some of these skills but lack others. In addition, poor transitions into a new job, which might arise from unrealistic expectations on both ends or may be due to the lack of onboarding for veterans, might hamper the success of newly hired veterans. This issue is not unique to veterans in the civilian workforce; poorly handled transitions are one of the leading causes of derailment among managers in general (Watkins, 2013).

Wilson (1978) noted that social skills reinforce a group's likelihood of survival. More cohesive groups are better able to survive threats from outsiders and control resources. Social skills also help individuals improve their relative positions within their groups by acquiring leadership positions and encouraging others to pursue common goals (Hogan & Sherman, 2020). We refer to building relationships as *getting along* and attaining leadership roles as *getting ahead*. There is a tension in any group between getting along and getting ahead, and the social skills that aid in building relationships are different from those that lead to status attainment. The social nature of humans has created a third tendency, *the need to find meaning*, through the rituals that provide a sense of order and predictability (Hogan, Jones, & Cheek, 1985), so that a sense of meaning and purpose is the reward for those who identify with the group. Supporting the values of the group is seen as a sign of good character (Hayes, Hogan, & Emler, 2016) for the individual and an indicator of esprit de corps at the unit level.

Although technical skills are relatively easy to train, nontechnical skills such as social skills (e.g., teamwork, behaving ethically, adaptability) may take a significant amount of time to train and learn from on-the-job experiences. Surveys of civilian employers indicate that they have difficulty finding individuals who meet their minimum technical qualifications and also have the social savvy to progress upward within an organization. Although these skills are difficult to find in the civilian population, the military prioritizes continuously building social skills in its staff and assessing them to gauge their progress and areas in need of improvement and then to encourage staff members to develop their skills. These characteristics of service members may be further honed through additional training while in the military. Leveraging personality predispositions is both efficient and good practice. The military leverages individual predispositions through various assessments both before and after people join the military. Likewise, using personality to select employees is a well-founded practice in civilian organizations. Civilian employers can then capitalize on the social skills, team-oriented mindset, and management experience of veterans that they bring to their civilian careers.

## How the Military Trains Soft Skills

The RAND Corporation (Hardison et al., 2017) conducted research on soldiers and Marines serving in combat arms occupations to identify when and how during their service they develop skills of interest to the civilian workforce employers. Table 6.1 lists and describes these skills.

RAND (Hardison et al., 2017) concluded that proficiency levels in the listed skills differ between service members and veterans based on their skill level when they entered the military. Service members and veterans also differ in the speed with which they gain skills due to individual differences in ability and experience. The RAND study also noted that certain nontechnical skills are so engrained in the military culture (e.g., teaching leadership and communication skills) that the development of those skills was not identified in some military training curriculums despite having requirements that they be taught (e.g., deliver a briefing, lead a team exercise). Of interest to employers who might hire veterans, the study also noted that many 'soft' skills and competencies are so embedded in military culture that veterans may not see them as marketable and will not mention them during interviews or promotion conversations. Civilian employers need to keep in mind this tendency for veterans to discount the cultural expectations of leadership, teamwork, and communication in the military and ask veterans specifically about their knowledge, skills, and abilities. This will allow employers to better understand the depth of experience and knowledge veterans have

**Table 6.1** Top Nontechnical Skills Gained in Army Training
Summary of the Top Nontechnical Skills Addressed in Army Courses

| Skill Addressed | Basic Combat Training (Entry-Level Personnel: E-1 and E-2)[a] | Basic Leader Course (Midlevel Personnel: E-4 and E-5)[a] | Advanced Leader Course (Mid- to Senior-Level Personnel: E-5 and E-6)[b] | Senior Leader Course (Senior-Level Personnel: E-6 and E-7)[b] |
|---|---|---|---|---|
| Handling work stress | ♠ | | | |
| Being dependable and reliable | ♠ | | | |
| Persistence | ♠ | | | |
| Conscientiousness and attention to detail | ♠ | | | |
| Interpersonal skills | ♠ | ♠ | | |
| Teamwork and team building | ♠ | ♠ | ♠ | ♠ |
| Oral communication | | ♠ | ♠ | ♠ |
| Managing and supervising the work of others | | ♠ | ♠ | ♠ |
| Decision-making/ decisiveness | | ♠ | | ♠ |
| Training others | | ♠ | | ♠ |
| Leading, motivation, and inspiring others to accomplish organizational goals | | ♠ | | |
| Critical thinking | | | | ♠ |
| Project planning | | | | ♠ |

*Note.* The absence of a ♠ does not Indicate that instruction in the skill is absent from the course, only that it was not among the "top skills" most emphasized in the course according to the subject matter experts interviewed. See https://www.rand.org/pubs/tools/TL160-1.html for a full description of the methodology used to construct the table. Table information describes the courses during the 2014 to 2015 time frame during which this study was conducted. Courses before or after that period may differ.

[a] Taken by all Army personnel.

[b] All combat arms personnel take a version of this course; however, some of the content and emphasis differ by job grouping (i.e., by occupational branch) and sometimes by job. Here, we report only those skills that instructors have indicated are common to all versions of the course for armor and infantry jobs.

*Source*: Adapted from Hardison et al., 2017, p. 12.

gained from their time in the military. Employers can use the RAND report to identify potential (unintentional) gaps in acknowledged experiences when interacting, interviewing, or working with veterans in civilian work settings.

## Measurement of Soft Skills: The Five-Factor Model

The model of personality known as the *five-factor model* or the *Big Five* is generally accepted by modern behavioral science researchers (Garras & Wong, 2016). The five components are (a) conscientiousness; (b) agreeableness; (c) negative emotionality; (d) openness to experience; and (e) extraversion. The five factors reflect the fact that the terms people use to describe other people cluster together in (about) five broad categories. Granular analyses (Judge, Rodell, Klinger, Simon, & Crawford, 2013; Soto & John, 2017) showed that these five themes all reflect aspects of social skill. For example, conscientiousness is composed of industriousness and orderliness and reflects positive attitudes toward authority. Agreeableness is composed of compassion and politeness and reflects charm and politesse. Negative emotionality (or neuroticism) is composed of moodiness and volatility; the other end of this dimension is emotional stability, and it is reflected in stable relationships. Openness is composed of curiosity and creative imagination and reflects an engaging interpersonal style. Finally, extraversion is composed of assertiveness and social self-confidence and reflects approachability. The value of the five-factor model is to predict aspects of social performance as outlined in Table 6.2.

Table 6.2  Typical Correspondence of Big Five Aspect Evidence to Getting Along, Getting Ahead, and Finding Meaning

| Big Five Aspect | Getting Along | Getting Ahead | Finding Meaning |
| --- | --- | --- | --- |
| Conscientiousness | Some evidence | Solid evidence | Solid evidence |
| Agreeableness | Solid evidence | Some evidence | Some evidence |
| Negative emotionality | Some evidence | Some evidence | Solid evidence |
| Openness to Experience | Some evidence | Some evidence | Some evidence |
| Extraversion | Solid evidence | Some evidence | Solid evidence |

*Note. Solid evidence*: There is consistent correlation between Big Five aspect and outcome class. *Some evidence*: The correspondence between the aspect and the outcome class may depend on the specific type of outcome or the level of employee.

## Evidence Relating the Big Five to Getting Ahead

Over 400 published studies, including research conducted in South Africa (van Aarde, Meiring, & Wiernik, 2017); Europe (Salgado & Táuriz, 2014); Asia (Oh, 2009); and the United States (Barrick & Mount, 1991; Barrick, Mount, & Judge, 2001; see also Schmidt & Hunter, 1998), link conscientiousness to higher supervisor ratings and to objective indices of productivity and training performance. The data clearly suggest that conscientious people are more successful in getting ahead—probably due to the integrity component of conscientiousness (Ones, Viswesvaran, & Schmidt, 1993; Van Iddekinge, Roth, Raymark, & Odle-Dusseau, 2012). People with integrity generally refuse to engage in counterproductive behavior such as stealing, shirking, or drug or alcohol use in school (Cuadrado, Salgado, & Moscoso, 2021) or on the job. A second likely path to success is the industriousness component of conscientiousness: Conscientious people tend to set and work toward and achieve goals (Barrick, Mount, & Strauss, 1993; Locke & Latham, 2002).

The role of conscientiousness is more variable for leaders, who are people who would be described as having "gotten ahead" of those trying to get ahead. DeRue, Nahrgang, Wellman, and Humphrey (2011, Table 3) found that conscientiousness was positively related to leadership outcomes such as objectively rated group performance and subordinate ratings of leader effectiveness. However, highly conscientious leaders are rated as engendering lower follower job satisfaction and lower satisfaction with the leader her- or himself.

The remaining four components of the five-factor model are also related to occupational performance, but their impact varies by occupational context and outcome. Agreeableness tends to predict performance in training for managers, professionals, human service providers (e.g., nurses), and police (Barrick et al., 2001, Table 3) but not for salespeople. Negative emotionality/emotional stability tends to predict supervisors' ratings and training performance for police samples (Barrick et al., 2001, Table 2; van Aarde et al., 2017). Openness tends to predict training performance for police (Barrick et al., 2001, Table 5; van Aarde et al., 2017). Extraversion is related to training performance, possibly specifically within police and managerial samples (Barrick et al., 2001, Table 1; van Aarde et al., 2017). Wilmot, Wanberg, Kammeyer-Mueller, and Ones (2019, see Table 3) found that extraversion was related to supervisor job performance ratings, organizational commitment, expatriate assignment adjustment, job satisfaction, going along with organizational change, and resistance to feeling burned out at work.

## Evidence Relating the Big Five to Getting Along

Organizational scientists refer to getting along with others as contextual performance, or how one acts within the context of work. Two ways getting along with others (contextual performance) is measured are through *organizational citizenship behavior* and *counterproductive work behavior*. Organizational citizenship behavior is reflected in being supportive of or helpful to coworkers. Counterproductive work behavior is reflected in disrupting teamwork, harassing or assaulting others, stealing or destroying property, personal deviance such as drug or alcohol use at school or on the job, or eating other people's food found in the office refrigerator. Chiaburu, Oh, Berry, Li, and Gardner (2011); Judge et al. (2013); van Aarde et al. (2017); and Van Iddekinge et al. (2012) showed that the components of the five-factor model consistently predicted contextual performance (more specifically prosocial organizational behaviors) and (negatively) counterproductive work behavior. Chiaburu and colleagues (2011) showed that it is useful to distinguish between behaviors related to coworkers, those related to the (impersonal) organization, and behaviors focused against management initiatives; these behavioral focuses have different relationships with contextual performance. Wilmot et al. (2019) found that correlations of extraversion to getting along with others, organizational citizenship behavior, and attendance were very small but positive.

Based on these reviews, conscientiousness, openness, and agreeableness are the best predictors of cooperation and putting in discretionary effort to improve the organization. Openness and extraversion are the best predictors of supporting organizational change initiatives.

## Evidence Relating the Big Five to Finding Meaning

Some people find meaning in their work, and others find meaning in their life as a whole. Judge, Heller, and Mount (2002) examined 163 studies using the five-factor model to predict life satisfaction and work satisfaction. Conscientiousness, extraversion, and (low) neuroticism predicted job satisfaction. Judge et al. (2002) also reviewed research regarding the determinants of life satisfaction, defined as subjective well-being. They found that all five factor dimensions predicted life satisfaction, but three aspects—conscientiousness, extraversion, and (low) negative emotionality—were related to job satisfaction. Extraversion was more related to job satisfaction than to life satisfaction, possibly because the workplace allows extraverts to work productively with others. In summary, people who are hard-working, able to work with others, and not socially anxious tend to be more satisfied at work.

## Utilization of the Big Five

The *Big Five* term is widely used in military assessment. The military uses a version of the five-factor model called the Tailored Adaptive Personality Assessment System (Nye et al., 2012) to select recruits using a "whole-person" model to identify individuals who will be exemplary service members given their motivational predispositions and soft skills. Similarly, the five-factor model informs the selection decisions of many companies that seek to select qualified applicants based on their predisposition for success in a job (Nye et al., 2012). In short, veterans entering the civilian workforce are familiar with a variety of assessments as they have spent much of their careers being assessed for both technical and nontechnical soft skills.

## Reputation in Action: Outside the Big Five

Social skill creates people's reputations, but reputations do not create social success. To understand successful social behaviors, we need to look at reputation in action, as found in political skill, ambition, and emotional intelligence.

## Political Skill

Social skills are the observable hard skills of the social world, and political skills are at the apex of the social skills. The big question concerns how to engage successfully in group politics (getting ahead) while maintaining support within the group (getting along). This requires political skill. Ferris et al. (2005, p. 127) defined political skill as "[T]he ability to effectively understand others at work, and to use such knowledge to influence others to act in ways that enhance one's personal and/or organizational objectives." There is nothing in this definition that implies manipulation as understood in the term *Machiavellian*; successful behavior within organizations requires dealing effectively with internal politics. This is considered one of the core qualifications for senior leaders in the federal government by both the DoD (U.S. DoD, 2014) and the U.S. Office of Personnel Management (2010).

Political skill has been studied in terms of how interpersonal influence works; this research identified four styles (Ferris et al., 2005): (a) social astuteness (cleverness in figuring out what others want); (b) interpersonal influence (interpersonal adaptability and flexibility); (c) networking ability (alliance building, positioning others for attainment of goals); and (d) apparent sincerity (projecting at least the appearance of what some might call "authenticity"). Political skill is meaningfully correlated with job performance (Munyon, Summers, Thompson, & Ferris, 2015). It seems to be the psychological process by which people apply their strengths and talents to achieve outcomes (Blickle, Wendel, & Ferris, 2010). Those with more political skill are better able to use their strengths and talents to achieve goals, while those with little political skill have difficulty using their strengths and talents. People who are better at politics seem to be more effective because they better understand the goals of their social group (e.g., squad, unit, organization) and their own personal goals and how to connect their goals with the organization's goals to create a "win–win" situation.

## Ambition

Personal motivation is an interaction of conscientiousness, extraversion, lower neuroticism/higher emotional stability, a parent's occupational prestige, and intelligence. Caveats on these results are important (Judge & Kammeyer-Mueller, 2012, p. 771) as the predictive nature of ambition measures have not been established in multiple occupational fields. It is obvious to the casual observer that some people want to get ahead (i.e., win) more than others do, and that is a function of ambition. An interesting question is whether ambition is about coming in first place (i.e., beating opponents), achieving difficult goals and personal records, moving forward against obstacles because of one's sense of mission, or some combination of these motivations.

## Emotional Intelligence

A step beyond agreeableness in the social skills hierarchy is empathy, which was defined by Hogan (1969) as "the intellectual or imaginative apprehension of another's condition or state of mind" (p. 307). Many people think of "emotional intelligence" when they think of empathy, though these terms are not synonymous (Ackley, 2016; Joseph, Jin, Newman, & O'Boyle, 2015; MacCann, Joseph, Newman, & Roberts, 2014). Emotional intelligence is actually at least three different skill sets: (a) identifying that other people are experiencing emotions, (b) understanding what those emotions mean, and (c) managing one's own emotions. Skill in these areas is related to higher job performance in jobs where the focus is on working closely with other people as opposed to, say, information technology or agriculture (Joseph & Newman, 2010), where work may not need to be done in close proximity to other people. But even then, emotional intelligence as measured in tests is itself a combination of basic human abilities, such as intelligence (for analytically reasoning about emotional cues) and the five-factor aspects of conscientiousness and lower negative emotionality/higher emotional stability. The implication for those seeking to understand social skills is that interpersonal emotional competence can be trained up to a point (Ackley, 2016), but eventually those with higher amounts of conscientiousness, cognitive ability, and self-control will be seen as more emotionally intelligent.

Veterans, especially officers, are trained to show and grow emotional intelligence as part of their daily service lives. For example, Taylor-Clark (2015) mapped the Army leadership requirements model to emotional intelligence competencies. Much as in the civilian employment realm, military occupations, where working closely with people and achieving results through the coordination of other people's efforts—basically, providing leadership—requires emotional intelligence. Taylor-Clark found that self-awareness, self-management, social awareness, and social skills development strategies—or as we have referred to them, developing intrapersonal and interpersonal skills—was consistent with developing leadership capacity. We speculate that, because military sector leadership models and well-known emotional intelligence competencies are aligned (Haynie, 2016; Korn

Ferry Institute, 2017), military personnel who have had successful leadership careers also can be effective civilian leaders by using soft social skills. Leadership and the skill set developed in veterans during their time in service is discussed in more detail in Chapter 10 of this book.

## Conclusion

It is much easier for an employer to list "hard skills" in terms of certifications and educational credentials in a job announcement than to advertise for emotional intelligence, conscientiousness, and political skill. However, it is exactly these soft skills that are key drivers of success for employees generally, and veterans have developed and demonstrated their soft skills throughout their military service. There are several ramifications of this for civilian employers as they review candidates with prior military service.

First, veterans have demonstrated success working in a system in which getting along with others is sometimes a matter of life or death. Teamwork and collaboration are ways to demonstrate soft skills. Employers can expect veterans to have these skills.

Second, veterans have been successful working in "strong" environments, that is, organizations with respected traditions, norms, and expectations to which members adhere. Promotion within a hierarchy, which is a version of getting ahead, is an indication of motivation and, possibly, competitiveness. This type of drive should be assessed relative to the needs of the target position and the organization's values to ensure a position is a good fit for both the organization and the veteran.

Third, veterans spend their time in the military being part of a broader community with its customs and values, a system that encourages finding meaning through continued participation, and a group of people that provides a strong sense of community and value-driven behaviors. This experience can make it difficult for veterans to move into civilian employment because most employers do not have strong values-based cultures compared to the military service branches. Onboarding programs that emphasize expectations, values, and mission are helpful for veterans as a way to transition into the organization he or she has just joined. Although military personnel have been trained for social skills, this training has come in organizations that intentionally reinforce these skills; many civilian organizations are not as diligent.

At the same time, it is possible for military personnel, especially officers, to hide behind the privileges conferred by rank. Employers cannot assume that veterans have the soft skills required for success, and veterans cannot assume that their soft skill advantages transfer to a civilian setting. Intentionally testing and hiring for soft skills thus will yield benefits for organizations by allowing them to identify the applicants with the soft skills needed for particular positions. Veterans will benefit from testing by being able to understand their soft skill sets more accurately.

Compared to their civilian counterparts, veterans often possess, whether or not they are aware of it, high levels of the soft skills most desired by hiring organizations.

# References

Ackley, D. (2016). Emotional intelligence: A practical review of models, measures, and applications. *Consulting Psychology Journal: Practice and Research, 68*, 269–286. http://dx.doi.org/10.1037/cpb0000070

Barrick, M. R., & Mount, M. K. (1991). The Big Five personality dimensions and job performance: A meta-analysis. *Personnel Psychology, 44*, 1–26.

Barrick, M. R., Mount, M. K., & Judge, T. A. (2001). Personality and performance at the beginning of the new millennium: What do we know and where do we go next? *International Journal of Selection and Assessment, 9*, 9–30. doi:10.1111/1468-2389.00160

Barrick, M. R., Mount, M. K., & Strauss, J. P. (1993). Conscientiousness and performance of sales representatives: Test of the mediating effects of goal setting. *Journal of Applied Psychology, 78*, 715–722.

Blickle, G., Wendel, S., & Ferris, G. R. (2010). Political skill as moderator of personality— job performance relationships in socioanalytic theory: Test of the getting ahead motive in automobile sales. *Journal of Vocational Behavior, 76*, 326–335. doi:10.1016/j.jvb.2009.10.005

Chiaburu, D. S., Oh, I.-S., Berry, C. M., Li, N., & Gardner, R. G. (2011). The five-factor model of personality traits and organizational citizenship behaviors: A meta-analysis. *Journal of Applied Psychology, 96*, 1140–1166. doi:10.1037/a0024004

Cuadrado, D., Salgado, J. F., & Moscoso, S. (2021). Personality, intelligence, and counterproductive academic behaviors: A meta-analysis. *Journal of Personality and Social Psychology, 120*(2), 504–537. https://doi.org/10.1037/pspp0000285

DeRue, D. S., Nahrgang, J. D., Wellman, N., & Humphrey, S. E. (2011). Trait and behavioral theories of leadership: An integration and meta-analytic test of their relative validity. *Personnel Psychology, 64*, 7–52. https://doi.org/10.1111/j.1744-6570.2010.01201.x

Dowd, T. P., & Tierney, J. (2005). *Teaching social skills to youth: A step-by-step guide to 182 basic to complex skills plus helpful teaching techniques.* Omaha, NE: Boys Town Press.

Ericsson, K. A. (2015). Acquisition and maintenance of medical expertise: A perspective from the expert performance approach with deliberate practice. *Academic Medicine, 90*, 1471–1486.

Ericsson, K. A., Krampe, R. T., & Tesch-Römer, C. (1993). The role of deliberate practice in the acquisition of expert performance. *Psychological Review, 100*, 363–406. doi:10.1037/0033-295X.100.3.363

Ferris, G. R., Treadway, D. C., Kolodinsky, R. W., Hochwarter, W. A., Kacmar, C. J., Douglas, C., & Frink, D. D. (2005). Development and validation of the political skill inventory. *Journal of Management, 31*, 126–152.

Garras, S. J., & Wong, L. (2016, March-April). Moving beyond the MBTI: The Big Five and leader development. *Military Review, 96*, 53–57.

Gobet, F. (2016). *Understanding expertise: A multi-disciplinary approach.* London, UK: Palgrave.

Hardison, C. M., McCausland, T. C., Shanley, M. G., Saavedra, A. R., Clague, A., Crowley, J. C., ... M. P Steinberg, P. S. (2017). *What veterans bring to civilian workplaces: A prototype toolkit for helping private-sector employers understand the nontechnical skills developed in the military* (Technical report # TL160-1). Santa Monica, CA: RAND. https://www.rand.org/pubs/tools/TL160-1.html

Hayes, T. L., Hogan, R., & Emler, N. (2016). The psychology of character, reputation, and gossip. In I. Fileva (Ed.), *Questions of character* (pp. 266–282). New York, NY: Oxford University Press.

Haynie, J. M. (2016). *Revisiting the business case for hiring a veteran: A strategy for cultivating competitive advantage* (Employment research series, paper 2). Syracuse, NY: Syracuse University Institute for Veterans and Military Families. https://ivmf.syracuse.edu/wp-content/uploads/2018/11/Revisiting-Business-Case-for-Hiring-a-Veteran-Full-Report.pdf

Hogan, R. (1969). Development of an empathy scale. *Journal of Consulting and Clinical Psychology, 33*, 307–316.

Hogan, R., Jones, W. H., & Cheek, J. M. (1985). Socioanalytic theory: An alternative to armadillo psychology. In B. R. Schlenker (Ed.), *The self and social life* (pp. 175–198). New York, NY: McGraw-Hill.

Hogan, R., & Sherman, R. A. (2020). Personality theory and the nature of human nature. *Personality and Individual Differences, 152*, 109561. https://doi.org/10.1016/j.paid.2019.109561

Joseph, D. L., Jin, J., Newman, D. A., & O'Boyle, E. H. Jr. (2015). Why does self-reported emotional intelligence predict job performance? A meta-analytic investigation of mixed EI. *Journal of Applied Psychology, 100*, 298–342. http://dx.doi.org/10.1037/a0037681

Joseph, D. L., & Newman, D. A. (2010). Emotional intelligence: An integrative meta-analysis and cascading model. *Journal of Applied Psychology, 95*, 54–78. http://10.1037/a0017286

Judge, T. A., Heller, D., & Mount, M. K. (2002). Five-Factor model of personality and job satisfaction: A meta-analysis. *Journal of Applied Psychology, 87*, 530–541. doi:10.1037//0021-9010.87.3.530

Judge, T. A., & Kammeyer-Mueller, J. D. (2012). On the value of aiming high: The causes and consequences of ambition. *Journal of Applied Psychology, 97*, 758–775. doi:10.1037/a0028084

Judge, T. A., Rodell, J. B., Klinger, R. L., Simon, L. S., & Crawford, E. R. (2013). Hierarchical representations of the five-factor model of personality in predicting job performance: Integrating three organizing frameworks with two theoretical perspectives. *Journal of Applied Psychology, 98*, 875–925. doi:10.1037/a0033901

Korn Ferry Institute. (2017). *Debunking myths in veteran hiring* (White paper). https://www.kornferry.com/content/dam/kornferry/docs/article-migration/VeteransMay2017.pdf

Locke, E. A., & Latham, G. P. (2002). Building a practically useful theory of goal setting and task motivation: A 35-year odyssey. *American Psychologist, 57*, 705–717. doi:10.1037//0003-066X.57.9.705

MacCann, C., Joseph, D. L., Newman, D. A., & Roberts, R. D. (2014). Emotional intelligence is a second-stratum factor of intelligence: Evidence from hierarchical and bifactor models. *Emotion, 14*, 358–374. doi:10.1037/a0034755

Macnamara, B. N., Hambrick, D. Z., Frank, D. J., King, M. J., Burgoyne, A. P., & Meinz, E. J. (2018). The deliberate practice view: An evaluation of definitions, claims, and empirical evidence. In D. Z. Hambrick, G. Campitelli, and B. N. Macnamara (Eds.), *The science of expertise: Behavioral, neural, and genetic approaches to complex skill* (pp. 151–168). New York, NY: Routledge.

Macnamara, B. N., Hambrick D. Z., & Oswald F. L. (2014). Deliberate practice and performance in music, games, sports, education, and professions: A meta-analysis. *Perspectives on Psychological Science, 25*, 1608–1618. doi:10.1177/0956797614535810

Meaden, J., & Kind, C. (2019, April). *Natural language processing & text analytics in organizational research.* Workshop presented at the 34th annual Society for Industrial/Organizational Psychology Conference, National Harbor, MD.

Munyon, T. P., Summers, J. K., Thompson, K. M., & Ferris, G. R. (2015). Political skill and work outcomes: A theoretical extension, meta-analytic investigation, and agenda for the future. *Personnel Psychology, 68*, 143–184. doi:10.1111/peps.12066

Nye, C. D., Drasgow, F., Chernyshenko, O. S., Stark, S., Kubisiak, U. C., White, L. A., & Jose, I. (2012). *Assessing the Tailored Adaptive Personality Assessment System (TAPAS) as an MOS qualification instrument* (Technical Report 1312). Ft. Belvoir, VA: United States Army Research Institute for the Behavioral and Social Sciences.

Oh, I.-S. (2009). *The five factor model of personality and job performance in East Asia: A cross-cultural validity generalization study* (Doctoral dissertation). University of Iowa, Iowa City, IA. http://search.proquest.com/dissertations/docview/304903943/

Ones, D. S., Viswesvaran, C., & Schmidt, F. L. (1993). Comprehensive meta-analysis of integrity test validities: Findings and implications for personnel selection and theories of job performance. *Journal of Applied Psychology, 78*, 679–703. http://dx.doi.org/10.1037/0021-9010.78.4.679

Salgado, J., & Táuriz, G. (2014). The five-factor model, forced-choice personality inventories and performance: A comprehensive meta-analysis of academic and occupational validity studies. *European Journal of Work and Organizational Psychology, 23*, 3–30. http://dx.doi.org/10.1080/1359432X.2012.716198

Schmidt, F. L., & Hunter, J. E. (1998). The validity and utility of selection methods in personnel psychology: Practical and theoretical implications of 85 years of research findings. *Psychological Bulletin, 124*, 262–274.

Soto, C. J., & John, O. P. (2017). The next Big Five Inventory (BFI-2): Developing and assessing a hierarchical model with 15 facets to enhance bandwidth, fidelity, and predictive power. *Journal of Social and Personality Psychology*, *113*, 117–143. http://dx.doi.org/10.1037/pspp0000096

Taylor-Clark, T. M. (2015). *Emotional intelligence competencies and the Army leadership requirements model* (Unpublished master's thesis). U.S. Army Command and General Staff College, Fort Leavenworth, KS.https://apps.dtic.mil/dtic/tr/fulltext/u2/a623911.pdf

U. S. Department of Defense. (2014). *Defense Senior Leader Development Program (DSLDP) Overview* (White paper). https://www.mcbbutler.marines.mil/Portals/189/Docs/CHRO/Training/Defense%20Senior%20Leader%20Development%20Program%20(DSLDP)/DSLDP%20Program%20Overview.pdf

U. S. Office of Personnel Management. (2010). *Guide to Senior Executive Service qualifications* (White paper). https://www.opm.gov/policy-data-oversight/senior-executive-service/reference-materials/guidetosesquals_2010.pdf

van Aarde, N., Meiring, D., & Wiernik, B. M. (2017). The validity of the Big Five personality traits for job performance: Meta-analyses of South African studies. *International Journal of Selection and Assessment*, *25*, 223–239. doi:10.1111/ijsa.12175

Van Iddekinge, C. H., Roth, P. L., Raymark, P. H., & Odle-Dusseau, H. N. (2012). The criterion-related validity of integrity tests: An updated meta-analysis. *Journal of Applied Psychology*, *97*, 499–530. doi:10.1037/a0021196

Vega, R. P., Xie, J., Halder, S., & Bumgardner, E. (2019, April). *How do employees feel about telework? An interdisciplinary approach*. Poster presented at the 34th annual Society for Industrial/Organizational Psychology conference, National Harbor, MD.

Watkins, M. D. (2013). *The first 90 days: Proven strategies for getting up to speed faster and smarter*. Cambridge, MA: Harvard Business Review Press.

Wilmot, M. P., Wanberg, C. R., Kammeyer-Mueller, J. D., & Ones, D. S. (2019). Extraversion advantages at work: A quantitative review and synthesis of the meta-analytic evidence. *Journal of Applied Psychology*, *104*, 1447–1470. http://dx.doi.org/10.1037/apl0000415

Wilson, E. O. (1978). What is sociobiology?. *Society*, *15*(6), 10–14.

# 7

# Hiring and Employing Wounded and Disabled Veterans

*Judy Young, Lisa Stern, and Daniel Geller*

The transition from military service to civilian employment can be a challenging process for veterans and their families. In addition to critical cultural adjustments, veterans are also reconnecting with family, reintegrating into their home communities, and beginning or resuming a civilian career. This process can be especially daunting for veterans with disabilities as there is often an additional and more formidable task at hand: adjusting physically, mentally, and emotionally to an injury and newly acquired disability. While ensuring that veterans obtain and sustain employment is significant to achieving and maintaining financial independence, employment is also essential to gaining a sense of purpose and pride and for reestablishing a wounded or disabled veteran's identity and self-confidence.

As the other chapters in the book demonstrate, employers are hiring veterans because the right veteran hire is a sound business decision. Companies with veteran and military hiring initiatives have capitalized on both the tangible and intangible diversity of skills and talents that veterans and veterans with disabilities bring to the workplace, including but not limited to the ability to quickly learn new skills and concepts; demonstrated flexibility to work in teams or independently; inherent leadership skills honed during their military service; and the self-discipline and respect for procedures that helped them perform exceptionally well under pressure and in stressful situations. In general, veterans are employees whose life experiences have taught them that the key to success is completing the mission and job. Veterans with disabilities have needed to acquire an added layer of resilience and problem-solving skills, as many must learn how to continually adapt and negotiate changing life circumstances. Not only will they establish a pathway to postmilitary employment and transition to functioning in the civilian

Judy Young, Lisa Stern, and Daniel Geller, *Hiring and Employing Wounded and Disabled Veterans* In: *Military Veteran Employment.* Edited by: Nathan D. Ainspan and Kristin N. Saboe, Oxford University Press. © Oxford University Press 2021. DOI: 10.1093/oso/9780190642983.003.0008 working world as an individual contributor, but also many need to determine if and how an acquired disability will impact career decision-making. Companies that know how to hire and retain veterans who obtained these additional skills of resilience, growth, and reflection will have a competitive advantage over others that do not know how to gain access to this population of veterans with disabilities.

This chapter offers business leaders and human resource professionals an overview of the intersection between disability, veteran status, and employment. First, some context is provided by discussing veterans and disability employment statistics. Next, some workplace challenges and common misperceptions often associated with veterans with disabilities in the civilian workforce are offered. The discussion continues to address disability disclosure and reasonable accommodation followed by promising practices for hiring and retaining veterans with disabilities. The chapter concludes by outlining federal laws pertaining to the employment of veterans with disabilities along with additional resources for employers.

## Veterans and Disability Employment Statistics

Approximately 200,000 service members leave the active duty military each year and return to civilian communities and workplaces. According to the Bureau of Labor Statistics (BLS), 4.1 million veterans served in uniform between September 11, 2001, and the end of 2018. Forty-one percent of these veterans report a service-connected disability (BLS, 2020). A service-connected disability is defined by U.S. Code as one that "was incurred or aggravated . . . in the line of the active military, naval, or air service" (38 U.S.C. § 101.16, https://www.govinfo.gov/content/pkg/USCODE-2011-title38/html/USCODE-2011-title38-partI.htm). It is important to note that not all service-connected disabilities present functional limitations in the workplace. In fact, the most prevalent service-connected disabilities experienced by this newest generation of veterans are tinnitus, hearing loss, and spine and knee injuries (VBA Annual Benefits (2020)). That said, traumatic brain injury (TBI) and post-traumatic stress disorder (PTSD) continue to be the injuries most often propagated by the media (Stone & Stone, 2015) and in the workplace, yet a veteran's susceptibility to post-traumatic stress is no greater than the average American (Office of the Chairman of the Joint Chiefs of Staff, 2014).

The Defense and Veterans Brain Injury Center (DVBIC) reports 383,947 veterans sustained a TBI between the years 2000 and the first quarter of 2018, and the National Center for PTSD estimates 11 to 20 percent of post-9/11 veterans are living with PTSD. As large as these numbers appear to be, they do not account for veterans who have not sought treatment for these injuries and therefore are not included in Department of Defense (DoD) injury reports or the Department of Veterans Affairs (VA) report of service-connected disabilities. The RAND Corporation estimated 19 percent of post-9/11 veterans have experienced a TBI, another 20 percent live with PTSD and/or depression, and about 7 percent have been diagnosed with both PTSD and TBI (Tanielian and Jaycox, 2008). To put this in perspective, the National Institutes of Mental Health reported that approximately 18 percent of the general population in the United States is affected by an anxiety disorder (including but not limited to PTSD and major depression), and according the Centers for Disease Control and Prevention, TBI accounts for approximately 30 percent of all injury deaths in the United States. In 2010, approximately 2.5 million TBIs occurred as either an isolated injury or along with another, and in 2013, there were 2.8 million TBI-related emergency room visits, hospitalizations, and deaths reported in the United States.

The BLS (2021) estimates 29% percent of working adults (ages 16–64) has a disability. The Social Security Administration highlighted the fact that more than one in four 20-year-olds will become disabled before they retire, yet estimates show only 8 percent of 18- to 64-year-olds report a work-related limitation. The Job Accommodation Network (JAN), a free service provided by the U.S. Department of Labor's Office of Disability Employment Policy, has seen an increase in the requests for information regarding employees acquiring disabilities later in life and continuing to work. JAN suggests employers have in place proactive policies and training related to disability and employment to address the likelihood that health-related issues will impact the context of the work environment.

## Challenges and Attitudes in the Workplace

Accessing and maintaining gainful and meaningful employment are critical factors to the successful transition of veterans from military careers to civilian life. While many employers consider military service a competitive advantage (see Chapter 2 of this book), negative perceptions related to military service and disability continue to pose concerns and barriers to achieving positive employment and career outcomes for both employers and veterans alike. Whereas senior corporate leadership may understand the benefits of hiring veterans and veterans with disabilities, more targeted training and education is often needed at the midmanagement and supervisory levels as well as for human resource professionals to dispel myths and misconceptions about military service, military occupations, disability, and reasonable accommodations. Addressing these topics openly may actually promote welcoming work environments for veterans with disabilities and help mitigate any perceived hiring barriers.

As outlined in the other chapters in this book, companies that are committed to hiring veterans use a wide range of sourcing and recruitment strategies, engage in veteran and disability-focused job fairs, post positions on veteran-specific websites, and conduct recruitment on military installations. Many have designated recruiters who previously served in the military, are military spouses, or have been trained specifically for outreach to the veteran community. In addition, the U.S. VA and the U.S. Department of Labor have coordinated efforts to support veterans in their transition, with both virtual and in-person assistance and employers with an online portal to post jobs and commit to hiring veterans (https://www.dol.gov/veterans/hireaveteran).

There are significant differences in how businesses communicate the value they place on military service and the corresponding skills and talent veterans bring to the workplace. Unfortunately, almost half of post-9/11 veterans understate or exclude their military service on their résumé and job application due to concerns that military service may have a negative impact on their ability to secure employment (Scanlon, 2016). Further, in a study by Disabled American Veterans and Monster, Military.com (2016), the majority of employers surveyed (73 percent) reported a commitment to hiring veterans; however, a significant group (45 percent) indicated that their work environment was not appropriate for veterans with disabilities in general, and 30 percent expressed specific concerns about employing veterans with PTSD. In the same study, while 38 percent of the veterans surveyed were not comfortable disclosing a disability on a job application, 84 percent believed their employers were willing to accommodate their impairments. A major finding from this study was the need for increased employer education regarding the hiring of veterans with disabilities.

In one study, 68 employers who participated in focus group sessions conducted by Cornell University's Yang-Tan Institute (YTI) on Employment and Disability highlighted the discrepancy between the interest in hiring veterans and concerns for accommodating disabilities (Lee, VanLooy, Young, & Stern, 2016). Overall, employers reported incorporating a wide variety of outreach and inclusion strategies to maximize recruitment, hiring, and retention efforts to specifically target veterans with disabilities. Veterans with disabilities who participated in the focus groups overwhelmingly expressed concern around the stigma associated with mental health impairments, PTSD, and TBI. Consequently, many chose not to disclose any type of disability, thereby not gaining access to potential accommodations that might have contributed to a successful employment experience.

The Americans With Disabilities Act (ADA), which applies to employers with a minimum of 15 workers, requires that organizations provide reasonable accommodations for qualified individuals with disabilities to allow them to perform the essential functions of their jobs. Reasonable accommodations, determined through an interactive process between the employee and employer, might include special equipment, such as a modified keyboard, an ergonomic chair, an elevated desk, or structural accommodations such as modified work schedules or more frequent breaks to allow employees to perform at optimum levels. While all accommodations are person and job specific, JAN can offer both employers and individual employees recommendations on accommodations for a broad range of workplace issues, as well as individualized consultation for specific cases.

If a veteran with a disability is unfamiliar with the ADA, he or she likely does not know about reasonable accommodations or the process for requesting them. Veterans who participated in the YTI focus groups mentioned above all received a disability determination as part of their VA rating for benefits, but they did not understand how, if at all, their specific service-connected disability could be considered a functional impairment at work or that it was possible to request an accommodation or modification to their job or work environment. Rarely, if at all, did a veteran understand the potential job-related limitations associated with a specific disability or the short- and long-term impact their disability might have on their employment situation. Most were uninformed about the ADA and their legal rights as an individual with a disability. Many were also reluctant to identify with the disability label. For some focus group participants, this lack of knowledge and awareness ultimately impeded their productivity, led to job abandonment, or resulted in the termination of employment (Lee et al., 2016).

## Misperceptions and Facts

An exploratory study (Stern, 2017) examined how the military-to-civilian career transition of post-9/11 veterans with disabilities was portrayed in the academic literature. Workplace stereotype and stigma were common themes identified as a barrier to employment for veterans and a barrier to recruitment and hiring for employers. While it is important to understand these common misperceptions, it is more important to highlight the facts. The following six stereotypes presented, along with the facts, are supported by a research-informed white paper from the Office of the Chairman of the Joint Chiefs of Staff (2014):

**Stereotype:** *Veterans suffer disproportionately from PTSD.*

*Fact:* While many veterans experience PTSD, their susceptibility to this condition is not significantly greater than that of the average American.

*Support for the facts:* The mental health of service members and veterans has garnered substantial attention in the media. Headlines often imply that service members and veterans are more likely to suffer from mental health issues than the general population. This misconception—specifically about post-9/11 veterans—can unfairly shape the impression many Americans have of the military community (National Commission on Military, National, and Public Service, 2019). It is important to understand and acknowledge that mental health conditions like PTSD are *not* unique to service members and veterans, and that they can be treated and accommodated as needed. The National Center for PTSD reports about seven or eight out of every 100 people will develop PTSD at some point in their lives (about eight million adults during any given year).

**Stereotype:** *Due to combat-connected post-traumatic stress, veterans are a liability at work.*

*Fact:* There are no data that confidently link PTSD with a propensity for violence.

*Support for the facts:* Although PTSD affects a comparatively small portion of the veteran community, misinformed concern can prejudice employers from hiring veterans. Despite this fact, a survey involving representatives from 69 companies of various sizes revealed that more than 50 percent of respondents believed that negative stereotypes, particularly concerning PTSD, adversely affected veteran employment prospects (Harrell and Berglass, 2012).

**Stereotype:** *Veterans who experience a TBI in combat are permanently damaged.*

*Fact:* More than 1.7 million mild TBIs occur each year in the civilian community, with most people experiencing minimal long-term effects.

*Support for the facts:* Common causes of TBI in the military are not necessarily different from those in the civilian community: vehicle accidents, falls, sports injuries, and recreational activities. Between 2003 and 2017, of TBI cases in the Defense Medical Surveillance System, 80.3 percent were classified as mild (DVBIC, 2017). The term *concussion* is often used to describe this injury in the civilian community. Most people who have experienced a TBI, or a concussion, experience no long-term effects. Stereotypes suggesting that all veterans have a brain injury or that a TBI should disqualify veterans from an employment opportunity constitute a rush to uneducated and misinformed judgment, especially when effective accommodation strategies are well understood and documented if employment-related challenges are present.

**Stereotype:** *Most veterans are not well educated or are not quality job candidates.*

*Fact:* The current generation of veterans exceeds, on average, national norms in education. In addition, more veterans seek some postsecondary education than do their nonveteran peers.

*Support for the facts:* Applicants for military service must meet academic, cognitive aptitude, ethical, and physical requirements. The Pentagon has reported that approximately 7 in 10 American youth (ages 17–24) would fail to qualify for military service because of reasons due to health, physical fitness, and educational background. In addition, 92 percent of veterans age 25 and older have at least a high school diploma, compared with 86 percent of the total population (Moore, n.d.). Thomas Meyer (2013) from Philanthropy Roundtable noted that the current service members also exceed national norms related to health and character qualities.

**Stereotype:** *Veterans do not possess relevant civilian jobs skills.*

*Fact:* Military experience imparts key vocational tasks, skills, experiences, and characteristics on service members that are highly valued and often required for success in business and industry.

*Support for the facts:* While common combat images and media representations of our Armed Forces might have those without military experience wondering how military skills translate to the civilian workforce community, the fact is more than 81 percent of military occupations have a direct civilian equivalent (Military Family Research Institute, n.d.). However, veterans often have difficulty in effectively translating their experiences into a civilian résumé. Over 40 years of peer-reviewed academic research from the fields of business, psychology, sociology, and organizational behavior demonstrated at least 10 key vocational tasks, skills, experiences, specific abilities, attributes, and characteristics required for success in business and industry that military experience imparts to veterans (Institute for Veterans and Military Families, 2012; RAND, 2017). Many of these attributes were discussed previously in this chapter and are presented in detail in other chapters of this book.

**Stereotype**: *Veterans are conditioned to follow orders and will lack initiative in the workplace.*

*Fact*: Service members are trained and expected to act on their own initiative consistent with their commander's intent; this empowerment breeds independence, maturity, and confidence in decision-making that should appeal to any prospective employer.

*Support for the facts*: Regardless of rank or occupational specialty, veterans have been trained to execute complex tasks in extremely challenging environments. When armed with a mission statement and the intent of their commander, these men and women have honed the skills to confidently make decisions based on their leader's guidance and intent. Unfortunately, those in the civilian workforce often fail to connect everyday responsibilities to the overall organizational purpose (Watson, Perry, Ripley, & Chittum, 2017). Ensuring veterans (and *all* employees) better understand how the work they do impacts the organization, its customers, and the community will go a long way to helping make this connection more tangible.

## Educating the Workforce

Educating managers, supervisors, and human resource professionals about military culture, disability, and more specifically about how reasonable accommodations can reduce the impact of an acquired disability is critical to improving employment outcomes for veterans with disabilities. Formal training and the dissemination of up-to-date, relevant information should be used when educating managers, executives, and human resource staff regarding the myths and facts about all disabilities, but specifically about the stigmatized impairments of PTSD and TBI to reduce concerns about employing veterans in general and, more importantly, employing veterans with disabilities.

In an effort to help the business community understand military cultural competency and how to support employees who are veterans and/or civilian soldiers (members of Reserve and National Guard units), the VA offers a Veterans Employment Toolkit. This toolkit targets managers and supervisors, human resource professionals, and employee assistance program (EAP) providers and includes a series of strategies and practices specifically focused on welcoming, orienting, and reintegrating veterans with disabilities into the civilian workforce. The toolkit is available online (https://www.va.gov/vetsinworkplace).

Hiring managers and supervisors should be regularly informed about company policies and practices related to the reasonable accommodation process. They should also be tasked with understanding the basics of the laws, regulations, and employer responsibilities that pertain to the recruitment, hiring, promotion, and overall inclusion of veterans (and other employees) with disabilities. Establishing a welcoming work environment that supports and appreciates the contributions of all employees benefits the entire workplace and may actually facilitate optimum job performance and reduce conflict, absenteeism, and turnover. To support outreach and recruitment efforts, many employers participate in veteran and disability-focused job fairs and develop partnerships with targeted local community-based organizations. Many proactive companies have designated outreach staff who are veterans themselves so they not only understand the transferable skills of potential recruits but also speak a common language. These staff can also provide mentoring for newly hired veterans as a strategy to assist in the adjustment to the civilian workplace.

Most employers report a high rate of satisfaction with the performance of veterans and veterans with disabilities hired by their organizations, according to a study of employer perceptions and hiring practices related to U.S. military personnel (Apollo Education Group, 2011, 2015). A random sample of over 20,000 employers representing a cross section of industries indicated that service members hired by their companies had typically outperformed their civilian counterparts in work ethic, reliability, and teamwork. One of the attributes most valued by survey respondents was leadership skills, yet most veterans fail to highlight this aspect of their service in their résumé or during the job interview process. It is noteworthy that while many employers found these qualities desirable, others considered them not sufficient enough for performing the majority of positions in the civilian workplace (O'Reilly, 2014). After all, hiring managers often find it easier to understand a résumé that highlights a college degree and civilian job titles than it is to understand what a field artillery surveyor, for example, might bring to the table. Many veterans also find it difficult to explain their military training, experience, and education in a way that makes it relevant to a civilian employer.

Finally, unless a disability is visible or a veteran has disclosed, an employer will likely not know if a veteran has a disability. This is, of course, no different from any other employee with undisclosed or nonvisible disabilities. As previously stated, veterans often do not correlate a disability incurred during military service with a disability that could potentially impact their work in the civilian workforce. Even if a disability is visible, employers must make no assumptions that the candidate or employee might need an accommodation. According to the Equal Employment Opportunity Commission (EEOC), while it is the responsibility of the candidate or employee to request an accommodation, an individual need not use the word *disability* in the request or need to reference the ADA or use the phrase *reasonable accommodation*. Therefore, it is important for managers, supervisors, human resource professionals, and other staff to receive ongoing training and professional development on how to recognize an accommodation request and how to respond appropriately. JAN (http://www.askjan.org) and the Employer Assistance and Resource Network for Disability Inclusion (EARN; https://www.askearn.org) are two trusted (and free) resources employers can contact for this type of training or information. Finally, while the ADA does not require employers to follow a specific policy to accommodate an applicant or employee with a disability, creating and sharing a formal reasonable accommodation policy and documenting procedures are highly recommended. Including this information in onboarding materials for all new employees is a promising practice.

## The Disclosure Dilemma

Most individuals with nonvisible disabilities are confronted with serious decisions concerning self-identification during their job search and while employed. This trepidation may be amplified for veterans with disabilities since many do not identify themselves as a person with a disability at work even though they might be adjusting to limitations imposed by their injuries. Those living with an "invisible" injury like PTSD or TBI are likely to be reluctant to share this information due to the stigma and fear often mistakenly associated with these specific conditions (Dalgin & Bellini, 2008). Disability notwithstanding, some service members are even reluctant to disclose their veteran status to prospective or current employers due to negative perceptions and specific misconceptions about the prevalence of psychological health and cognitive injuries (e.g., PTSD, TBI) among the veteran population. Given these concerns, it is not surprising that the decision to disclose a disability or veteran status may be one of the most significant challenges veterans make as they transition to the civilian workforce. Unfortunately, avoiding such disclosure may have a significant impact on effective job performance due to the additional stress of hiding this information. Concealing disability may also have major implications on an employee's well-being in terms of both psychological and physical health, especially if he or she is continuing treatment and needs a flexible work schedule as an accommodation. While not specifically focused on veterans, a study on disability disclosure was conducted whereby survey respondents described their process for evaluating the timing and need for self-identification (von Schrader, Malzer, & Bruyère, 2014). The following considerations were most often revealed:

- assessing the workplace culture and comfort level with direct supervisors
- needing a reasonable accommodation for successfully performing job tasks
- reducing stress associated with keeping the disability secret
- desire for employees to be accepted for who they were
- fear of disparate treatment in terms of hiring, firing, and advancement opportunities
- being subjected to bullying or harassment

Eighty percent of employee respondents who self-identified did so primarily due to their need for an accommodation or a desire to be honest and forthcoming about their disability. Therefore, an effective strategy that employers might use to encourage the disclosure of disability (by both applicants and employees) is to highlight their commitment to providing reasonable accommodations during all stages of employment. This may include specific references to their interest in hiring individuals with disabilities, inclusive of veterans, in the company's diversity statement and promotional materials and participating in veteran and disability-specific online and in-person job fairs and recruitment events. Since visible cues are important in attracting desired candidates, it is not uncommon to have veterans wear their military uniforms to these events or to have employees with visible disabilities staffing booths and interacting with job seekers. Furthermore, some recruitment events may also include a separate workshop for veterans with disabilities in an effort to attract and educate them on their employment rights (as both a veteran and a person with a disability) along with the company's commitment to reasonable accommodation.

While the disclosure study (von Schrader et al., 2014) sought information on perceptions related to disclosure practices of individuals with disabilities in general and not specifically of veterans, the themes and conclusions were not significantly different from those expressed by veterans with disabilities (Lee et al., 2016). When prompted to share strategies for encouraging disability disclosure and accommodation dialogues, most employers stated they asked *all* job applicants if any modifications were needed to facilitate the performance of essential functions for the position in consideration. Other employers sponsored corporate special events to demonstrate their commitment to disability and veteran inclusion, often during October to support National Employment and Disability Awareness Month and November to honor Veterans Day. These designated recognition events present excellent opportunities to remind employees about the benefits of disclosing disability and veteran status, the process for doing so, and the confidentiality that is granted to those who self-identify and disclose a disability. Special events like these also provide a great opportunity to disseminate information about the organization's reasonable accommodation process, including how, when, and where requests may be submitted. Lee et al. (2016) found that employer participants reported an appreciable increase in self-identification and accommodation requests after such reminders and celebratory events.

Sodexo Incorporated is an example of a company that has done this and is presented as a case study. It is a world leader in food services and facilities management and has expressed its committed to ensuring an inclusive environment for all employees regardless of race, age, gender, ethnicity, ability, sexual orientation, or any other personal characteristics. The company's commitment to diversity and inclusion is cornerstone to their values and fundamental to their overall growth strategy.

As of 2017, more than 18,000 managers and 24,000 nonmanagement employees in the United States alone participated in at least one awareness program regarding nondiscrimination. Sodexo also focuses on building cultural competency and educating employees on various dimensions of diversity, including veterans, military families, and individuals with disabilities. Some examples include the following:

- Each year, Sodexo's "Remember Everyone Deployed" (RED) Friday Initiative shows support for veterans. In 2017, it included a special month-long promotion that raised funds for the Armed Services YMCA. Sodexo team members wear red to show support and solidarity for veterans and, through special promotions, raised money for veteran causes.
- The company uses its CareerBlog to regularly highlight stories of veteran employees and how their military experiences have helped contribute to their success with the company.
- Employees volunteer for Stand Down events for homeless veterans in their communities and offer on-site résumé assistance and recruitment opportunities.
- "SOAR With HONOR: A Day of Discovery, Development, and Dialogue," an event hosted by two of Sodexo's business resource groups, HONOR (Honoring Our Nation's finest with Opportunity and Respect) and SOAR (Sodexo Organization for disAbilities Resource), brings together internal and external speakers, organizes a resource fair promoting the company's community-based partners, and provides information about disclosure and reasonable accommodation.

## Recruiting and Retaining Veterans With Disabilities

Employers seeking to target veterans with disabilities in their recruitment efforts have multiple resources at their disposal. These include specific programs for wounded warriors sponsored by each of the five military service branches, such as the U.S. Army Wounded Warrior Program (AW2) and the U.S. Department of Labor's American Job Centers (AJCs), which operate in over 1,600 locations across the country. Most AJCs have a local veterans employment representative and a Disabled Veterans Outreach Program (DVOP) representative, whose collective charge is to connect employers with qualified veterans, both with and without disabilities. While AJCs are often name-branded by the communities they serve, they can be found at the Department of Labor's CareerOneStop website (https://www.careeronestop.

org). Employers who also meet the definition of federal contractor or sub-contractor are also obligated to list their available positions with their state or local AJC.

In an effort to increase referrals and applications from qualified veterans with disabilities, employers can also take proactive steps to ensure they are attracting these candidates. Certainly, companies are making it easier for veterans to find them by joining veteran and disability groups on social media sites such as LinkedIn, Twitter, and Facebook. Many are also building authentic veteran-committed portals on their company career site; however, often overlooked is accessibility for all potential users. For example, can your company website be accessed by a veteran who might have lost his or her sight and uses a screen reader? Are videos subtitled for those who might have auditory injuries? Does the website allow for moving, blinking, or flickering content to be turned off for those who have experienced a cognitive or neurological injury? How might a job applicant who cannot use his or her arms use your website? Often, poor website design unintentionally eliminates qualified applicants from applying for jobs. Website accessibility should be a critical consideration for any company desiring a truly diverse applicant pool and certainly one that is inviting for all veterans with disabilities. The Web Accessibility Initiative (W3C) offers evaluation tools, resources for inclusive designs, principles of website accessibility, and other services to help determine if website content meets accessibility guidelines and standards (https://www.w3.org/WAI/). In addition, JAN offers strategies for checking online application and website accessibility (https://askjan.org/topics/onlineapps.cfm).

An additional consideration for employers actively recruiting veterans with disabilities is to partner with community-based, military, and veterans service organizations (VSOs) that support service member and veteran career transition. Many of these organizations also offer training and job placement assistance specifically for veterans with disabilities. A directory of VSOs can be found on the VA website (https://www.va.gov/vso). Some veterans with disabilities receive employment services from the VA's Vocational Rehabilitation and Employment (VR&E) program or a state vocational rehabilitation agency (see the Resources section of this chapter for state information). These programs offer skills training, placement assistance, and job coaching support (if needed) once a veteran is hired. Employers that partner with an AJC can connect with state vocational rehabilitation practitioners and DVOP representatives, often at the same location. Employers can find the AJC in their area by visiting https://www.servicelocator.org and entering a zip code.

Each military service branch sponsors an employment resource for veterans who were wounded, ill, or injured during their time in service. These programs also actively work to connect employers with the veterans they serve. Information about these branch-specific programs can be found using the Education and Employment Initiative (http://warriorcare.dodlive.mil/carecoordination/e2i/), part of the DoD Office of Warrior Care Policy. In addition, employers can reach out to service-specific Transition Assistance Centers, participate in military job fairs such as *Hiring Our Heroes* (sponsored by the U.S. Chamber of Commerce at https://www.hiringourheroes.org), or by posting open positions with the National Labor Exchange (https://usnlx.com). Bring materials that clearly communicate a commitment to hiring veterans, including those with disabilities, to all recruitment events. Describing your company's commitment to workplace accommodations, flextime, or access to an EAP might be a differentiator that generates interest. These materials could also highlight the value of self-identification, the process for requesting reasonable accommodations, and information about disability and veteran-focused employee resource groups (ERGs; if these are available).

Employers who are federal contractors or subcontractors have additional recruitment obligations. The Vietnam Era Veterans' Readjustment Assistance Act (VEVRAA) prohibits federal contractors and subcontractors from discriminating in employment against protected veterans and requires employers to take affirmative action to recruit, hire, promote, and retain these veterans. Categories of protected veteran status include disabled veteran, recently separated veteran, active duty wartime or campaign badge veteran, and Armed Forces service medal veteran (for more information and detailed definitions on protected veterans, see https://bit.ly/2OYTCg2). These employers are required to establish annual hiring benchmarks for protected veterans and to invite applicants to self-identify as protected veterans at both the pre- and posthire phases of the application process. It is a promising practice to invite all applicants to self-identify as a person with a disability at pre- and post–job offer as federal contractors and subcontractors may count veterans with disabilities for their obligations under both the VEVRAA and Section 503 of the Rehabilitation Act (which prohibits discriminating against individuals with disabilities).

The majority of veterans with disabilities are recruited like all other veterans—using traditional veteran recruitment and hiring strategies. By simply including some of the targeted strategies discussed in this section as an overlay to what is already being done, organizations will likely see an increase in the number of qualified veteran applicants who also happen to be veterans with disabilities.

## Interviewing Veterans With Disabilities

The purpose of a good interview is to find out if a candidate is a good match for a potential position in terms of skills, experience, and company culture. In this regard, interviewing veterans and veterans with disabilities is no different from the processes used with any other candidate. When interviewing a veteran, focus on how the candidate's education, training, and military experience align with the skills and background required for the position of interest. Some specific suggestions for interviewing a veteran who has *disclosed a disability*, either before or during an interview, are discussed next.

To allow a candidate to assess whether he or she is able to perform the essential functions of the job, a thorough explanation of specific tasks and job requirements should be provided. Share the job description itself since having detailed information about the position and related tasks may allow an applicant to determine whether a reasonable accommodation might be needed to perform the essential functions. Veterans may not be familiar with disability laws and accommodation policies; therefore, questions such as "Might you need special equipment to do this job?" or "Would you need a flexible work schedule?" could start a productive conversation to more accurately determine modifications that would help the veteran be most productive. Even if the candidate discloses a disability during the interview process, the focus of subsequent questions should relate strictly to the job requirements rather than attempting to explore how the injury occurred or what limitations it may pose under circumstances that are not job related. The JAN provides a general overview of the "do's and don'ts" of medical inquiries and the ADA (https://askjan.org/articles/Job-Application-Interview-Stage-Dos-and-Donts.cfm). Employers can also contact JAN directly at (800) 526-7234 (voice) or (877) 781-9403 (TTY) to confidentially discuss a specific situation.

There is added sensitivity to posing questions if the disability disclosed is a TBI or PTSD due to the misconceptions related to these impairments and the stigma associated with them. Again, interviewers must refrain from asking question beyond the scope of determining fitness for the position. For example, rather than asking if an applicant experiences fatigue during the day because of nightmares or flashbacks, the interviewer should explain the work schedule and follow up with a question related to the candidate's ability to meet this requirement. If the answer is related to a concern around schedules, flexible start and end times might be suggested as a reasonable accommodation. In addition, showing candidates in the final round of interviews the actual work site is also a good practice as it would allow a candidate who happens to have a disability to assess the potential need for an accommodation that may facilitate better concentration. For example, repositioning furniture or providing special equipment to mitigate the effect of loud noises are low-cost solutions to address such concerns and may also increase productivity. JAN has been studying accommodations since 2004 and has found 59 percent of accommodations cost absolutely nothing (JAN, 2017). For more information and additional examples of low-cost, high-impact accommodations, visit http://bit.ly/3sjLaq4.

A qualified veteran (or any other job candidate) with a significant disability might bring a job coach to an interview as a reasonable accommodation. Interviewers should keep in mind that regardless of the presence of the job coach, the candidate is the one being interviewed and all questions should be addressed directly to him or her. Job coaches are professionals that support some job seekers and employees who are receiving services from a vocational rehabilitation agency; as such, these individuals are typically paid by these agencies. In addition to serving in a support role during an interview, a job coach can assist with new employee orientation, help the employee learn effective strategies for completing tasks efficiently, and facilitate acclimation to a new work environment. Job coaches typically focus on understanding all of the essential job requirements and can often identify potential accommodations to help the employee enhance his or her performance.

## Supervising and Retaining Veterans With Disabilities

While recruiting and hiring a veteran with or without disabilities is an important first step, retaining all good employees is often a challenge and a concern. A significant number of veterans with disabilities who participated in the focus group sessions discussed in Lee et al. (2016) indicated difficulties adjusting to the civilian work environment and subsequently changed jobs multiple times. There are several strategies that employers could implement to address this issue and increase the likelihood of job retention. As with other veteran hires, successful retention starts with the onboarding process. Providing insight on the differences between military culture and language and those of the civilian workplace is often a good first step. Explaining the lines of communication, promotion practices and criteria, performance expectations, and the workplace "chain of command" is another important step in the orientation process. The assignment of mentors, both veterans and nonveterans, is also an effective strategy to support adjustment to the work environment, increase the likelihood of success, and reduce turnover. Organizations that have an EAP should provide information about its availability and services during the onboarding process and explain how to access these services. It is also important to highlight the confidentiality that is guaranteed for employees seeking support from an EAP. Additional information on EAPs is provided further in this chapter.

The RAND Corporation's study of the 100,000 Jobs Mission designed to increase veteran employment opportunities found that most participating companies expanded significant effort on recruitment but were less focused on effectively managing and retaining the new hires (Hall, Harrell, Bicksler, Stewart, & Fisher., 2014). While good supervisory practices are critical for maintaining a productive workforce and positive work environment for all employees, some strategies may be especially effective for enhancing and supporting the performance and job retention of veterans. For individuals who have recently transitioned from the military to the civilian workforce, early assessment of their job performance is especially critical. This includes clear feedback to address any performance issues in a timely manner as well as affirmation for tasks well done. It is also important to modify communication styles to accommodate for differences in learning styles and also to bridge any language and cultural gaps that exist between the military and civilian work environments.

If accommodations have been put into place, more frequent communication will aid in assessing the effectiveness of the accommodation or identifying others to further enhance job performance. These discussions may also reveal challenges that could be mitigated by referring employees to confidential counseling services of an EAP, reaching out to peer mentors, or calling for the assistance of ERG members or human resources. A best practice and key strategy is to address any productivity or workplace behavior concerns in a timely manner to implement job-saving interventions, whenever feasible and appropriate. A good job fit between employer and employee increases the likelihood of a new hire remaining in the first job for a longer period of time, increases the probability that veteran will have a positive beginning to civilian work life, and arguably enhances the overall quality of life as well as financial readiness for the veteran and their family. Maury, Stone, Bradbard, Armstrong, and Haynie (2016) found that "a good job fit between employer and employee increases the likelihood of a new hire remaining in the first job for a longer period of time, increases the probability that veteran will have a positive beginning to civilian work life, and arguably enhances the overall quality of life as well as financial readiness for the veteran and their family" (p. 14).

## Mentoring

Given the success mentoring holds for grooming executives and high-potential employees, mentorship programs have been seen as a facilitator to a veteran's successful transition to the civilian workforce. There is robust research support for mentoring programs demonstrating utility in the workplace generally and growing support for veteran-friendly mentoring programs specifically (Schafer, Swick, Kidder, & Carter, 2016). Organizations considering the establishment of a veteran mentoring program can access a mentoring handbook from American Corporate Partners (ACP), a nationwide mentoring program dedicated to the transition of veterans into the civilian workforce (https://www.acp-usa.org/). Mentoring is also discussed in greater depth in Chapter 9.

Due to the unique and often multiple cultural identities of veterans (with and without disabilities), there may be a benefit to accessing multiple mentors. These mentors might include managers or coworkers who have chosen to serve as a disability advocate, veteran employees from any branch or same branch of service, and civilian employees who could provide insight and support about the culture and operation of the workplace. One promising practice is to assign mentees to mentors with similar experiences. In addition, mentors who have successfully completed the transition process to civilian employment can be found as another best practice as the guidance, support, friendship, and advice one veteran receives from another is irreplaceable.

## Veteran or Military Employee Resource Groups

Employee resource groups have emerged in the past two decades as a key diversity and inclusion strategy across U.S. workplaces (Githens & Aragon, 2009; Welbourne, Rolf, & Schlachter, 2015). Going well beyond the support group mentality that characterized their early development, ERGs have extended their reach and play an active role in changing organizational cultures, environments, workplace practices, and business strategies. ERGs are employee-led groups that are typically formed around common issues, interests, and/or similar characteristics or life experiences. According to DiversityInc, ERGs are often key to improving and enhancing the company's employee engagement, talent development, and recruitment efforts.

Over the years, ERGs have evolved from a social network membership focus to a business function. In fact, many organizations have renamed these groups as business resource groups to better reflect their role. Both veteran and disability-focused ERGs have increased in popularity in recent years and are often open to any employee with an interest regardless of disability or veteran status. As a result, employees who may be reluctant to self-identify as a person with a disability or a veteran can join these groups without compromising their privacy and can enjoy the benefits and camaraderie they offer. ERGs are especially suited for veterans who are used to functioning in group settings and place a high value on peer support. While a company of any size can implement an employee or business resource group, it is typically larger companies that use them to bridge cross-functional employee relationships and enhance professional development opportunities. DiversityInc (https://www.diversityincbestpractices.com) has identified additional promising practices with regard to creating and sustaining veteran, military, and disability ERGs:

Companies that participated in the 100,000 Jobs Mission shared information about the specific activities in which veteran ERGs have engaged (https://veteranjobsmission.com). These include, but are not limited to, targeted philanthropic efforts to support veterans and family members in their communities, assisting homeless veterans, and supporting families of deployed service members. ERG member support might be especially helpful to new veteran hires who are making the transition to work, especially for those who are also adjusting to an acquired disability. ERG members can also serve as mentors and take an important role in helping veterans adjust to the workplace culture by enhancing their understanding of workplace structures, business hierarchy, and strategies for how to access opportunities for promotion and advancement. Another suggestion is to consider equipping your military/veteran ERG with the information they need to help educate veterans in your workforce about the ADA, reasonable accommodations, disability disclosure, with the booklet *Know Your Employment Rights Under the ADA: A Guide for Veteran*, written by the Southeast ADA Center for veterans and can be accessed at https://bit.ly/3lEOObC.

Disability and veteran-focused ERGs are also instrumental for providing information about reasonable accommodations and employee rights and responsibilities. They can offer advice to other employees about veteran or disability self-identification and explain the potential pitfalls and advantages for doing so. More importantly, ERG members with disabilities may help ease the adjustment to work by helping a veteran learn how to mitigate any impact of disability, not only at the workplace but also in the community and at home. As such, they may be an important resource for those veterans who are still accepting and understanding an injury and any perceived loss of identity.

The ERG members often play a significant role in company outreach and recruitment efforts by attending job fairs, visiting military bases to share information about employers' veteran and disability-friendly practices, and offering testimonials on company websites. ERG members frequently take part in special veteran-focused networking events and promote their company's brand and reputation as an "employer of choice" for service members and their families. Many participate as mentors in the onboarding process for newly hired veterans to ease adjustment to the job and the civilian work environment. By providing support and fostering morale, the engagement of ERG members has a decidedly strong impact on the job retention of veterans and veterans with disabilities.

## Employee Assistance Programs

Employee assistance programs have a long history of offering resources to assist employees with personal and job-related issues, addressing workplace challenges, and promoting healthy lifestyles. EAPs are especially important to ensuring that veterans with disabilities, particularly those with TBI or PTSD, remain employed and avail themselves of needed support and appropriate professionals. EAP programs typically compile and disseminate resources related to obtaining accurate diagnosis and treatment options for a variety of impairments and offer listings and contact information for recommended practitioners for further consultation. They may also administer mental health screening assessments to identify appropriate resources for further assistance.

Aside from offering direct services to employees, EAP staff also provide education and training for managers about dealing with performance and behavior issues for workers under their supervision. Staff may disseminate materials about specific disabilities prevalent among veterans, the workplace impact of such disabilities in the context of employment, information about the availability and nature of EAP services, and the manner by which referrals can be made. Additionally, EAP staff may educate managers and supervisors about military transition challenges and advise them on how to address workplace behavioral issues and concerns about job performance. The VA offers a resource for EAP providers with specific information about targeted services to veterans and their families at https://www.va.gov/vetsinworkplace/docs/em_EAP_practices.asp.

## Federal Laws Protecting Veterans' Employment in the Private Sector

While hiring veterans has been found to be a good business practice by most employers, there are also a number of legal requirements worth mentioning. These include federal, state, and local laws that impact private and public organizations as they recruit, hire, and promote veterans, employees with disabilities, and returning members of the National Guard and Reserve. Below is a summary of major federal statutes. Companies should also review their obligations under state and local laws as these often provide greater protections. Furthermore, it is important to note that companies that recruit and hire veterans with disabilities can count such individuals toward multiple compliance benchmarks and goals. Additional information regarding the federal laws referenced in this section can be found in in the Resources section of this chapter.

## The Vietnam Era Veterans' Readjustment Assistance Act

The Vietnam Era Veterans' Readjustment Assistance Act prohibits federal contractors and subcontractors with at least $100,000 or more in contracts from discriminating in employment against protected veterans and requires affirmative action to recruit, hire, promote, and retain these veterans. Regulations (which went into effect on March 24, 2014) also require meeting specific hiring benchmarks, annual data collections, invitations for applicants to self-identify as protected veterans both pre- and post–job offer, the listings of available positions with the appropriate state or local job service, and the use of specific language when incorporating the equal opportunity clause into a subcontract.

## Section 503 of the Rehabilitation Act (Section 503)

Updates to Section 503 regulations (effective on March 24, 2014) prohibit federal contractors and subcontractors from discriminating in employment against individuals with disabilities and requires affirmative action to recruit, hire, promote, and retain such individuals. The new rule also makes changes to the nondiscrimination provisions of the regulations to bring them into compliance with the ADA Amendments Act of 2008. Some of the key features of Section 503 include a nationwide utilization goal of 7 percent for qualified individuals with disabilities, an invitation to self-identify at both the preoffer and postoffer phases of the application process using a form suggested by the Office of Federal Contract Compliance Programs (OFCCP), and collecting data annually to document comparisons for the number of individuals with disabilities who apply for positions with the number hired.

## The Americans With Disabilities Act

Enacted in 1990 and amended in 2008, the ADA prohibits discrimination against qualified individuals with disabilities in the private sector and in state and local governments that employ more than 15 workers. The ADA defines a person with a disability as someone with a physical or mental impairment that substantially limits a major life activity, has a record of such impairment, or is regarded as having such an impairment. While the 2008 ADA Amendments Act maintained this three-prong definition, it expanded the meaning of major life activities to include bodily functions such as the immune and digestive systems, normal cell growth, and respiratory, circulatory, cardiovascular, endocrine, and reproductive functions. The amendments also include impairments that are episodic or in remission, such as cancer, if during its active phase would be substantially limiting.

The ADA requires employers to provide reasonable accommodations to the known physical or mental limitations of otherwise qualified applicants and employees with disabilities to facilitate and support the performance of essential job functions unless doing so would impose an undue hardship. Essential functions are those job tasks that the individual who holds the position must be able to perform with or without the assistance of a reasonable accommodation. Essential functions are addressed by the Equal EEOC in the following manner: (a) whether performance of a job function is the reason the position exists; (b) the number of employees available to perform the function; and (c) the degree of expertise or skill required to perform the function. Undue hardship is defined as an action requiring significant difficulty or expense to an individual business. It is determined based on several factors, including the type of business operation, the cost or nature of the accommodation, and overall financial resources of the organization.

The ADA is not a hiring preference or mandate, and it does not entitle an individual with a disability to employment. What it does is prohibit employment-related discrimination based on disability or the assumption of disability. Many employers believe that once hired, an employee with a disability can never be fired. This is simply not true. Employees with disabilities are held to the same performance and behavior standards as all other employees, can be subjected to the same disciplinary processes and termination as all other employees, and their employment can be terminated as long as it does not merely relate to their disability. If the employee with a disability experiences difficulties performing essential job tasks, he or she may request an accommodation or modification to the work environment at any time during the employment life cycle. Once known, it is then the responsibility of the employer to engage in an interactive process to determine, jointly with the employee, the most effective job accommodation or modification to the work environment. For additional information regarding the interactive process, refer to the EEOC. JAN also provides free resources and individualized consultation to employers on this topic. If you have questions about workplace accommodations or the ADA and related legislation, JAN should be your first resource. Contact JAN at (800) 526-5234 voice or (877) 781-9403 (TTY), on the web at https://askjan.org by email at jan@askjan.org, or by text at (304) 216-8189 and via Skype at janconsultants.

There is a wide range of employer-focused ADA resources: The U.S. Department of Labor's Office of Disability Employment Policy offers a series of informational materials on disability-related myths and facts, the implications of ADA, and employer best practices; the EEOC has created an *Veterans and the Americans With Disabilities Act: A Guide for Employers* (2020) and the National ADA Network provides information employers can use to help employees who are veterans understand their rights and responsibilities under the ADA (see the Resources section of this chapter for more detail). It is important to remember, however, that veterans may not be aware of reasonable accommodations and the ADA, and even if they are, they may not consider their service-connected disability to be a disability in the workplace. To ensure that all of your employees are educated and informed on the ADA and your company's accommodation procedures, consider incorporating this material into your company's onboarding process. Remember, if any employee has trouble performing his or her job tasks and the difficulties are related to a known (disclosed) disability or medical condition, he or she may request an accommodation at any time during the employment life cycle. See the Resources section of this chapter for a sample reasonable accommodation request form for new employees.

## The Uniformed Services Employment and Reemployment Rights Act

The Uniformed Services Employment and Reemployment Rights Act (USERRA) prohibits discrimination against individuals who serve or have served in the Armed Forces, Reserves, National Guard, or other uniformed services. USERRA is intended to ensure these employees are not disadvantaged in their civilian careers because of their service, are promptly reemployed in their civilian jobs on return from duty, and are not discriminated against in employment based on past, current, or future military service. It also provides protection of civilian job rights and benefits and requires that returning Reservists and Guardsmen be promptly reemployed in the same position that they would have attained had they not been absent for military service. This includes seniority status, pay, and other rights and benefits. Employers are also prohibited from retaliation against an individual for action taken to exercise USERRA rights. The Employer Support of the

Guard and Reserve (ESGR) is a free resource that offers virtual and in-person briefings and resources to help educate employers on USERRA as well as the benefits of military-connected employees. ESGR provides outreach and ombudsmen services in communities across all 50 states, the District of Columbia, Guam, Puerto Rico, and the U.S. Virgin Islands. In fiscal year 2015, ESGR helped to successfully mediate approximately 75 percent of the 1,802 USERRA cases reported, meaning all of these cases were resolved without going to court.

## Tax Credits and Incentives Available to Private Sector Employers

Employers who make a strategic decision to target, hire, and train service-disabled veterans may qualify for incentives and tax credits, such as the Work Opportunity Tax Credit (WOTC), the Disabled Access Credit, the Architectural Barrier Removal Tax Deduction, and the Special Employer Incentives program.

The *WOTC* is a federal tax credit available to private sector employers who hire veterans and individuals from other eligible target groups, such as people with disabilities and others who have experienced a significant barrier to employment. While the future of the WOTC is unclear, at the time of this publication tax credits were available for employers that hire veterans with the following employment or circumstantial criteria (see IRS.gov Section 52—Special Rules; Section 3111(3)—Credit for Employment of Qualified Veterans: https://bit.ly/2NMouQk):

- a veteran who is a member of a family that received food stamps for at least a 3-month period during the previous 15-month period ending on the hiring date;
- a disabled veteran entitled to compensation for a service-connected disability, who has been
  - hired within 1 year of discharge or release from active duty, or
  - unemployed for at least 6 months in the year ending on the hiring date;
- a veteran who has been unemployed for
  - at least 4 weeks in the year ending on the hiring date; or
  - at least 6 months in the year ending on the hiring date.

To qualify for the WOTC incentive, the veterans' eligibility must be verified. That means the prospective veteran employment candidate must have

- served on active duty in the U.S. Armed Forces for more than 180 days, OR have been discharged or released from active duty for a service-connected disability; AND
- not have a period of active duty of more than 90 days that ended during the 60-day period ending on the hiring date.

Because WOTC and other related tax credits can be confusing, the U.S. Department of Labor (2020) has created a fact sheet to help employers better understand employee eligibility, calculate tax credits, and address the steps necessary for application. WOTC state coordinators are also available to answer any questions and can likely keep employers informed of any additional veteran tax credit programs. Employers should also contact their state VA Office (listed at https://www.va.gov/statedva.htm) to keep abreast of any additional industry or region-specific incentives available for hiring veterans and veterans with disabilities.

The *Disabled Access Credit* and the *Architectural Barrier Removal Tax Deduction* are tax credits designed for small businesses that incur expenses to provide access to individuals with disabilities. Qualified small businesses are those that earned $1 million or less or employed no more than 30 full-time employees during the previous year. Credit may be taken every year when such expenses are incurred. Employers should consult IRS Form 8826, "Disabled Access Credit" for further information (http://bit.ly/393AcNV). The Architectural Barrier Removal Tax Deduction encourages a business of any size to remove architectural and transportation barriers for individuals with disabilities. A deduction of up to $15,000 annually may be taken for qualified expenses that would otherwise be capitalized, and deductions can be claimed as a separate expense on the income tax return. The Disabled Access Credit and the Architectural Barrier Tax Deduction can be combined in the same tax year if expenses meet the criteria for both.

*Veteran Readiness and Employment* is a program of the VA that works to match job-seeking veterans to employers with job openings. Salary subsidies and reimbursements and the provision of assistive technology (AT) are used as employer incentives. Through the on-the-job training programs, VR&E subsidizes veterans' salaries so that employers pay an apprentice-level wage while veterans are in training. As the veteran progresses, the employer pays a larger portion of the salary until the training is completed, and then the employer pays the full salary. VR&E can also provide specialized tools, equipment, and workplace modifications to eligible veterans, allowing them to effectively perform their duties. These are valuable services that help eligible veterans without additional cost to employers. Finally, the Special Employer Incentive program offers employers an inducement to hire veterans who are facing extraordinary obstacles to employment, including reimbursement of as much as 50 percent of the veteran's salary for up to 6 months. More information about VR&E's employer resources and VR&E employment coordinators can be found in the Resources section of this chapter and online at https://www.benefits.va.gov/VOCREHAB/employers.asp.

## Employing Veterans With Disabilities in the Government

Several resources are available to help local, state, and federal government offices connect with veterans with disabilities and provide an opportunity for a meaningful work experience. These include the Non-Paid Work Experience program, Operation Warfighter, Veterans' Preference, special hiring authorities, and the Computer/Electronic Accommodations Program (CAP).

The *Non-Paid Work Experience Training* program allows local, state, and federal government offices to temporarily employ a veteran without having the position count against the agency's full-time equivalent allocation. VR&E pays the veteran a monthly subsistence allowance while he or she learns valuable work-related skills and experience. VR&E can provide employers with information about other federal programs offering incentives to companies that employ veterans.

*Operation Warfighter* is a DoD internship program that matches qualified wounded, ill, and injured service members with nonfunded federal internships to gain valuable work experience during their recovery and rehabilitation. This process assists with a service member's reintegration back to military duty or as he or she transitions into the civilian work environment, where the person can employ the newly acquired skills in a nonmilitary work setting.

*Veterans' Preference* is available to veterans with disabilities, those who served on active duty in the Armed Forces during certain specified time periods, or participated in military campaigns. Veterans' Preference does not guarantee a job or apply to internal actions such as promotions, transfers, or reassignments. What it does, however, is give eligible veterans a preference in appointment over many other applicants. In the federal government, Veterans' Preference eligibility includes a 10-point preference for disabled veterans and a 5-point preference for nondisabled veterans. All 50 states offer qualified veterans preferential hiring (Lewis & Pathak, 2014), and many local governments have adopted similar systems as well.

*Special hiring authorities* are tools that government agencies can use to hire veterans with disabilities without going through the full application process. These veterans are also eligible for jobs under special hiring authorities (https://www.fedshirevets.gov/job-seekers/special-hiring-authorities/) that override the customary hiring process. There are five special hiring authorities that pertain to veterans' employment in the federal sector: Veterans Recruitment Appointment, the Veterans Employment Opportunity ACT, 30 Percent or More Disabled Veterans, Disabeled Veterans Enrolled in a VA Training Program, and the Schedule a Appointing Authority, which allows federal agencies to apply special hiring preferences for eligible candidates with severe disabilities under specific categories.

The *Computer/Electronic Accommodations Program* provides ATs) and accommodations to support individuals with disabilities and wounded, ill, and injured service members throughout the federal government. CAP's Wounded Service Member Initiative (https://www.cap.mil/wsm/) works closely with medical providers, therapists, case managers, military treatment liaisons at military treatment facilities (MTFs), and AW2 representatives to increase awareness and availability of ATs. CAP provides needs assessments, AT, and training to wounded, ill, and injured service members with cognitive, dexterity, hearing, and visual impairments. Once the appropriate AT has been identified, CAP not only provides the solutions free of charge to support the service member's medical recovery and rehabilitation, but also the service member can retain the equipment on separation from active duty. CAP also offers a series of online training modules to help federal employers better understand how to hire employees with disabilities and wounded, ill and injured service members and how to provide reasonable accommodations after they are hired. More information can be found at https://www.cap.mil/NewsEvents/Training.aspx.

## SkillBridge: A Unique Partnership From the Department of Defense

The DoD SkillBridge program provides an opportunity for service members to gain valuable civilian work experience through specific industry training, apprenticeships, or internships during the last 180 days of service. While the program does not specifically target active duty service members with service-connected disabilities, they are certainly in the mix of applicants. Training must offer eligible service members an experience to acquire the knowledge, skills, and abilities to obtain job opportunities in the civilian workforce. This unique partnership provides service members a chance to refine the skills they acquired during military service and adapt them as they learn and work in civilian career areas (before transitioning to veteran status). For employers and industry partners, SkillBridge provides an opportunity to offer real-world training and work experience for in-demand fields and a pipeline to highly capable and motivated candidates. The program provides an important opportunity for both the service member and employer to evaluate fit, suitability, and desire for specific jobs and civilian work environments. More information for employers and industry partners can be found at http://bit.ly/2OQASzn.

## Conclusion

Veterans leave the military with a diverse skill set and a wealth of professional experience amassed during their time in service. Some also leave with an injury and subsequent service-connected disability that may or may not impose a functional limitation in the workplace. While this chapter offers an overview to the intersection of disability, veteran status, and employment, it is important to remember that every veteran with or without a disability is unique. Company-wide commitment to training (and retraining) human resource and management staff on the ADA and accommodations is critical; however, the ADA does not legislate attitudes. Employers that make a concerted effort to proactively demystify common stereotypes about veterans, military service, and disability will go a long way—and will likely lead to increased employee performance and greater job satisfaction, which ultimately impact productivity, engagement, and the bottom line.

# Resources

*American Corporate Partners*
https://www.acp-usa.org/
Founded in 2008, ACP aims to ease the transition from the military to the civilian workforce. ACP is a nonprofit organization engaged in national corporate career counseling for our returning military.

*American Job Centers*
https://www.careeronestop.org/
American Job Centers provide free help to job seekers for a variety of career and employment-related needs. More than 2,500 AJCs, funded by the U.S. Department of Labor's Employment and Training Administration, are located throughout the United States.

*BrainLine*
https://www.brainline.org/
BrainLine is a national multimedia project offering information and resources about preventing, treating, and living with TBI. BrainLine includes a series of webcasts, an electronic newsletter, and an extensive outreach campaign in partnership with national organizations concerned about TBI.

*Traumatic Brain Injury Center of Excellence*
https://health.mil/About-MHS/OASDHA/Defense-Health-Agency/Research-and-Development/Traumatic-Brain-Injury-Center-of-Excellence
The Traumatic Brain Injury Center of Excellence is a part of the U.S. Military Health System. Specifically, it is the TBI operational component of the Defense Centers of Excellence for Psychological Health and Traumatic Brain Injury. Founded in 1992 by Congress, its responsibilities have grown as its network of care and treatment sites has grown.

*Psychological Health Center of Excellence*
http://bit.ly/2NPKnyg
The mission of the Psychological Health Center of Excellence is to improve the lives of our nation's service members, veterans, and their families by advancing excellence in psychological health and TBI prevention and care.

*Department of Defense | Office of Warrior Care Policy | E2I Initiative*
http://warriorcare.dodlive.mil/carecoordination/e2i/

The Education and Employment Initiative (E2I) is a program that assists wounded, ill, and injured service members early in their recovery process to identify their skills and match them with the education and career opportunities that will help them successfully transition to civilian life. Regional coordinators establish and maintain relationships with private, public, and nonprofit sector employers with an interest in helping veterans with disabilities begin a civilian career.

- A list of E2I regional coordinators can be accessed here: https://goo.gl/p67T68

*Employer Assistance Resource Network for Disability Inclusion*
https://askearn.org/

The Employer Assistance and Resource Network on Disability Inclusion (EARN) is a free resource that helps employers tap the benefits of disability diversity. EARN educates public and private sector organizations on ways to build inclusive workplace cultures, empowering them to become leaders in the employment and advancement of people with disabilities.

*Employer Support of the Guard and Reserve*
https://www.esgr.mil/

The ESGR, a DoD program, was established in 1972 to promote cooperation and understanding between Reserve Component Service members and their civilian employers and to assist in the resolution of conflicts arising from an employee's military commitment.

*Equal Employment Opportunity Commission Resources*
https://www.eeoc.gov/eeoc/index.cfm

The U.S. EEOC is responsible for enforcing federal laws that make it illegal to discriminate against a job applicant or an employee because of the person's race; color; religion; sex (including pregnancy, gender identity, and sexual orientation); national origin; age (40 or older); disability; or genetic information.

- ADA: Your responsibilities as an employer: http://bit.ly/3f5EKqT
- Resources for Employers and Small Businesses: http://bit.ly/3siDt3i

- Enforcement Guidance on Reasonable Accommodation and Undue Hardship: http://bit.ly/3tMES2G
- Guide to Veterans and the ADA for employers: http://bit.ly/2Piui4n

*Federal Laws Protecting Veterans*
- Section 503 of the Rehabilitation Act (Section 503): http://bit.ly/2PlXnMs
- Uniformed Services Employment and Reemployment Rights Act: https://www.dol.gov/vets/programs/userra/
  - USERRA outcomes (http://bit.ly/31cmOTo)
- Vietnam Era Veterans' Reemployment Adjustment Act: http://bit.ly/319ZxkP
- Work Opportunities Tax Credit: http://bit.ly/3rirJwu

*Job Accommodation Network*
https://askjan.org/
The JAN is the leading source of free, expert, and confidential guidance on workplace accommodations and disability employment issues. Working toward practical solutions that benefit both employer and employee, JAN helps people with disabilities enhance their employability and shows employers how to capitalize on the value and talent that people with disabilities add to the workplace.
- Sample customizable forms, including onboarding accommodations request form, plan of action, accommodation approval/denial, and more: http://bit.ly/3sguTCn
- Vocational rehabilitation agencies listed by state: http://bit.ly/31ctPDr

*Just-in-Time Disability Toolkit*
https://disabilitytoolkit.edi.cornell.edu/
Cornell University offers 10 tools to help mangers as they deal with disability issues within their work teams. Each tool is based on a disability issue managers typically encounter in the workplace, and each has been designed to be used in about 5 minutes—and contains links to test knowledge, print out a one-page sheet of reminders, or pursue further resources.

*Military Transition Assistance—Service Specific*
https://www.dodtap.mil/

Each branch of the military coordinates transition services for its service members. Transition counselors are located in the following offices at local military installations:

- Air Force–Airman & Family Readiness Center: https://www. myairforcebenefits.us.af.mil/Benefit-Library/Federal-Benefits/ Airman-and-Family-Readiness-Center-(AandFRC)

*Hire Heroes USA*
https://www.hireheroesusa.org/
Hire Heroes USA provides free, expert career coaching and job sourcing to more than a thousand transitioning U.S. military members, veterans, and military spouses each week.

*National Center for PTSD*
http://www.ptsd.va.gov
The National Center for PTSD is dedicated to research and education on trauma and PTSD, working to ensure that the latest research findings help those exposed to trauma.

*National Resource Directory*
http://nrd.gov/
The National Resource Directory is a resource website that connects wounded warriors, service members, veterans, their families, and caregivers to programs and services that support them. It provides access to services and resources at the national, state, and local levels to support recovery, rehabilitation, and community reintegration.

*Society for Human Resource Management*
https://bit.ly/3seo4kN
The Society for Human Resource Management offers a series of helpful resources for integrating and engaging veterans in the workforce, including but not limited to employer FAQs and resources; how to begin hiring veterans; military employment resources; and more.

*U.S. Chamber of Commerce Hiring Our Heroes*
https://www.uschamberfoundation.org/hiring-our-heroes

The U.S. Chamber of Commerce Hiring Our Heroes is a nationwide initiative to help veterans, transitioning service members, and military spouses find meaningful employment opportunities.

*U.S. Department of Labor | Office of Federal Contract Compliance Programs*
https://www.dol.gov/agencies/ofccp
As a part of the OFCCP's ongoing efforts to support federal contractor compliance with Section 503 of the Rehabilitation Act (Section 503) and the VEVRAA regulations, the agency offers resources that federal contractors may find useful.

*U.S. Department of Labor | Veterans Hiring Resources*
- Employer Guide to Hire Veterans (2018): https://bit.ly/3lJxEcT
- Hire a Vet: https://www.dol.gov/veterans/hireaveteran/
- State and regional Department of Labor veterans employment representatives can be found at http://bit.ly/2NMBLIE

*U.S. Department of Veterans Affairs | Vocational Rehabilitation &*
*Employment*
https://benefits.va.gov/vocrehab/
Information for employers on salary subsidies, AT, salary reimbursement, and federal tax credits for hiring eligible veterans with disabilities.
- VR&E employment coordinator list available as Excel download in resource tab on site.

*U.S. Department of Veterans Affairs | Veterans Employment Toolkit*
https://www.va.gov/vetsinworkplace/
This toolkit provides a variety of outside resources for employers, managers or supervisors, and human resource professionals.
- Resources for EAP providers: http://bit.ly/2PoxUBK

*W3C Web Accessibility Initiative*
https://www.w3.org/WAI/
The W3C Web Accessibility Initiative (WAI) develops guidelines widely regarded as the international standard for web accessibility; support materials to help understand and implement web accessibility; and resources through international collaboration.

- Evaluation tools: http://bit.ly/3lGIBf6
- Resources for inclusive design: http://bit.ly/2OZazqG
- Principles of website accessibility: http://bit.ly/3r9RXBr

# References

Apollo Education Group. (2011, 2015). *Hiring heroes: Employer perceptions, preferences, and hiring practices related to U.S. military personnel.* https://bit.ly/2RASFY4

Dalgin, R. S., & Bellini, J. (2008). Invisible disability disclosure in an employment interview. *Rehabilitation Counseling Bulletin, 52*(1), 6–15.

Disabled American Veterans & Monster, Military.com. (2016). *Disabled veterans talent survey.* https://is.gd/WewOnu

Defense and Veterans Brain Injury Center (DVBIC). *DoD worldwide numbers for TBI.* https://www.biami.org/department-of-defense-tbi-numbers/

Githens, R. P., & Aragon, S. R. (2009). LGBT employee groups: Goals and organizational structures. *Advances in Developing Human Resources, 11*(1), 121–135.

Hall, K., Harrell, M. C., Bicksler, B., Stewart, R., & Fisher, M. P. (2014). *Veteran employment: Lessons from the 100,000 jobs mission.* Santa Monica, CA: RAND. https://www. rand.org/pubs/research_reports/RR836.html

Harrell, M. C., & Berglass, N. (2012). *Employing America's veteran: Perspectives from businesses.* Washington, DC: Center for New American Security. https://www.issuelab.org/ resources/17932/17932.pdf

Institute for Veterans and Military Families. (2012). *The business case for hiring a veteran: Beyond the clichés.* Syracuse University. https://bit.ly/2xe8g6L

Job Accommodation Network. (2020). *Workplace accommodations: Low cost, high impact.* https://askjan.org/topics/costs.cfm?csSearch=3222525_1

Lee, K., VanLooy, S., Young, J., & Stern, L. (2016). *Strategies for gaining insight to the employment challenges of veterans with disabilities: Final report to the Bob Woodruff Foundation.* Ithaca, NY: Yang-Tan Institute on Employment and Disability. http:// digitalcommons.ilr.cornell.edu/edicollect/1358

Lewis, G. B., & Pathak, R. (2014). The employment of veterans in state and local government service. *State and Local Government Review, 46*(2), 91–105.

Meyer, T. (2013). *Serving those who served: A wise givers guide to assisting veterans and military families.* Washington, DC: Philanthropy Roundtable.

Maury, R. V., Stone, B. M., Bradbard, D. A., Armstrong, N. J., and Haynie, J. M. (2016, August). *Workforce readiness alignment: The relationship between job preferences, retention, and earnings.* Syracuse, NY: Syracuse University Institute for Veterans and Military Families. https://is.gd/6c1aRW

Military Family Research Institute (MFRI). (n.d.). *How to help military and veteran families: For employers.* https://bit.ly/2xfGpD4

Moore, W. (n.d.). *Coming back with Wes Moore.* https://to.pbs.org/2xhrSGQ

National Commission on Military, National, and Public Service. (2019, January 2019). *Interim report: A report to the American people, the Congress, and the President.* Washington, DC: National Commission on Military, National, and Public Service. https://is.gd/uj0GAO

Office of the Chairman of the Joint Chiefs of Staff, Office of Reintegration. (2014, October). *Veteran stereotypes: A closer look*. Washington, DC: Office of the Chairman of the Joint Chiefs of Staff, Office of Reintegration. https://www.jcs.mil/Portals/36/Documents/CORe/141024_veteran_stereotypes.pdf

O'Reilly, S. (2014). *Veteran unemployment: Causes, consequences and remedies*. Baltimore, MD: Johns Hopkins University. https://is.gd/xP17jA

Scanlon, S. A. (2016). How employers can recruit and retain veterans. Hunt Scanlon Media. (2016, November 8). https://huntscanlon.com/employers-can-recruit-retain-veterans/

Schafer, A., Swick, A., Kidder, K., & Carter, P. (2016). *Onward and upward: Understanding veteran retention and performance in the workforce*. Washington, DC: Center for a New American Security. https://is.gd/6BVyUC

Stern, L. (2017). Post 9/11 veterans with service-connected disabilities and their transition to the civilian workforce. *Advances in Developing Human Resources, 19*(1), 66–77.

Stone, C., & Stone, D. L. (2015). Factors affecting hiring decisions about veterans. *Human Resource Management Review, 25*, 68–79.

Tanielian, T., & Jaycox, L. H. (Eds.). (2008). *Invisible wounds of war: Psychological and cognitive injuries, consequences, and services to assist recovery*. Santa Monica, CA: The Rand Corporation. https://t.ly/H66Y

U.S. Bureau of Labor Statistics (BLS). (2019). *Employment situation of veterans sum-2018* (USDL-19-0451). Washington, DC: Bureau of Labor Statistics. https://is.gd/0kl5MH

U.S. Bureau of Labor Statistics (BLS). (2016). *Persons with a disability: Labor force characteristics summary* (USDL-17-0857). Washington, DC: Bureau of Labor Statistics. https://is.gd/BLZNbT

U.S. Department of Labor Bureau of Labor Statistics. (2020). Employment situation of veterans – 2019. Washington, DC: U.S. Department of Labor Bureau of Labor Statistics. https://www.bls.gov/news.release/pdf/vet.pdf

von Schrader, S., Malzer, V., & Bruyère, S. M. (2014). Perspectives on disability disclosure: The importance of the employer practices and workplace climate. *Employee Responsibilities and Rights Journal, 26*(4), 237–255.

Watson, K. W., Perry, M., Ripley, B., & Chittum, R. (2017, July 11). How your company can better retain employees who are veterans. *Harvard Business Review*. https://is.gd/3jAvtG.

Welbourne, T. M., Rolf, S., & Schlachter, S. (2015, September). Employee resource groups: An introduction, review and research agenda. In *Academy of Management Proceedings* (Vol. 1, No. 1, pp. 15661–1594). Briarcliff Manor, NY 10510: Academy of Management.

# 8

# Veteran Hiring and Retention

Lessons on Organizational Culture, Shared Expectations,
and Leadership Practices

*Sherri Eiler, Ren Nygren, Sandra Olivarez, and Gary M. Profit*

Employers have realized the value of veteran hiring for many decades
(Collins et al. 2014; Farley, 2010; King, 2011) and have realized that veterans
bring to these organizations a competitive advantage due to their skills, education, and experience acquired during military service. But while many
companies understand the benefits of hiring military veterans (Baruch &
Quick, 2007; Faurer, Rogers-Brodersen, & Bailie, 2014; King, 2011), many
of these companies find that retaining these employees can be challenging.
These challenges can be overcome with an understanding of the military's
culture, your organization's corporate culture, and how veterans coming
from the military's culture fit in with your corporate culture. We provide
examples from our experiences directing Walmart's military programs. These
programs share some commonalities with the veterans hiring programs set
up by other Fortune 500 companies; however, each organization encounters
unique opportunities and challenges regarding veteran hiring and retention,
with the opportunities and challenges based in part on the nature of their
business, the jobs they offer, and the career paths available to veterans. In this
chapter, we review several examples of Walmart's military programs, associated metrics, and our partnerships with additional nonprofits in the community. We also share the experiences, insights, and knowledge garnered from
Walmart's veteran hiring efforts and offer examples and ideas that smaller
companies may be able to use as they consider and deploy veteran hiring
initiatives.

A proponent of veteran hiring for decades, Walmart formally launched
the Veterans Welcome Home Commitment in 2013. This commitment guaranteed a job offer to veterans honorably discharged from active duty with
the expectation of hiring 100,000 veterans by 2018. In May 2015, when it

Sherri Eiler, Ren Nygren, Sandra Olivarez, and Gary M. Profit, *Veteran Hiring and Retention* In: *Military Veteran
Employment*. Edited by: Nathan D. Ainspan and Kristin N. Saboe, Oxford University Press. © Oxford University Press 2021.
DOI: 10.1093/oso/9780190642983.003.0009

became clear that this expectation was not ambitious enough, Walmart announced the expansion of the commitment with a goal of 250,000 new veteran associates by 2020. (At Walmart, all staff are identified as associates instead of employees, personnel, and the like. As such, we use the term *associates* throughout.) A milestone was reached at the end of January 2020, with more than 250,000 veterans hired in Walmart stores, Sam's Clubs, distribution centers, and the Walmart home office in Bentonville, Arkansas, and 42,000 have been promoted in since joining the Walmart team. As a natural next step, on Veterans Day of 2018, Walmart announced the launch of the Military Spouse Career Connection, giving hiring preference to military spouses seeking employment with Walmart or Sam's Club. Since launch, and as of January 2020, more than 19,000 military spouses had been hired.

In fact, Walmart is the largest private sector employer of veterans and military spouses—second only to the combined hires of federal and state governments—with more than 100,000 associates who are veterans and more than 150,000 who are members of veteran families and military families. As it has been throughout the company's history, the commitment to service members and their families will continue for decades to come.

Preliminary analyses of the careers of these Walmart associates have produced some interesting, high-level patterns. Table 8.1 lists such patterns for veterans compared to nonveterans hired into managerial and hourly positions at Walmart.

The patterns listed in Table 8.1 are generally encouraging, yet they highlight the need for further work to ensure veterans are well supported as they join the civilian workforce. Our experience has offered us some important lessons, and the focus of this chapter is to share those lessons involving organizational culture, shared expectations, and leadership as they relate to the important issue of hiring and retaining veterans.

## Organizational Culture

Corporate culture refers to the beliefs and behaviors that determine how a company's employees and management interact and handle outside business transactions. Recent research on veteran perspectives regarding organizational culture indicated that compared to the general U.S. workforce, veterans are slightly more likely to prioritize aspects of the organization's culture and people and are slightly less likely to prioritize those related to

**Table 8.1**  High-Level Patterns for Veterans Hired Into Managerial and Hourly Positions

| Management Hires | Hourly Hires |
| --- | --- |
| More promotions than nonveteran peers | More promotions than nonveteran peers |
| More likely to succeed to upper level positions | Fewer disciplinary actions |
| Higher geographic flexibility on hiring | More willing to stay in roles for longer periods of time |
| Progressively less willing to relocate as they rise—They did this in the military already | Less call-in absenteeism |
| Less difficulty (compared to nonveteran associates) adapting to a company that is the largest in the Fortune 500 in size and scope | More likely to convert from part-time to full-time employment |
| Fewer disciplinary actions | Higher exit rates—finding other opportunities or returning to school |
| More willing to stay in roles for longer periods of time | |

work, rewards, and opportunity (CEB Corporate Leadership Council, 2014). Always evolving, corporate culture is often implied, not expressly defined, and develops organically over time from the cumulative traits and observable patterns of behavior of the people the company hires (Katzenbach, Oelschlegel, & Thomas, 2016; Watkins, 2013). People join companies for many reasons, from compensation and prestige in the corporate sector, to passion and filling unmet needs with entrepreneurial start-ups. For new hires, onboarding activities for their new organization vary and are as simple as filling out the appropriate paperwork up to and including attending a multiday orientation class to learn the high points of the employee handbook and the company culture. Additionally, some organizations offer outward signs of culture/belonging such as badges, company-issued equipment, and/or colorful vests such as those worn by Walmart associates.

Like corporate culture, military culture also involves a set of beliefs and behaviors that are fundamental to the individual and collective military experience. With the end of the military draft and the start of the all-volunteer force, service to the nation has been voluntary since 1973. Those that make up the U.S. Armed Forces are demographically, geographically, and ethnically diverse and share a common set of values and beliefs that today underscore their voluntary service to the nation (Substance Abuse and Mental Health Services Administration [SAMSHA], 2010). The military, like any profession, has its own practices and language. People join the military for a variety of reasons, ranging from family tradition, honor, and duty to securing full-time employment with educational benefits that can last a lifetime.

Entry into military service is designed and structured to create discipline, focus, and control. Regardless of how someone enters, service members spend their first weeks in uniform at initial training ("basic training") immersed in the military lifestyle and culture (SAMHSA, 2010). They learn about the history of their service, military customs and courtesies, proper wear of the uniform, military bearing, military values and ethics, and other information that is critical to their success in the service, including how to listen to and follow orders and how to function within the military chain of command. The initial training also teaches how to focus and maintain awareness in challenging situations—situations where they are lacking sleep, are physically exhausted, or are under unaccustomed and extreme stress (SAMSHA). Initial training is also intended to teach recruits to fire a weapon and most importantly put country, service, unit, and buddy before self. Service members' first introduction to military service during initial training is also where they learn that there is no greater bond than the one they share with the people "to their left and their right" (SAMSHA). For many, this bond of brotherhood/sisterhood lasts throughout their military career and beyond. This bond is highly valued, nurtured, and protected; however, the loss of identity and camaraderie on leaving the military can be a detriment in transitioning into the civilian community (SAMSHA; Junger, 2016).

Military values and the values of each of the services are deeply engrained during initial training and reinforced during the length of service. While there are clear differences in the level of commitment, military values and corporate values for many companies may be similar and aligned and even use the same words. For example, Table 8.2 shows a comparison of Walmart values and the military services values, demonstrating notable similarity and alignment.

Knowing that our veteran candidates bring these deeply engrained values, Walmart understands the importance of the alignment of these values and clearly demonstrates the compatibility of Walmart and military culture. To help bring values to life, Walmart defines the behaviors that demonstrate our culture. One of our associates, during a meeting, told the team, "I saw Walmart's values, how much they aligned to my service values,

Table 8.2  Comparison of Walmart Values and Military Service Values

|  |  | Walmart Values | | | |
|  |  | Act With Integrity | Service to the customer | Strive for Excellence | Respect for the Individual |
| --- | --- | --- | --- | --- | --- |
| Air Force Values | Integrity first | X | | | |
|  | Service before self | | X | X | |
|  | Excellence in all we do | | | X | |
| Army Values | Loyalty | X | X | | X |
|  | Duty | | X | | |
|  | Respect | | | | |
|  | Selfless service | | X | | |
|  | Honor | X | | | X |
|  | Integrity | X | | | |
|  | Personal courage | X | | | |
| Navy and Marine Corps Values | Honor | X | | | |
|  | Courage | X | | | |

and I knew I had found the company where I wanted to work after I left the service." Walmart has a larger mission, to help people save money so they can live better, and encourages veteran associates to support the "save money" part of the mission by being focused on their job and also to embrace and activate the "live better" part of the mission through empowering partnerships. Given our success with this mission within Walmart, we recommend other companies review the mission of your company and ensure there is a greater purpose to which veterans can connect. Once this is identified, promote the purpose and organization's values in your recruiting messages to veterans.

An example of how Walmart helps veteran associates build a sense of engagement and purpose is through metric-driven, public/private partners such as Team Red, White, and Blue (Team RWB), a national, nonprofit veteran service organization that seeks to connect veterans to communities through physical and social activity. Through a partnership with Walmart Benefits, the teams have engaged veterans, associates, and community members across the nation with the ZP Eagle Charge. Research drawn from a 2014 survey conducted by Team RWB involving more than 4,000 veteran, active duty military, and civilians showed this type of engagement has multiple benefits (Team RWB, 2014):

- Nearly half (45 percent) of "less active" Team RWB organization veterans felt part of something bigger than themselves.
- The percentage jumped to 94 percent for those Team RWB organization veterans who defined themselves as "active."
- Active Team RWB organization veterans feel an increased sense of brotherhood/sisterhood in their lives (66 percent).
- A majority of veterans (73 percent among active members) reported sharing the challenges they face as a veteran with civilians, and 87 percent demonstrated the strengths they have as a veteran to civilians. Of equal importance, 75 percent of civilian members stated that they better understand both the challenges and strengths of veterans in their communities.

Training deeply engrains service identification, and it is difficult to replicate it in a civilian organization. Veterans' paths forward after leaving their military service must address the loss of the military service identification and support the creation of a new community aligned with the company's culture (Junger, 2016). While your company might not be able to provide such extensive experiences as a large company like Walmart to your veteran associates, you can develop programs and offer opportunities that can provide a similar sense of engagement and purpose to your veteran associates.

## Shared Expectations

Cultural compatibility is a foundational building block in the transition process for a service member. At Walmart, we have found that engaging, supporting, and facilitating feelings of belonging to our associate base for our veteran hires helps us benefit from the loyalty, innovation, and leadership of this highly skilled talent pool. Equally important is consideration of achieving shared expectations in order to ensure a positive associate experience.

Veterans represent the largest, most diverse, and talent-rich pool in the world and offer a distinct competitive advantage to the organizations that hire them. Walmart leverages military candidates' best-in-class training, unique skill sets, and experience to strengthen our workforce. As veterans enter into the civilian workforce, Walmart assists in a smoother transition for both parties by establishing shared expectations. Regardless of whether veteran talent is sourced or a veteran applies for a job independently, an important first step in facilitating a smooth integration is to create shared expectations. Shared expectations can also be considered social contracts. A *Harvard Business Review* white paper explains that "social contracts have their roots in social capital theory, which emphasizes information exchange and reciprocity between employees, mutual trust and fairness, and shared values and expectations" (Riordan & O'Brien, 2012, Harvard Business Review.com). By doing this purposefully, organizations are able to raise the bar and strengthen their workforce while simultaneously validating that veterans' opportunities for career growth are within their grasp. This may be achieved by providing a clear path of training and development that allows an associate to progress, over a period of time, into a role of increased responsibility.

Figure 8.1 shows the four key steps generally associated with the process for transitioning veterans into an organization. As the largest employer with the most veteran hiring experience in our industry, Walmart has captured several lessons across these four steps as displayed in Figure 8.1.

It is important that employers are cognizant that they should create a positive experience for veterans by establishing shared expectations throughout all four steps. Clear and consistent communication throughout each phase is essential to facilitating a positive transition for veteran candidates/associates. Figure 8.2 is an example previously used by Walmart to relay such messages to veterans that are prospective Walmart associates.

*Talent acquisition* (illustrated in Figure 8.3) incorporates everything from attraction through an organization's employment brand; to the selection process (application, screening, and interviews); and job offer and concludes with a candidate ultimately being hired. Furthermore, our veteran screening experience has illustrated the importance of careful understanding and translation of the veteran rank/grade (e.g., sergeant first class/E-7, lieutenant colonel/O-5) and skill set in relation to civilian jobs. More specifically,

**Figure 8.1** Key steps for transitioning veterans into an organization.

**Figure 8.2**  Marketing message to potential Walmart associates.

recruiters and leaders without military experience need to develop their understanding of each branch of the services (e.g., Air Force, Army) in order
to accurately assess whether a candidate is fit for positions in the organization. Many tools and resources exist online and may be easily found using an
Internet search engine. For example, when reviewing a military résumé, you
may want to utilize the O*NET OnLine resource (https://www.onetonline.

## Transition With Support

Take advantage of the programs and organizations that have your back as you return home. Look into the Department of Defense's Transition Assistance Program, Student Veterans of America or online networks like RallyPoint and LinkedIn. Plus, of course, our own resources on WALMARTCAREERSWITHAMISSION.com – including the Transition Timeline.

## Discover Civilian Opportunities

Join the veterans who've been hired under our Veterans Welcome Home Commitment, where we guaranteed a position to every veteran honorably discharged since Memorial Day 2013. You just have to meet our standard hiring criteria. It's as simple as that.

## Pick Your Next

With our goal of hiring 250,000 veterans by 2020 ,we're bound to have an opprtunity that's right for you, too. Whether you're joining our Asset Protection team as a Customer Host, taking the lead in Store Operations as an Assistant Manager, putting your service-learned mechanical talents to work as a Maintenance Technician or guiding the business in a Corporate career, the next chapter of your story is up to you.

Get started with our Find Your Fit tool at
**WALMARTCAREERSWITHAMISSION.COM**

Careers  |  Community  |  Commitments    *Walmart is an Equal Opportunity Employer – By Choice.*

**Figure 8.2**  Continued

org/crosswalk) to assist in translating a Military Occupational Code into a civilian counterpart.

At Walmart, a decision has been made to nest the military employment brand (see Figure 8.4) within the overarching employment brand. We have done this by integrating our military microsite into our corporate careers website, synthesizing the language on the military pages to resonate with both the Walmart brand and the military audience. Additionally, we have

**Figure 8.3** Talent acquisition.

**Figure 8.4** Talent acquisition.

updated our minimum qualifications in some of our key job descriptions to include options for alternative experience in lieu of traditional retail experience, empowering hiring teams to leverage soft skills (e.g., leadership, mission focus, results-driven goals, and cultural alignment) that veteran talent often brings to the table. Soft skills are discussed in greater depth in Chapter 6 in the discussion of personality factors of veterans and skills training. With this holistic approach, a veteran's integration into the corporate culture is activated at the outset.

*Onboarding* (illustrated in Figure 8.5) encompasses a very purposeful process of introducing a new associate to the organization; it includes sharing history and culture and also setting employer expectations. Onboarding, which is more or less organizational socialization, refers to how new associates attain the essential information, behaviors, and skills deemed necessary to transition effectively into an organization. Walmart believes it is important to integrate veteran and civilian associates in the same manner, creating a singular new hire associate experience from Day 1. Tactics utilized in an onboarding process frequently include the following:

**Figure 8.5** Onboarding.

- *Orientation* is a formally scheduled "kickoff" to onboarding a new associate. Introductions to the business and culture are made, and official new hire paperwork is completed.
- *Culture* and organizational histories are brought to life using tactics such as guest speakers, videos, or, in some cases, computer-based learning, often during orientation.
- *Training* helps newly hired associates to feel capable and empowered to successfully complete the responsibilities they are hired to perform. Some level of baseline training may be completed during orientation with all new associates and then followed up with more specialized training within their work department.
- *Expectations* should be clearly defined and established between the new associate and their leadership. This is especially important for the veteran new hires who may still be used to very direct guidance, an artifact of military culture, for their job and responsibilities.
- *Role clarity* can assist in the new hire's understanding of their new job responsibilities and how their role impacts the larger organization as a whole, helping to set a veteran up for early success. Ideally, this piece of the onboarding process will support newcomers in reducing ambiguity and uncertainty so that it is easier for them to get their jobs done correctly and efficiently.
- *Adjustment* is a key achievement of onboarding. In order to increase the success of an onboarding program, it is important to monitor how well new hires are adjusting to their roles, responsibilities, peers, leadership team, and the organization through some sort of metric or survey. One specific tactic that has been effective is identifying a sponsor or advocate whose responsibility is aimed at assisting in a smoother integration into the organization for veteran new hires.

*Experience* (illustrated in Figure 8.6) involving the transition from military to civilian work is truly unique for veterans. Their experience embodies the entire transition process from still in uniform, all the way through the candidate experience, offer acceptance, orientation, and sponsorship or advocacy on the job. The transition for veterans into civilian roles is easier when they have a peer who can assist them in their new role. Walmart offers new associates a sponsorship program with a dedicated peer to introduce them

**Figure 8.6** Experience.

to Walmart and connect them with the work location, facility, and so on. As an extension of that, the Veteran Champion program provides a veteran peer as a go-to person to help ensure a smoother transition into their new roles. It may also be described as a formal, institutionalized onboarding process that positions new veteran associates for success and makes them confident in us and in their ability to succeed in the work environment. Walmart's initial research indicated that veteran associates utilizing the Veteran Champion program are more engaged and have a more optimistic view of their opportunities with the organization.

*Retention* (illustrated in Figure 8.7) involves realizing the actual return on investment and/or leveraging the value that a veteran associate's experience adds to the business through longevity, growth, and development. Organizations may be able to increase their veteran retention by taking steps to address veteran associates' needs and their reasons for leaving. Employers wishing to increase veteran associate retention should therefore offer specific programs (i.e., opportunities for associates to take part in more advanced or diverse activities; effective compensation programs, which may include healthcare and family friendly benefits; effective communications with senior management; and opportunities for contributions to the organization) to aid in associate retention in the civilian workforce (Maury, Stone, and Roseman, 2014). Chapter 13 in this book includes more details on retaining veteran associates in your organization.

These four key steps—talent acquisition, onboarding, experience, and retention—for transitioning veterans into the organization deserve careful attention. In addition to the important work associated with these four steps, leaders and supervisors play an important role in veteran retention and are encouraged to welcome, teach, connect, check in, and support.

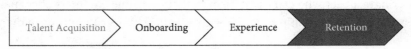

**Figure 8.7** Retention.

## Leadership and Supervisory Practices

When combined with the benefits discussed in the previous sections of this chapter, it is clear that significant business opportunities are evident through military veteran hiring. While the organizational and societal benefits associated with veteran hiring are clear, the role that leaders and supervisors need to play in ensuring veteran success in the organization has received relatively less attention.

A primary leadership imperative is to retain these flexible and adaptable team players who think systematically under pressure and deadlines. In their 2014 Veteran Job Retention Survey (Maury et al., 2014), VetAdvisor and the Institute for Veterans and Military Families at Syracuse University offered some insights. Included in their primary findings were the following:

- Nearly half of those surveyed stayed in their first postseparation position 12 months or less. Further, there is a relationship between job tenure and job alignment with the respondents preferred career field, with closer alignment driving initial tenure.
- The three employment-related issues of greatest importance to respondents were (a) opportunities to apply their skills and abilities, (b) adequate benefits and pay, and (c) meaningfulness of the work.
- Respondents' biggest obstacle to obtaining initial employment was finding opportunities that matched their military training and experience.

The researchers at Syracuse University's Institute for Veterans and Military Families also asked the following questions to veterans who left a civilian sector job or were considering leaving their current job: "Please indicate the reasons you are considering changing employer/career fields"; "Please indicate the reason(s) you left your first postmilitary job"; "For which reason(s) would you have stayed at this position/job?" They received the following responses:

- Reasons for leaving: The top five were new employment opportunity (43 percent); lack of career development/advancement (31 percent); quality of work (30 percent); inadequate compensation/benefits (28 percent); and inadequate professional development opportunity (23 percent).

- Reasons for staying: The top five were increased salary/benefits (61 percent); opportunity for career development/advancement (45 percent); opportunity for professional development (34 percent); quality of work (33 percent); and work environment/culture (31 percent).
- Important aspects of employment: Accounting for 92 percent the top four were opportunities to use skills and abilities; compensation/pay; meaningfulness of the job; and job security.

With the consistency in the top reasons offered for leaving and staying and the important aspects of employment, the survey results captured lessons and hold opportunities for organizational learning. Clearly, there is an important role for the supervisor and leaders of a newly hired veteran amidst all of these aspects of employment. In fact, the immediate supervisors of newly hired veterans need to be fully aware of the career/development interests, feelings about environment/culture, satisfaction with coworkers, and any concerns related to job security/employment status and quality of work for the veteran new hires. Ideally, this supervisor–new hire relationship begins in the talent acquisition process and is fostered through onboarding and continuing engagement, building a solid foundation of trust, and understanding.

Supervisors are also in a unique position to link their understanding of organizational culture to the interests and motivations of newly hired veterans. As with the military experience, it all begins with an idea: a purpose larger than self. Simply, in all things, in all tasks, and beyond any debate, the American military's purpose is to serve and protect America. Equally simple, organizations have missions and visions that drive daily business efforts. For example, Walmart's mission is to save people money so they can live better. Both are big, enduring ideas to which people can commit themselves. The idea and purpose are brought to life by the values that define the organization. Those accepted behaviors are the essence of the organization's culture. A supervisor and the newly hired veteran can link their individual personal interests and motivations to organizational culture merely through an informal conversation or by sharing experiences.

As demonstrated previously in this chapter in Table 8.1, the values of the four services are comparable and align well with the Walmart values. Those values are the bedrock, the foundation, of both the military professions and the Walmart culture. This alignment of values assists veterans as they transition into a new job and organizational culture. As in military service, a primary responsibility of leaders and supervisors is to clearly inculcate foundational values and beliefs to ensure a shared understanding that underlies thoughts and actions in the workplace.

An understanding of organizational mission and purpose and an appreciation of the culture are at the root of a successful transition from military service to a civilian organization. It is the foundation of a values-based process of aligning each candidate, and ultimately each associate, with Walmart's organizational expectations. With alignment between value systems, the practical question of how candidates find where they fit in the organization still needs to be answered. A critical question for talent acquisition professionals is how to help veteran candidates match their career aspirations and personal brand with available organizational entry points. It is clear that the answers are found in the shared responsibilities of the candidate and the organization, and, at Walmart, it is a combination of technology and human touch. Faced with this challenge, Walmart has developed a technology-enabled tool called "Fit Finder" (https://www.walmartcareerswithamission.com/content/people-experience/military.html), which combines career aspirations and personal branding to assist veteran candidates in their job search. In addition to this technology-enabled assistance, Walmart offers basic career counseling through PeopleScout, a recruitment process outsourcing partner, providing a high-touch candidate experience to address employment questions. The candidate experience includes not only his or her job in the organization, but also the promise of career opportunity. Notably, career opportunity, or the lack thereof, is one of the principal reasons identified by research for staying with or leaving an organization.

A second supervisory imperative involves achieving and managing shared expectations between candidate experience and associate experience. Full transparency when attracting, recruiting, and hiring a new veteran associate leads to the pivotal process of onboarding the new team member into the organization. At Walmart, we begin with sponsorship and advocacy for new veteran associates, institutionalized in the Veteran Champion program. This formal, associate–sponsor-focused program is designed to support veteran assimilation into the new employment setting and to ensure early success. It is led principally by Walmart veterans and members of veteran and military families who have a natural affinity for those with similar experiential portfolios.

Finally, supervisors who empower their associates are critical in growing and developing, managing, and retaining veteran associates. It is fair to say that, at Walmart, we may view retention somewhat differently from others: While we want all veteran associates who have a passion for retail to find a home at Walmart, we are even more committed to ensuring that all veteran associates' experiences with us are positive and equally support those whose aspirations take them to different opportunities as productive members of our communities. We also know that too often, rather than quitting an organization, employees quit their bosses. Engaged and engaging leaders and supervisors who serve their customers and their associates make the difference in helping to make sure that good associates stay with the organization.

In summary, leaders and supervisors play a critical role helping newly hired veterans identify a common purpose and culture alignment; find a job that fits their career aspirations as well as personal brand; match their initial entry into the organization with future career opportunities; ensure shared expectations throughout the candidate and associate experiences; and link them to engaging sponsors during and after onboarding.

## Conclusion

The successful hiring and retention of military veterans is a complex yet extremely important imperative for employers. Recruiters, hiring managers, team members, and executive leadership in organizations with veteran hiring programs must work together to ensure that newly hired veterans receive clear communication and support regarding organizational culture, shared expectations, and leadership practices. In addition to the insights we have shared on these three specific areas throughout our chapter, there are several additional takeaways to consider.

First, the best recruiters of veterans are often those who have an affinity for and knowledge of military service. These recruiters are able to readily match a candidate's military experience to the needs of their organization. Knowing that not all recruiters will have such military experience, it is essential to equip those recruiters with insights into military service. These insights and knowledge can be shared between military and nonmilitary recruiters via training and development planning. The following sources/ideas are suggested for talent acquisition professionals seeking development in this area:

- Review the chapters and references provided within this book and select two or three resources regarding military culture and experiences—remember that there are differences between the military branches with regard to culture and experiences.

- Scan your associate base for individuals with military experience— invite them to spend time with recruiters and/or hiring managers to share nuances of their experiences being hired into civilian roles and any suggestions to improve that experience for other veterans.
- Reach out to any nearby military installations and request a meeting with their community relations officer(s); explain what your organization is planning with regard to military hiring and ask for their ideas/ involvement regarding your initiative.

Second, employers need to actively manage the onboarding of veterans into their organizations. Such active management would likely include training leaders and supervisors to recognize and address veterans' interest in organizational mission/culture as well as expectations they likely have regarding development, advancement, and the work they are asked to perform. Mentoring programs that link already employed veterans with newly hired veterans can improve new hire engagement, performance, and ultimately retention. See Chapter 9 in this book for more information on mentoring and affinity groups.

Third, employers need to proactively consider and plan for transparency regarding career path opportunities. Naturally, fairness for both veteran and nonveteran associates needs to be achieved; however, there appears to be a heightened need for clarity with veterans regarding promotion pipelines and other forms of career development/advancement.

Finally, it is critical for employers to gather and maintain data on where veterans serve within their organization. Tracking this information may be difficult in some settings as providing information on previous military experience may be voluntary. Organizations may be able to improve their tracking information if they take steps to engage associates with military backgrounds, explain the organization's programs and intent, and ask for their ideas and involvement. Ultimately, it is important to have veteran information in order to track movement, understand needs, and leverage this unique talent in the onboarding and retention of newly hired veterans.

In summary, at Walmart, we believe that it is not only our duty, but also our honor to support the men and women in uniform when they are on the battlefield and when they return home and transition to civilian life. Our experience has offered us some important lessons, and the focus of this chapter has been to share those lessons involving organizational culture, shared expectations, and leadership as they relate to the issue of hiring and retaining veterans so that you can apply them to your organization. We admire your interest in this topic and offer encouragement for the continued practical and research-oriented focus on this important work.

# References

Baruch, Y., & Quick, J. C. (2007). Understanding second careers: Lessons from a study of U.S. Navy admirals. *Human Resource Management, 46*, 471–491.

Collins, B. C., Dilger, R. J., Dortch, C., Kapp, L., Lowry, S., & Perl, L. (2014). *Employment for veterans: Trends and programs*. Washington, DC: Congressional Research Report. https://fas.org/sgp/crs/misc/R42790.pdf

Corporate Executive Board Recruiting Leadership Council. (2014). *Meeting veteran goals for branding by influence.*

Farley, J. I. (2010). *Military to civilian career transition guide: The essential job search handbook for service members* (2nd ed.). Indianapolis, IN: JIST.

Faurer, J., Rogers-Brodersen, A., & Bailie, P. (2014). Managing the re-employment of military veterans through the Transition Assistance Program (TAP). *Journal of Business and Economics Research, 12*, 55–60.

Junger, S. (2016). *Tribe: On homecoming and belonging.* New York, NY: HarperCollins.

Katzenbach, J., Oelschlegel, C., & Thomas, J., (2016). *Ten principles of organizational culture. Strategy+Business: Organizations & People, Spring*, issue 82. https://selecthealth.org/-/media/selecthealth82/pdf-documents/wellness-materials/culture/10-principles-of-organizational-culture.ashx

King, E. (2011). *Field tested: Recruiting, managing, and retaining veterans.* New York, NY: AMACOM.

Maury, R., Stone, B., and Roseman, J. (2014). *Veteran job retention survey.* Syracuse, NY: Institute for Veterans and Military Families and VetAdvisor.

Riordan, C. M., & O'Brien, K. (2012). *For great teamwork, start with a social contract.* Harvard Business Review. https://hbr.org/2012/04/to-ensure-great-teamwork-start

Substance Abuse and Mental Health Services Administration (SAMHSA). (2010). *Understanding the military: The institution, the culture, and the people.* Washington, DC: Author.

Team Red, White, and Blue. (2014). *Team RWB metrics survey.* Tampa, FL: Author.

Watkins, M. D. (2013). What is organizational culture? And why should we care? *Harvard Business Review.* https://hbr.org/2013/05/what-is-organizational-culture

# 9

# Veteran Affinity Groups and Mentoring Programs

*Mark L. Poteet and Tammy D. Allen*

Military members are provided with a vast range of opportunities to develop professional skills during their service that can translate to the civilian workplace. Specifically, the training and experience that military members receive can equip them with technical skills (e.g., hardware operations, computer programming, medical device technology); leadership capabilities (e.g., influence, directing others); personal attributes (e.g., conscientiousness, integrity, adaptability); interpersonal skills (e.g., communication, teamwork); and problem-solving skills (e.g., decision-making) (Abrams & Kennedy, 2015; Boutelle, n.d.; Wirthman, 2014). Without question, these capabilities are needed in today's workplace and are transferable from military settings to a variety of roles in a range of industries, such as manufacturing, technology, or healthcare.

With an estimated average of 200,000 talented and experienced military members transitioning from the military to the civilian workplace each year, U.S. companies and organizations have responded in concerted fashion to assist with this transition and take advantage of this strong source of talent. Programs such as the U.S. Chamber of Commerce's Hiring Our Heroes campaign (https://www.hiringourheroes.org/) and the Veterans Job Mission (https://www.veteranjobsmission.com/), a cross-organizational initiative that began with 11 companies and has grown to well over 200 companies, provide transitioning veterans with several resources (e.g., training courses; career planning tools; résumé-building assistance; transition guides; online networking programs). Government organizations such as the Department of Defense's Employer Support of the Guard and Reserve (ESGR; http://www.esgr.mil/About-ESGR/Who-is-ESGR) and the Department of Veterans

Mark L. Poteet and Tammy D. Allen, *Veteran Affinity Groups and Mentoring Programs* In: *Military Veteran Employment.* Edited by: Nathan D. Ainspan and Kristin N. Saboe, Oxford University Press. © Oxford University Press 2021. DOI: 10.1093/oso/9780190642983.003.0010

Affairs' Veterans Employment Services Office (https://www.vaforvets.va.gov/veso/Pages/default.asp) also provide both veterans and their employers with resources (including job fairs, support programs, employer briefings, military skills translators, and job search tools) to help bolster the employment of U.S. military members, reservists, and veterans (Box 9.1).

These programs, in conjunction with changing attitudes about employing retired military service members (Constantine, 2016), have played a key role in the increased hiring of veterans. According to statistics released by the Bureau of Labor Statistics (2020), the unemployment rate of all veterans dropped in recent years (3.2 percent to 2.8 percent from December 2018 to December 2019, e.g.), bettering the comparative nonveteran unemployment rate. As a specific example, as a result of overwhelmingly exceeding its initial hiring goals, the 100,000 Jobs Mission recently was renamed to Veterans Job Mission, with a revised goal of hiring one million veterans. Thus, while there are still pockets of military veterans who have higher than average unemployment, overall more and more veterans are successfully entering the workforce.

---

**Box 9.1  Case Study: Supporting Veteran Employees Through Multiple Services**

---

*NASA's Lyndon B. Johnson Space Center (JSC)* plays a key role in human space exploration, having led human space flight programs such as Mercury, Gemini, Apollo, and the space shuttle. With approximately 10,000 civil servant and contractor employees on site, it is currently involved in a host of operational and research programs, including mission control, the International Space Station, and the *Orion* space exploration vehicle. Its Connected Veterans Employee Resource Group (ConVERG) offers a variety of benefits and services, such as providing assistance to military employees who are on deployment, serving as a support network for their families, helping military members returning from deployment to transition back to the workplace, providing education to all employees on veteran-related issues, and providing networking, mentoring, and relationship-building opportunities for new and current veteran employees. All of these activities are centered on the goal of building a strong veteran community and supporting veterans to be effective members of the JSC workforce.

## Challenges Remain

Despite the encouraging news about veterans entering the civilian workplace, veterans may still face a number of challenges once they have entered employment. These include the following:

- Adjusting to the civilian workplace culture, including a company's reporting structure (e.g., hierarchical vs. matrix); diverse roles and operations; power distance (e.g., central vs. decentralized decision-making); internal and external relationships; and different levels of uniformity and formality in language, dress, conduct, and the like. For example, companies we interviewed for this chapter noted that civilian companies generally provide more autonomy and personal responsibility with regard to issues such as career development—seeking training, driving promotions, obtaining coaching, and so on, whereas in the military a member's career path is generally more controlled (Wirthman, 2014).
- The potential of veterans can be invisible to influential leaders in the organization, and few veterans have senior leader sponsors (Abrams & Kennedy, 2015). Some companies with which we spoke noted that veterans may encounter challenges seeing how their skills and experience translate to different roles within a civilian workplace. Matos and Galinsky (2013) noted that unfamiliarity with organizational hierarchies can make it difficult for newly hired veteran employees to obtain support needed to drive strong performance.
- The strong sense of purpose and mission that veterans feel during their military service can be more difficult to obtain within civilian workplaces (Abrams & Kennedy, 2015).
- Veterans can face perceptual challenges in the civilian workforce. Veterans may encounter beliefs from employers and managers that are seen as overly inflexible or regimented (Abrams & Kennedy, 2015). Abrams and Kennedy also outlined a number of false assumptions that organizational colleagues may hold about veterans, such as their political leanings, mental and emotional states, and values.
- Missing a strong sense of brotherhood and camaraderie, some veterans at times may perceive a civilian workplace that values individual contribution rather than dedication to one's team or the organization as a whole. The tight bonds that form through intensive and prolonged

contact within the military may be less pronounced in a civilian work-place, where less time is spent among fellow employees (Boutelle, n.d.).

Outcomes of these challenges are relatively easy to conceive—a limited sense of engagement or commitment to an organization a veteran perceives does not value their experience or skills, makes unfounded assumptions about them, or is perceived to provide limited opportunity to be of service to others. Retention subsequently suffers as the veteran employees may choose to leave a company if they do not feel appreciated. In a recent survey of vet-erans, it was found that the average tenure of a veterans' first job postmilitary was 25.59 months. Additionally, 43 percent left their first job within a year or less, and an even greater number left within 2 years. Common reasons for leaving their first job included lack of career development and advance-ment opportunities, lack of meaningful and quality work, lack of profes-sional development opportunities, insufficient recognition, challenges with management relationships, and work environment and culture issues. Increased opportunities for career advancement and professional develop-ment were among the top three reasons a veteran would have stayed within a job (Maury, Stone, & Roseman, 2014).

For these reasons, organizations have begun to focus on strategies that can increase the retention, engagement, and satisfaction of veteran employees (Box 9.2). For example, the Veterans Job Mission has begun to place greater focus on helping veterans acclimate to the civilian workplace, enhance their career development, and facilitate stronger organizational retention (Veterans Job Mission, 2015). A study by RAND Corporation (Hall, Harrell, Bicksler, Stewart, & Fisher, 2014) and the experiences of several organiza-tions have identified two programs that help increase veteran retention: *affinity groups* and *mentoring programs*.

This chapter describes these two programs in greater depth and discusses their potential impact for a company's veteran workforce population. We begin by defining mentoring programs and affinity groups and outlining their benefits in general. We then outline specifically how such programs can address challenges veterans face in the workplace, thus benefitting both com-panies and veteran employees. After this, we discuss specific issues to con-sider and steps to take in creating such programs. Finally, we end with some overall recommendations and best practices companies can follow to lev-erage the power of these programs. Throughout the chapter, we include short case examples of different companies' programs to further illustrate some

---

**Box 9.2  Case Study: Fulfilling Multiple Needs**

---

*Exelon Corporation* is a Fortune 100 energy company with around 34,000 employees and a presence throughout the United States and Canada. A multiple time recipient of *Military Times*' "Best for Vets" workplace, its Exelon Militaries Actively Connected (E-MAC) affinity group serves a number of distinct purposes. First, E-MAC exists in part to provide a support network for veterans and those interested in veterans' issues. It also gives members an opportunity to network with colleagues from other business units and functions, allowing them to better understand the organization. Members of E-MAC also provide guidance and support to the company's veteran recruiting and onboarding efforts, for example, helping recruiters review résumé and understand veterans' issues, attending virtual career fairs, and helping potential employees understand career paths, salary requirements, and benefits. There is also a volunteer community outreach focus to E-MAC, such as participating in fundraising events or painting local American Legion Halls. In a related manner, by interacting and communicating with external stakeholders and representing the company at events, E-MAC members contribute to the company's brand as a veteran-friendly organization.

---

key points. In compiling information for this chapter, we reviewed available peer-reviewed research, examined technical reports and publications from organizations and authors who have researched veterans' retention issues or implemented these programs, and interviewed several organizations that are or have implemented programs for veterans in their workplaces, many of whom have been awarded and recognized by veterans organizations for their efforts.

## The Role of Mentoring Programs and Affinity Groups

### Mentoring Programs

Mentoring is a relationship between two individuals (a mentor and a protégé) whereby one is focused on helping the other enhance their job or career-related success and well-being (Allen, Finkelstein, & Poteet, 2009). Typically, the mentor is more experienced, skilled, competent, or knowledgeable than the protégé on the specific issue(s) or topic(s) of the mentoring relationship. A classic description of mentoring outlines two broad types of activities that mentors provide: career support (e.g., job-related guidance, visibility on projects, networking opportunities) and psychosocial support (e.g., friendship, role modeling, counseling) (Kram, 1985). This definition does not cover broader types of mentoring such as group mentoring (whereby one mentor works with an intact group of multiple people), but does recognize other forms of one-on-one mentoring, such as peer mentoring (peer to peer) and reverse mentoring (junior to senior employees).

A mentoring program is a structured program, often run within and with the official sanctioning and support of a company, designed to initiate, facilitate, and support mentoring relationships. Companies typically support and facilitate such formal programs by providing policies, budgetary and personnel resources, program management, training, guidelines, manuals, and/ or other forms of support to mentors and protégés. The type of relationships that result from these programs are considered "formal," to be distinguished from "informal" mentoring relationships that are naturally occurring without any formal support or sanctioning from an organization.

A substantial body of research supports the overall benefits of mentoring for protégés, mentors, and organizations (Allen, Eby, Poteet, Lentz, & Lima, 2004; Allen, Lentz, & Day, 2006; Allen & O'Brien, 2006). Specific benefits for protégés include career development, improved job attitudes, and improved job performance (Eby et al., 2013). Because of the benefits associated with mentoring, numerous organizations have implemented formal mentoring programs (Allen et al., 2009). While in general research generally attributes more benefits to informal versus formal mentoring relationships, when designed well, formal programs provide many of the same benefits as naturally occurring mentorships (Ragins & Cotton, 1999). Although a robust literature has developed on best practices for formal mentoring programs, and the benefits of mentoring for active duty military have been documented, research focused on organizational programs specifically designed to support veterans' transition to the civilian workforce is nonexistent. However, research has demonstrated the positive impact that mentoring programs can have with other types of transitions, such as school to work (Renn, Steinbauer, Taylor, & Detwiler, 2014) and new employee socialization (Chao, Walz, & Gardner, 1992).

## Affinity Groups

An affinity group can go by several names, including affinity network, business resource group, employee resource group, affiliation group, networking group, or internal caucus group (Kravitz, 2008). At its most basic level, an affinity group is a formal association of people who share common goals, issues, interests, characteristics, or backgrounds (Salemi, 2015). Focusing more specifically on affinity groups as a mechanism of employee involvement, Van Aken, Monetta, and Sink (1994) defined an affinity group as "a collegial association of peers that meets on a regular basis to share information, capture opportunities, and solve problems that affect the group and the overall organization" (pp. 41), with several features such as having formalized roles, holding regular meetings, and being self-managing.

Affinity groups in general can serve a variety of purposes and roles for veteran employees and organizations (see Competitive Edge Services Inc., Burton Blatt Institute at Syracuse University, & Department of Veteran Affairs, 2013; Matos & Galinsky, 2013; Van Aken et al., 1994, for examples). They can identify and address workplace issues that are relevant to and/or affect its members, for example, by providing input to programs, policies, or initiatives that affect veterans or by discussing and creating programs or resources themselves to address veterans' issues (Matos & Galinsky, 2013). Affinity groups can also serve as a powerful networking tool, helping members broaden their relationships and enhance coordination, both inside and outside the organization (Network of Executive Women, 2006). These groups can also serve an outreach component; for example, they can help with recruiting efforts, provide a means for members to volunteer in community projects, or provide assistance to families or communities directly impacted by veterans' issues. Finally, affinity groups can help acclimate new employees to the organization, as well as provide support for individuals to share their ideas, concerns, and feedback (Matos & Galinsky, 2013).

When comparing mentoring programs and affinity groups, there are a few differences. For example, mentoring is often a one-on-one relationship, whereas affinity groups are group based. In general, the learning experience within mentoring relationships can be more focused and structured on specific goals. Affinity groups may focus on a broader range of activities, such as helping with recruiting efforts or engaging in community outreach. Thus, there are ample reasons why an organization would choose to implement both types of programs and consider them as separate initiatives, as they can impact veteran employees in different ways.

However, both types of programs share several characteristics: Both are formally sanctioned by the organization, both are typically extrarole learning experiences, both rely heavily on interpersonal relationships as a means of achieving their respective goals and purposes, both possess some degree of structure, and both rely on the concerted and dedicated efforts of their participants to drive success. Therefore, for the purposes of this chapter, we review these two programs in tandem, yet where appropriate we highlight where differences between the programs mandate different design and implementation considerations and recommendations.

## The Benefits of Mentoring Programs and Affinity Groups for Veterans

Overall, we were not able to locate research published in the gold standard of research publications—peer-reviewed journals and publications—looking at the benefits of mentoring and/or affinity groups focused on veteran employees. However, there is little reason to expect that the career-related benefits that come from mentoring programs for employees in general (described previously) do not apply to veterans. That said, based on the practice literature (e.g., best practice guides; technical reports), our conversations with program managers and stakeholders, and our general understanding of mentoring programs and affinity groups, it is our contention that these initiatives can have multiple benefits for the veteran employee population.

As noted in 100,000 Jobs Mission's guide on veterans' business resource groups, benefits of using affinity groups can include improved recruitment of veterans, increased retention, professional development, company branding, and networking (100,000 Jobs Mission, 2014). Affinity groups and mentoring programs can help with veterans' adjustment to the climate and culture of civilian workplaces (Matos & Galinsky, 2013) by providing seasoned, knowledgeable colleagues to "teach them the ropes"; help them understand unwritten rules, norms, and organizational culture; and provide guidance on how to build relationships, take control of one's own professional and career development, establish credibility, and perform in a successful manner.

According to Maury et al. (2014), a chief concern of military members is professional development. Mentoring programs, and more specifically an individual's mentor, can provide the veteran protégé with coaching and guidance on how to transfer and leverage their skills and experience to their job duties, projects, and responsibilities. Affinity groups can also expand the range of activities that a veteran can become involved with outside of their formal job roles (e.g., volunteering at internal or external community events), allowing the veteran to potentially tap competencies that are unused in the work environment while also strengthening the skills and abilities that are used in that environment (Salemi, 2015). Such opportunities may also provide a greater sense of purpose and meaning to the veteran's employment with a company.

In terms of career growth, mentoring programs and affinity groups can help provide the career development opportunities that recently hired veterans state are at the top of their wants and needs from their employers (Kravitz, 2008; Maury et al., 2014). Mentors can introduce veteran employees to key stakeholders in the organization, sponsor them for high-potential development opportunities, and provide support when promotional opportunities arise. For veteran employees with ongoing military service commitments such as Reservists or National Guardsmen, Matos and Galinsky (2013) noted that mentors with similar experience can help these employees "successfully manage the entire deployment experience from departure to return" (p. 13). For example, these authors described one company that uses sponsors to help deploying employees transition between civilian and military roles, provide guidance on balancing the dual roles, and assist with deploying employees' families as needed.

Benefits go beyond the veteran employee as well. Specifically, affinity groups and mentoring programs can help nonveteran employees and managers learn how to work effectively with and understand perspectives of their veteran colleagues (Kravitz, 2008). Through the two-way nature of the one-on-one mentoring relationship, a mentor can learn about the veteran protégé's communication style, problem-solving approach, experience, and perspectives. Many of the companies we spoke with permitted both veteran and nonveteran employees to be members of veteran affinity groups—thus providing another avenue for knowledge transfer about veterans' issues. Some affinity programs also provide services to the families of veteran employees who may be on active deployment.

As noted by Kravitz (2008), affinity groups can also serve an advocacy role in providing leaders and employees with information and education related to the group's issues. For example, at Cintas Corporation, a key component of its Veterans Network is its focus on developing and delivering education to managers, executives, and employees on topics such as how veterans prefer to be engaged and how to communicate with veterans on various organizational topics (e.g., differences between military vs. operations or sales cultures).

Matos and Galinsky (2013) noted that some companies use mentoring as an outreach component to help new veterans learn the skills and take the actions necessary to find employment opportunities (e.g., résumé writing, interviewing skills, conducting job searches). In addition to serving the veteran community, this can provide the organization with a broader pool of veteran talent from which to recruit and select.

Rider (2014) noted that affinity groups provide an avenue for sharing ideas with others outside of the immediate group. This is consistent with Van Aken et al.'s (1994) framing of affinity groups as a method of employee involvement. Affinity groups can provide a valuable outreach role, such as assisting with veteran recruiting efforts, participating in local community events, and addressing veterans' issues within their respective workplaces (Matos & Galinsky, 2013). For example, at BAE Systems its Veterans Support Network has implemented multiple avenues for recognizing the contributions of its veteran workforce, such as issuing lapel pins, facilitating recognition communication from the chief executive officer, and issuing challenge coins (a tradition in the military that demonstrates membership in a group)—all of which help build a greater sense of camaraderie. By partaking in these activities, organizations can tap into the veteran employee's strong service orientation while also increasing the diversity of ideas presented. An increased sense of inclusion and satisfaction may result (Rider, 2014).

Mentoring programs and affinity groups can provide substantial access to different team-building and networking opportunities, which can have several benefits for the veteran employee. For instance, these programs can help increase the number and strength of bonds an employee forms with both veteran and nonveteran employees. For affinity groups in particular, this can help to strengthen team relationships (Salemi, 2015) and potentially facilitate the strong camaraderie that veterans experience during their military service. Networking also provides more access to key decision-makers who can influence the veteran's career growth. It can also increase social and professional support (Kravitz, 2008). Networking also helps expand the veteran's knowledge of other corporate functions, roles, departments, and more, which broadens their business perspective while also providing the veteran with more perspective into potential career paths (Salemi, 2015).

## Establishing and Maintaining Mentoring Programs and Affinity Groups

Given the relationship-oriented nature of both affinity groups and mentoring programs, the impetus for how these programs evolve can start at multiple levels. For example, some programs can be initiated from a grassroots perspective, such as when an existing informal group of colleagues with similar interests decides to formalize their efforts into a sanctioned affinity group, or from a more top-down approach when leadership initiates the creation of a formal mentoring program to address a strategic talent management issue or need. Regardless of how the program or group is initiated, it is advisable to take a careful, methodical, and inclusive approach to design and implementation. Below we outline issues to consider and summarize steps and methods to take when designing these programs, drawing on our own research and experience. Readers are referred to Allen et al. (2009) and U.S. Office of Personnel and Management (USOPM; 2008) for more detailed information.

1. *Perform a Needs Assessment.* Conducting a thorough analysis of the underlying needs and context behind these programs is a key first step. Gather (a) the organization's strategy, business objectives, available resources, level of support for the program, culture, and existing programs that might address the needs; and (b) the stakeholder group's interests, goals, and support (Box 9.3). As communicated by Blue Cross Blue Shield of Michigan, connecting with other organizational departments in the company can help one learn about their issues, concerns, and opportunities; help identify areas where an affinity group can contribute; and establish the foundation for joint collaboration in building and integrating the program throughout the company. This information provides the foundation for the program design decisions and ensures that the program is aligned with business strategy and company culture.

2. *Incorporate Best Practices.* As done by Exelon in the design of its employee resource group, benchmarking other companies with successful affinity groups or mentoring programs can provide a valuable source of information on the challenges, benefits, and real-world issues associated with

## Box 9.3  Needs Assessment to Expand Programs

JPMorgan Chase provides a range of financial services, including investment and commercial banking, asset management, and consumer and small business banking. Through its over 230,000-member workforce, it is a leading financial services firm serving customers across the world. A cofounder of the Veterans Job Mission, its VETS (Voices of Employees That Served) business resource group has traditionally been used for relationship building, communication, and networking activities, along with providing members with several community outreach volunteer opportunities (e.g., natural disaster relief and career or job transition assistance). Desiring to make a greater impact on retention and to tap into the veteran employees' need to serve, the company embarked on a series of focus groups and research to better understand retention and performance across business lines and regions. From this research, it has developed and is piloting a more holistic and integrated approach to enhancing veteran employees' acclimation, retention, networking, career development, and job success. Specifically, through its Pathfinder mentoring program, new veteran employees will be paired with a seasoned employee for 1 year to learn about specific topics related to their transition (e.g., communication; military and corporate value integration), followed by having non-veteran managers sponsor one or more new veteran employees. The VETS group is also looking to provide more career development education for members, such as holding professional development web sessions on topics like conducting effective performance appraisals or preparing for interviews.

implementing and maintaining these programs. Reading company technical reports, reviewing best practice guides, conducting interviews with peer companies, and reviewing the literature are all helpful activities.

3. *Set Goals and Objectives.* Research in the goal-setting literature underscores the need for specific and achievable goals in order to motivate one's efforts (Locke & Latham, 2006). This concept is universal across a wide range of activities, including mentoring and affinity projects. As outlined by Allen et al. (2009), targeted, detailed objectives for mentoring can enhance the chances of achieving strong results (Box 9.4). Creating a clear, realistic, and achievable set of goals and objectives for the program helps

---

**Box 9.4  Case Study: Multiple Objectives—Multiple Programs**

---

*Cintas Corporation* is a leading provider of corporate uniforms, restroom supplies, and cleaning, first aid, safety, and fire protection products and services, operating over 400 facilities and employing about 40,000 individuals, with more than 1 million customers worldwide. Cintas has embarked on a multiple-program approach to enhance the orientation, connections, and acclimation of newly hired and tenured veterans, with the overall aims of enhancing retention and engagement of its veteran workforce. To complement its veteran recruiting strategies, it has recently formalized an ERG from an existing informal network of military veterans as a way to further connect veterans and involve them in related issues, such as educating nonveteran managers on how to engage and communicate with new veteran employees. Cintas also operates a veteran-focused mentoring network, called the Quick Reaction Force, that pairs a new veteran hire with a tenured employee to provide additional education and resources to help the new employee orient, acclimate, and succeed in the organization. Consistent with its decentralized culture, participants are provided some latitude and creativity on how best to structure and implement their mentoring engagements.

---

in several ways. Goals provide direction for the program's activities; they set the parameters for several program structure decisions (e.g., who will participate, how often meetings will be held);and they inform the specific outcomes that are desired as well as how those outcomes can be tracked and evaluated.

4. *Design the Program.* In Table 9.1 are several issues to consider and address when determining how to create structure and processes for these programs. In general, there are no "right or wrong" answers to these questions. Rather, the appropriate answers to these questions will vary depending on the organizational context (i.e., the goals of the program, the strategic need it is intended to address, the available resources for the program, and the culture of the organization). Nevertheless, having clear structure, rules, roles and responsibilities, requirements, protocols, and processes can be important for ensuring an effective and sustainable program (100,000 Jobs Mission, 2014).

5. *Communicate the Program.* Communicating information about the program is an important step for building support and increasing participation

**Table 9.1** Design and Implementation Issues to Address

| Affinity Groups | Mentoring Programs |
| --- | --- |
| • Will an employee's participation be considered as "time on clock" or activities to be completed outside of the formal allocated work time period?<br>• What type of governance structure will be used (e.g., governing board; presidential structure)? What specific duties and responsibilities will these positions hold?<br>• What level of leadership support will be provided, and how?<br>• How often will the affinity group's governing structure meet?<br>• What scope and range of activities will the affinity group undertake, and how often?<br>• How will potential members be informed about the program? How will the program be marketed internally and externally?<br>• How will program success be defined and measured? By whom?<br>• What resources, such as budget, meeting space, etc., can be provided? | • What population will serve as mentors? How will these individuals be recruited and screened?<br>• What level of structure will be provided or required? For example, will there be a required number of mentor–protégé meetings? How often will they occur? Will there be formal mentoring agreements used? How long will mentoring relationships last?<br>• How will mentoring relationships be monitored and program success evaluated?<br>• Who will have responsibility for managing the mentoring program?<br>• How will matches between mentors and protégés be made? On what criteria? By whom?<br>• How will mentoring relationship challenges and issues be handled and resolved?<br>• What training will be provided to mentors and protégés? |

from targeted populations (Box 9.5). Companies may benefit from creating a formal marketing plan that incorporates multiple communication vehicles, including communications during new employee orientation, workplace posters, emails, newsletters, or announcements (Competitive Edge Services Inc. et al., 2013; USOPM, 2008). Designing processes for recruiting qualified mentors, working with internal human resources staff to identify appropriate methods for notifying veteran employees about mentoring and affinity group opportunities, and determining vehicles for publicizing information to other related internal and external groups and organizations are important components of a communication plan.

6. *Implement the Program.* Implementation of an affinity group or mentoring program becomes relatively straightforward to the extent that the preceding steps have been undertaken in a careful and comprehensive manner. Generally speaking, ensuring that adequate resources are obtained and provided to participants is a key step for smooth implementation. Having a leader or team dedicated to overseeing the implementation can

---

### Box 9.5  Case Study: Structure and Communicate the Program

*Blue Cross Blue Shield of Michigan*, a mutual nonprofit insurance company, has over 8,100 employees and is the largest health insurer in the state of Michigan. Its recently established Veterans Employee Resource Network provides veteran employees with engagement, professional development, transition support, and networking opportunities, as well as educational and informational awareness activities for nonveteran employees. To help manage its activities, the resource groups employ a formal governance structure, with an executive sponsor, two cochairs, liaisons at regional offices, and volunteer subcommittees who plan the group's activities and educational sessions. It also uses multiple communication channels to publicize its events and activities, including electronic board messaging, internal newsletters, direct flyers, and email. Through these efforts, the organization has seen promising attendance at the group's sessions while its membership goals are being met.

---

help ensure quick resolution of any barriers or obstacles experienced, as well as facilitate clear communications between all involved stakeholders. Some companies we spoke with recommended conducting a pilot test as a way to determine the potential benefits and obstacles to mentoring or affinity groups.

Key actions important for successful implementation of mentoring programs include (a) careful matching of mentors with protégés and (b) providing training to participants. Research has demonstrated that training benefits mentors and protégés in terms of perceptions of the program's effectiveness, greater understanding of the program, more mentor commitment, and the amount of mentoring received (Allen, Eby, & Lentz, 2006a, 2006b). Furthermore, research has indicated that mismatches are often a key problem among the participants (Eby & Lockwood, 2005). Specific recommendations for these two activities are provided in the next section.

7. *Monitor, Evaluate, and Revise.* It is important to include processes or methods for tracking and evaluating program performance. This allows the organization to determine whether the goals and objectives of the programs are being met, to spot early onset problems that need to be resolved, to identify opportunities for improvement, and to develop

success stories that can be used for further marketing and promotion. For mentoring programs, this could involve periodic check-ins with mentors and protégés to gauge how well the mentorships are going (e.g., are meetings being held, are goals being met, is communication effective) as well as end-of-program/mentorship evaluations (e.g., What results were achieved? How effective were the relationships? Were perceptions of the program positive?). Similarly, evaluations of affinity groups can take place at the event level (e.g., Was the group's participation in the job recruiting fair impactful?); at the group level (e.g., Do group members feel more satisfied, included, and engaged?); or the organizational level (e.g., Are retention rates for veterans improving?). A variety of methods can be used depending on the goals of the program, available resources, and types of information gathered (e.g., interviews, surveys, focus groups, or organizational/business metrics). The specific measures/metrics to be evaluated should be aligned with the goals and objectives of the program. At NASA's Johnson Space Center, for example, employee resource groups are required to report twice a year to the organization's Inclusion and Innovation Council—a midterm report of activities and projects and a year-end report of highlights and successes. This process allowed the Connected Veterans Employee Resource Group (ConVERG) to demonstrate its cross-program impacts, such as helping Johnson Space Center's Employee Assistance Program prepare a presentation on considerations specific to supervising veteran employees.

## Best Practice Recommendations

Based on existing literature and our conversations with companies, there are several recommendations and guidelines we can offer to organizations wishing to use these mentoring and affinity group programs to assist veterans in making the transition to a civilian workforce to become successful, long-term employees. These recommendations are first presented for affinity and mentoring programs in general, then recommendations specific to affinity groups or mentoring programs are provided. In no way is this list complete, and does implementing one or more of these guidelines does not guarantee the success of a program. However, we feel confident that chances of program success are increased to the extent these recommendations are adopted.

## Mentoring Programs and Affinity Groups

### Build and Sustain Support

It almost goes without saying that building, gaining, and sustaining internal support for these efforts is important to ensuring success (Network of Executive Women, 2006; USOPM, 2008). This is important at multiple levels: At one level is commitment from senior leadership to provide necessary funding, personnel, facilities, and authority to officially sanction and legitimize such programs (Box 9.6). Ensuring that members of mentoring programs or affinity groups have support from their direct supervisor or line of management is often a prerequisite for the veteran to get the dedicated time needed to participate in the programs. Still further is focused support for the program from specific stakeholders or internal champions (Network of Executive Women, 2006). For example, some organizations have executive(s) serve as sponsors for their programs. This has multiple benefits, such as ensuring that the program has a voice at the senior leadership table; that program managers and participants have a point of contact to convey program information; that a strong leadership presence is available that can facilitate decision-making, garner resource support, and implement changes to the program; and that, perceptually, the program is seen as important throughout the company.

To build internal leadership support, it is important to demonstrate the importance, benefit, and value of such programs—in other words, to make

---

**Box 9.6  Case Study: The Power of Executive Support**

*BAE Systems* is a global organization located worldwide with over 80,000 employees; it designs, develops, manufactures, and supports technology-focused defense, security, and aerospace systems, solutions, and products. For its Veterans Support Network affinity group, having an executive sponsor has helped to initiate changes that have benefited the organization's veteran workforce. For example, the group proposed installing parking signs designated for combat-wounded veterans at the organization's facilities across several locations. Despite obstacles (e.g., limited parking availability at some locations), within a few weeks the signs were installed at 25 different locations, some with multiple signs and multiple buildings through the support of the executive sponsor.

the business case (USOPM, 2008). At Cintas Corporation, collecting and continuously presenting impact data help to inform executives who might not be able to regularly observe firsthand the natural camaraderie that forms and strengthens between former military members or the direct impact the program's activities have on the company. This helps to build initial support for creating a program (e.g., using impact data from other companies' programs or estimating impact numbers internally) as well as to ensure long-term sustainability. Similarly, selling the program to participants is an important step in building initial support and commitment to participate. This can include explaining how the program operates and what it is intended to accomplish (for both participants and the company), as well as outlining the benefits and outcomes that mentors and protégés may expect to achieve.

## Align Program With the Culture

Although mentoring programs and affinity programs can both focus on helping veteran employees to adapt a specific company's culture, it is also important to embed the design and implementation of the programs themselves with the company culture. Companies that value flexibility and bottom-up decision-making may benefit from programs with fewer boundaries, policies, and structure; conversely, companies that value tradition, structure, and formal top-down decision-making may wish to model their programs with these components. Exelon Corporation, for example, recognized the potential for veteran interest groups that were occurring at local business units to contribute to the company's broader strategy. Therefore, oversight and administration of the veteran's resource group program was rolled up to the corporate level to provide some level of consistency, while each chapter in the local business unit retains authority for determining its activities and operations in a manner that best fits the local business unit culture, location, and stakeholders.

## Have a Clear Charter, Mission, and Purpose Linked to Business Needs

It is important for mentoring and affinity programs to think carefully about the goals they want to accomplish to ensure that they are aligned with business goals and add value to both veteran employees and the organization (Network of Executive Women, 2006; USOPM, 2008). This can help build initial support for the program as well as ensure its long-term sustainability. Additionally, as was communicated by representatives from Johnson Space Center's ConVERG program, it helps groups "cut through the noise" and focus on what matters.

## Remain Adaptable

There are certain components of these programs that will generally be fixed and relatively consistent. For example, parameters outlining what populations are eligible to be mentors and protégés within a mentoring program or company policies and procedures around the operation of affinity groups may be foundational for such programs and change little over time. However, as noted by some companies, it is important not to overburden such programs with too many rules, regulations, and procedural components. Similarly, it can be beneficial to allow participants a level of creativity and flexibility to adapt the program. Changes to programs might be required for a variety of reasons:

- New needs of the veteran population may emerge (e.g., moving from a goal of acclimating new veteran employees to also providing support for family members).
- Feedback might indicate areas of inefficiency or opportunities for improving the structure of operations of the program.
- The success of a program may garner support from senior leaders to expand the size or reach of the program or assist in creating similar programs in other business units.

In each of these instances, ensuring participants are empowered to identify potential needs or concerns, develop relevant solutions, communicate these to appropriate stakeholders, and act to address them is important for long-term success.

## Ensure Adequate Resources

Long-term sustainability of mentoring and affinity programs is enhanced when the program's goals are consistently aligned with available internal resources. Such support can be multilayered and go beyond the more obvious mechanisms. For example, mentoring programs focused on acclimating new veteran employees should ensure that, at a minimum, enough mentors are available to be paired with incoming veterans. However, it is also critical to ensure that the mentors have bandwidth to take on these additional responsibilities, have the core interpersonal skills and knowledge needed to be effective mentors, and have the right internal connections to help new veteran employees build relationships.

Similarly, for affinity groups, having structured parameters for the group (e.g., frequency of meetings per year), meeting space, financial support for group activities, determining whether attendance/participation in group meetings is on or off company paid time, and gaining support from external organizations (e.g., community organizations) whose assistance may be needed, are critical resources to consider and plan for up front. As participation in these types of programs is typically voluntary, ensuring there is a relatively large group of enthusiastic and committed members willing to contribute can help to ensure the program's activities move forward when some members are unable to participate due to increased job-related demands.

## Model Inclusion in Program Design

A common goal among veteran affinity groups and mentoring programs is to encourage a strong sense of engagement and inclusion. A first step in making this happen is to use input from veterans to help design and implement programs. Gaining their insights, ideas, feedback, and concerns can help ensure that the program's objectives are linked to their needs and that its activities have value for the target audiences. As noted by General Dynamics Information Technology, seeking feedback from transitioning veterans regarding how to best structure the mentoring program can help ensure that it provides a meaningful experience.

## Improve Continuously

Programs do not always perform as designed, and the needs of target populations and the organization change over time. For this reason, it is key to continually assess performance and use feedback to make changes (Box 9.7). For some mentoring programs, particularly those early in their tenure,

---

**Box 9.7  Case Study: Monitor Performance and Adjust to Increase Impact**

---

*General Dynamics Information Technology (GDIT)* provides information technology, systems engineering, professional services, and simulation and training to customers in the defense, federal civilian government, health, homeland security, intelligence, state and local government, and commercial sectors. In 2015, GDIT introduced a mentoring program to assist newly hired veterans with their transition into the company. The program involves helping new hires understand what to expect in a new culture, discussing how their skill sets bring value to the business and mapping out a career path. Each newly hired veteran is matched with a GDIT mentor who has gone through a similar transition. The program was not intended to be prescriptive, and once participants are provided a description of the program's goals, protégés are empowered to drive the structure and frequency and define barometers of success with their mentors. In order to expand and enhance the program, innovative changes are being considered, such as automating assignments based on similarities in military branches and rank, building more structure to the mentoring process and providing training related to fostering successful mentorships. These prospective changes were identified as a result of analyzing participant feedback, assessing the program's performance, and reviewing the effectiveness of other programs as a means to incorporate best practices.

---

companies we spoke with noted a desire for greater participation from its veteran protégé population. To do so, they were in the process of adjusting based on the feedback received and research into other programs.

## Affinity Groups

### Don't Limit Them to Veterans

Consistent with the work of Abrams and Kennedy (2015), many of the companies with whom we spoke allow for both veteran and nonveteran employees to join their veterans' affinity groups. For example, at NASA's Johnson Space Center, current and former military members, as well as

family and friends of military members—essentially anyone who wants to
support veterans' issues—are welcome and at times are some of the most engaged affinity group members. Nonveteran employees may have a natural interest in veterans' issues, or may have had family members or friends serve in
the military, and thus feel compelled to contribute. Including committed and
motivated nonveterans can help to further broaden the reach and impact of
the group across the organization and further sustain the success of largely
volunteer-driven affinity groups.

## Target Outcomes to Multiple Levels

For affinity groups, it can be a good practice to ensure its objectives and
outcomes address the needs and interests of multiple stakeholders—in effect,
to have a win-win for all involved. For example, as noted elsewhere in this
chapter, affinity groups can have benefits for its members (e.g., recognition,
increased acclimation to organization); for the company's resources (e.g.,
assisting with veteran recruiting efforts); for the company's operations and
business (e.g., providing input into new products or services); and for the external community (e.g., via outreach efforts). Ultimately, all of these benefits
can help to further strengthen the company's brand.

## Partner With Other Organizations

As is evident in this chapter, the types of activities with which a veteran affinity group can undertake are wide ranging. For some groups, particularly
those in the early stages of existence, it can make sense to team up with other
organizations that may have more resources to offer, provide a more comprehensive set of services and activities outside of work, or do certain things
better (Box 9.8). At General Dynamics Information Technology, partnering
with the USO-Metro has enabled employees to assist service members as
they transition home from active duty and allowed its veteran employees
to get more involved in assisting veterans outside of the workplace. While
this may not have a direct impact on the bottom line, these types of activities can help to build the company's brand, strengthen the local community,

---

**Box 9.8  Case Study: Partner for Success**

---

The *University of Maryland's full-time MBA program* is home to the SmithVet professional club. This group was designed to facilitate networking opportunities between veteran students and employers and between veteran students across different MBA programs, as well as to help veterans acclimate to working with nonveteran students and to assist in outreach efforts to recruit prospective veteran students. Currently in the early stages of operation, the program has successfully partnered with other existing clubs to conduct team-building exercises, facilitate empowerment activities, provide interviewing and résumé building mentoring to other students, and hold networking events. It has found this partnership approach valuable to help the SmithVet members increase their channels for finding employment while also helping to establish the credibility of the new club.

---

and further build the engagement, motivation, and satisfaction of its veteran employees.

## Mentoring

### Matching Mentors and Protégés

The importance of the age-old question of "how do we best match our mentors with protégés" cannot be overstated. An appropriate match helps ensure that a strong bond will form, which will serve as the basis for a successful long-term mentoring relationship characterized by trust, open communication, and commitment (Allen et al., 2009). Unfortunately, the answer to this question is—it depends. It depends on the objectives of the program, the culture of the organization, and the characteristics of the participants. For mentoring programs designed to help new veterans acclimate to a civilian workplace, build relationships with colleagues, connect with other veteran employees for support, or work through the challenges of succeeding in new roles, it is important to pair a new veteran employee with a senior employee who has the experience of making a similar transition. To encourage a strong bond and sense of camaraderie between military colleagues, matching participants on common background and interests is important. For example, General Dynamics Information Technology looks at matching mentors and protégés who were in the same branch of service and at similar ranks. At NASA's Johnson Space Center, consideration is given to match mentors and protégés based on similarities between their military rank (for the protégé) and organization level (for the mentor), and in their employing function. Geographical proximity is another factor used to match participants—mentors and protégés generally prefer being close in proximity to one another (Eby & Lockwood, 2005), as this may enhance the frequency with which mentors and protégés interact (Allen et al., 2006a).

Matching is often a time-consuming process to the extent it is handled manually, so some companies use technology to assist with this task. Veterati produces one such tool for this purpose. Veterati assists organizations seeking to help or hire veterans and veterans looking for employment. Their technology leverages algorithmic matching, automated scheduling, best-in-class practices deployed via text message, automated phone calls to connect mentees to mentors, and just-in-time text messages to capture reviews from each meeting and longer term community success metrics, to provide a user experience that is seamless from signup to completing a phone call with the mentor. The company's ultimate mission is to leverage their technology to connect 100 million employed Americans to 1.5 million transitioning veterans and 5.5 million underemployed or unemployed military spouses.

## Provide Training and Resources

Particularly relevant for mentoring programs due to their focused one-on-one learning relationship, ensuring participants have the requisite training, knowledge, and resources to fulfill their responsibilities is key (Box 9.9). As outlined by Allen et al. (2009), there are multiple levels of training topics that can be covered, ranging from basic, foundational information about the program to advanced skill building, such as how to handle relationship challenges. The choice of training goals, topics, and design should be integrated with the program's goals, available resources, and organization culture. Beyond training, other resources that mentors and protégés could find useful include instruction guides, manuals, and toolkits.

---

**Box 9.9  Case Study: Provide Resources for Support**

---

One large leading national retailer with whom we spoke operates a mentoring program designed to help newly hired veterans transition from a military to civilian culture. Operating alongside a management training program for these veterans, the mentoring program pairs veteran protégés with a senior mentor who coaches and guides the veteran in dealing with issues related to the transition. Once mentoring assignments are made, the program manager informs protégés of their match and then gives guidance on how to establish and structure the relationship (e.g., how often to reach out to mentors). Protégés are also provided with background information on their specific mentor (e.g., biography, corporate experience, company role, military background), as well as a toolkit containing guidelines for an introductory call (e.g., questions they can ask to initiate conversations with their mentor). Mentors are provided with a mentor guide that reviews information such the program's goals and operations, their role and responsibilities within the program, and tips and questions for engaging conversations with protégés. Mentors are also provided with an outline of the development program's curriculum to help them stay informed about the protégé's areas of learning.

---

## Additional Recommendations

### Integrate Programs

When considering implementing affinity or mentoring programs for veterans, organizations are encouraged to take a holistic perspective and determine how these initiatives can complement existing programs, as well as each other. For instance, organizations might want to use affinity groups and mentoring programs in concert after considering the unique advantages of each program. While an affinity group can provide the veteran with an outlet for maintaining the strong camaraderie and bonds that develop through their service, one-on-one mentoring can supplement this with more focused attention to each veteran's skill development and job performance. This approach is being taken at BAE Systems, where its Veterans Support Network is paired with a Veteran Mentorship Program. While the affinity group engages members with opportunities to share information with fellow veterans, develop new programs for veterans, and recognize the veteran workforce, members who want more focused guidance or opportunities to develop can self-nominate for the mentoring program. Through this program, the veteran protégé can receive tutelage from a more senior or peer colleague, helping both the mentor and the protégé to learn more about the protégé's skills, capabilities, and potential, thus serving as a tool for talent identification.

## Align With Existing Programs

Similarly, organizations should consider how an affinity group and/or mentoring program complements or adds to existing initiatives. Doing so avoids duplication of efforts, makes maximal use of available resources, furthers the success of multiple programs, and targets and sharpens the goals and structure of the program. Aligning a veteran's affinity group with other internal groups and networks may help address any internal obstacles and enhance impact and influence (Network of Executive Women, 2006). At NASA's Johnson Space Center, the ConVERG affinity group assists its Pathways Intern Program, one of the center's major vehicles for hiring new employees, by pairing current veteran employees with interns who are experienced and tenured former military members seeking advanced degrees, to ensure that they have a peer group they can relate to as they complete their work rotations.

## Conclusion

The employment outlook for veterans has become increasingly positive over recent years, with the veteran unemployment rate of 3.5 percent in 2017 being the lowest in 16 years (U.S. Department of Labor, 2017). However, challenges remain to acclimating and retaining transitioning veteran employees within the civilian workforce. Affinity groups and mentoring programs are ideally suited to help veterans learn about and adjust to the unique challenges and considerations that come with working in civilian workplaces, to sharpen existing skills and develop new competencies that will enable their success, to develop relationships with internal colleagues and external stakeholders, and to provide opportunities for inclusion that can enhance veterans' commitment and engagement. Along with the career-related benefits that veterans may receive, organizations may benefit from increased veteran employee retention, strengthening of its competitive and brand positioning, and enhanced diversity of ideas and perspectives. Despite the relative lack of peer-reviewed research on veteran-based mentoring and affinity programs specifically, the case studies highlighted in this chapter and research from the mentoring literature in general point to several recommendations that can help organizations design, develop, implement, and sustain effective mentoring programs and affinity groups for its veterans workforce:

- Build support for the programs
- Align program with the organization's culture
- Link the charter, mission, and purpose of the program to business needs
- Keep the program adaptable
- Ensure adequate resources are allocated
- Include veterans in the program design
- Practice continue improvement
- Partner, integrate, or align with other programs where possible

## Veterans Employee References

- Hiring Our Heroes: https://www.uschamberfoundation.org/hiring-our-heroes
- Employer Support of the Guard and Reserve: https://www.esgr.mil/About-ESGR/Who-is-ESGR
- Team Red, White, and Blue: https://www.teamrwb.org
- VA for VETS: https://www.vaforvets.va.gov/veso/Pages/default.asp
- Non-Commissioned Officers Association: https://ncoausa.org/about/
- Veterans Job Mission: https://www.veteranjobsmission.com/
- Feds Hire Vets: https://www.fedshirevets.gov

## References

Abrams, M., & Kennedy, J. T. (2015). *Mission critical: Unlocking the value of veterans in the workforce*. Los Angeles, CA: Vireo Books/Rare Bird Books.

Allen, T. D., Eby, L. T., & Lentz, E. (2006a). Mentorship behaviors and mentorship quality associated with formal mentoring programs: Closing the gap between research and practice. *Journal of Applied Psychology, 91*, 567–578.

Allen, T. D., Eby, L. T., & Lentz, E. (2006b). The relationship between formal mentoring program characteristics and perceived program effectiveness. *Personnel Psychology, 59,* 125–153.

Allen, T. D., Finkelstein, L. M., & Poteet, M. L. (2009). *Designing workplace mentoring programs: An evidence-based approach.* Oxford, UK: Wiley-Blackwell.

Allen, T. D., Lentz, E., & Day, R. (2006). Career success outcomes associated with mentoring others: A comparison of mentors and nonmentors. *Journal of Career Development, 32,* 272–285.

Allen, T. D., & O'Brien, K. (2006). Formal mentoring programs and organizational attraction. *Human Resource Development Quarterly, 17,* 43–58.

Allen, T. D., Eby, L. T., Poteet, M. L., Lentz, E., & Lima, L. (2004). Career benefits associated with mentoring for protégés. A meta-analysis. *Journal of Applied Psychology, 89,* 127–136.

Boutelle, C. (n.d.). *Veterans bring key skill assets to the civilian workforce.* https://www.siop.org/Research-Publications/Items-of-Interest/ArtMID/19366/ArticleID/5029/Veterans-Bring-Key-Skill-Assets-to-the-Civilian-Workforce

Bureau of Labor Statistics. (2020). *Table A-5: Employment status of the civilian population 18 years and over by veteran status, period of service, and sex, not seasonally adjusted.* https://www.bls.gov/news.release/empsit.t05.htm

Chao, G. T., Walz, P. M., & Gardner, P. D. (1992). Formal and informal mentorships: A comparison on mentoring functions and contrast with nonmentored counterparts. *Personnel Psychology, 45,* 619–636.

Competitive Edge Services, Inc., Burton Blatt Institute at Syracuse University, & Department of Veteran Affairs. (2013). *Veterans in the workplace: Recruitment and retention.* https://www.va.gov/vetsinworkplace/docs/Veterans_in_Workplace_Final_Report.pdf

Constantine, J. (2016, February 19). Why 2016 is the year for veterans in the workplace. *Industry Week.* http://www.industryweek.com/workforce/why-2016-year-veterans-workplace

Eby, L. T., Allen, T. D, Hoffman, B. J., Baranik, L. E., Sauer, J. B., Baldwin, S., . . . Evans, S. C. (2013). An interdisciplinary meta-analysis of the potential antecedents, correlates, and consequences of protégé perceptions of mentoring. *Psychological Bulletin, 139,* 441–476.

Eby, L. T., & Lockwood, A. (2005). Protégés' and mentors' reactions to participating in formal mentoring programs: A qualitative investigation. *Journal of Vocational Behavior, 67,* 441–458.

Hall, K. C., Harrell, M. C., Bicksler, B. A., Stewart, R., & Fisher, M. P. (2014). *Veteran employment: Lessons from the 100,000 Jobs Mission.* Santa Monica, CA: RAND. http://www.rand.org/pubs/research_reports/RR836.html

JPMorgan Chase & Company. (2015). *Military and veterans affairs fact sheet.* https://www.jpmorganchase.com/corporate/Corporate-Responsibility/document/MilitaryandVeterans-Affairs-FactSheet_20141110.pdf

Kram, K. E. (1985). *Mentoring at work: Developmental relationships in organizational life.* Glenview, IL: Scott Foresman.

Kravitz, D. A. (2008). The diversity-validity dilemma: Beyond selection-the role of affirmative action. *Personnel Psychology, 61,* 173–193.

Locke, E. A., & Latham, G. P. (2006). New directions in goal-setting theory. *Current Directions in Psychological Science, 15,* 265–268.

Matos, K., & Galinsky, E. (2013). *Employer support for the military community.* Families and Work Institute and Society for Human Resource Management. http://familiesandwork.org/site/research/reports/www_military_spprt.pdf

Maury, R., Stone, B., & Roseman, J. (2014, September). *Veteran job retention survey: Summary.* Syracuse, NY: Institute for Veterans and Military Families and VetAdvisor, Syracuse University. https://ivmf.syracuse.edu/wp-content/uploads/2016/06/VeteranJobRetentionSurveySummaryACC_03.16.18.pdf

Network of Executive Women. (2006). *Affinity networks: Building organizations stronger than their parts: Best practices from the Network of Executive Women Consumer Products and Retail Industry.* https://docplayer.net/10689423-Affinity-networks-building-organizations-stronger-than-their-parts.html

100,000 Jobs Mission. (2014, December). *Leading practice: Business resource groups—your force multiplier.* https://www.veteranjobsmission.com/content/dam/veteran-jobs-mission/documents/Business%20resource_groups%20_your_force_multiplier.pdf

100,000 Jobs Mission. (2015, October). *Leading practice: Performance and retention.* https://www.mchra.org/resources/Documents/Vets/Performance%20and%20Retention.pdf

Ragins, B. A., & Cotton, J. L. (1999). Mentor functions and outcomes: A comparison of men and women in formal and informal mentoring relationships. *Journal of Applied Psychology, 84*(4), 529–550.

Renn, R. W., Steinbauer, R., Taylor, R., & Detwiler, D. (2014). School-to-work transition: Mentor career support and student career planning, job search intentions, and self-defeating job search behavior. *Journal of Vocational Behavior, 85,* 422–432.

Rider, D. (2014, July). Workplace affinity groups. *Human Resource Executive Online.* http://www.hreonline.com/HRE/view/story.jhtml?id=534357294

Salemi, V. (2015, December). 5 ways affinity groups can boost your career. *U.S. News & World Report.* http://money.usnews.com/money/blogs/outside-voices-careers/2015/12/08/5-ways-affinity-groups-can-boost-your-career

U.S. Department of Labor. (2017, August). *Lowest July veteran unemployment rate since 2001.* Washington, DC: U.S. Department of Labor. https://www.dol.gov/vets/newsletter/

U.S. Office of Personnel Management (USOPM). (2008, September). *Best practices: Mentoring.* Washington, DC: U.S. Office of Personnel Management. https://www.opm.gov/hrd/lead/BestPractices-Mentoring.pdf

Van Aken, E. M., Monetta, D. J., & Sink, S. D. (1994, Spring). Affinity groups: The missing link in employee involvement. *Organizational Dynamics, 22*(4), 38–54.

Veterans Job Mission. (2015, November). *Veterans Jobs Mission: New name, new goal for hiring one million U.S. military veterans.* https://www.veteranjobsmission.com/news/830

Wirthman, J. (2014, February). Military vets bring talent, leadership to the workforce. *ForbesBrandVoice.* http://www.forbes.com/sites/northwesternmutual/2014/02/05/military-vets-bring-talent-leadership-to-the-workforce/#2a3ef3221740

# 10

# The Key Role of Supervisors
# for Supporting Veterans in the Workplace

*Leslie B. Hammer, Krista Brockwood, and Sarah N. Haverly*

This chapter focuses on leadership—both the leadership experience and abilities a veteran brings to an employer and the importance of civilian workplace supervisors. Supervisors are key in supporting and recognizing the unique knowledge, skills, and abilities that our former and current service members bring to the workplace, enhancing not only the quality of business outcomes, but also the social relationships within organizations. This chapter begins with a focus on the importance of managers and supervisors providing a culture of support for veterans by addressing how such support leads to improvements in self-efficacy, health, well-being, and job outcomes such as increased retention of veterans in the civilian workplace. This chapter then addresses the importance of both the leadership skills and qualities brought to the workplace by our veterans—and how organizations can recognize, utilize, and maximize the leadership skills that these veterans offer.

## Supporting Veteran Transitions to the Workplace

As U.S. troops from domestic overseas military operations exit military life and transition to a nonmilitary way of life, many veterans must adapt to civilian jobs. Service members have exceptional skills and experiences that make them extremely valuable members of the workforce and, in particular, for leadership positions. Organizations, with the proper leadership support and resourcing, can be well situated to support military veterans to leverage these leadership skills. Adler, Zamorski, and Britt (2011) have argued that research is needed to expand the focus from postdeployment mental health to a broader application of the psychology of transition to include home, work,

Leslie B. Hammer, Krista Brockwood, and Sarah N. Haverly, *The Key Role of Supervisors for Supporting Veterans in the Workplace* In: *Military Veteran Employment*. Edited by: Nathan D. Ainspan and Kristin N. Saboe, Oxford University Press.
© Oxford University Press 2021. DOI: 10.1093/oso/9780190642983.003.0011

and social factors that impact the transition process. Supervisors are a key part of successful transitions into the workplace, and recognizing and capitalizing on the unique skills that veterans bring to the workplace can only enhance the success of organizations as well as enhance the success of our veterans' transitions.

There are many examples of military personnel making successful transitions to civilian workplace leadership. In fact, a report by the employment recruitment and talent management company Korn/Ferry International revealed that 8.4 percent of Fortune 500 Company chief executive officers have a background of military experience (compared to only 3 percent of the male general population; Duffy, 2006), and approximately one third of all federal workers are veterans. We also see higher numbers of veterans more generally in the state public sector compared to private sector organizations. Veterans are also more likely to be found in police and fire departments, as well as other first-responder types of jobs. Likewise, in the private sector many companies have been successful with hiring and retaining veterans.

Recognizing the leadership skills of our military veterans is critical for today's human resources departments and top management to take full advantage of some of our best trained and most valuable leaders entering the workforce. Furthermore, policies and practices should be put in place to allow for our veterans to maximize their contributions to the workplace and, in turn, increase the workplace retention of some of our most skilled men and women who have served our country. If the organizational context is not supportive of veterans entering and/or returning to civilian jobs, with many of these veterans having remaining state and federal obligations on their multiyear contracts (as National Guardsmen and Reservists), they will likely experience high levels of stress and work–family conflict (Hammer, Cullen, Marchand, & Dezsofi, 2005). More research will be needed as we broaden perspective from one focused on postdeployment factors to the more general psychology of transition, to include home, work, and social factors that impact the transition process. Supporting these transitions includes facilitating our veteran's shift into leadership positions in civilian employment and also providing the necessary training and programs to employers to create a culture of support for veterans who are currently part of the civilian workforce. Supportive environments for veterans in the workforce can lead to a greater likelihood of success on the job.

## The Role of Supervisors and Leaders in the Workplace

Supervisors and leaders in organizations can have a significant impact on the success and retention of military veterans in the civilian workplace. Supervisors have unique responsibilities for workers in their workgroups in terms of directing performance outputs and in terms of impacting employee health and well-being. Supervisors are also the gatekeepers to top organizational leaders and to accessing—and utilizing—key organizational programs and policies. Thus, supervisors have significant power over workers.

Research shows (e.g., Pielstick, 2000) that leadership can occur in many different settings, both formal (as in the case of a designated leader position) and informal (as in the case of taking initiative and leading by example but without a named leadership role). In formal organizational settings, the leader, often a supervisor, has an opportunity to support and improve the workplace via their position of authority and through their designated role.

Generally, leadership occurs when one person influences another. Early leadership research focused on exceptional leaders and looked for common characteristics. However, the many characteristics of effective leaders throughout history yields an impractically long list of traits, including many that contradict one another. Over time, research shifted focus from the traits of leaders to their behaviors (Lord, Day, Zaccaro, Avolio, & Eagly, 2017) and has successfully identified some of those behaviors that relate to important outcomes like group productivity and satisfaction. Specifically, the behaviors of effective leaders include initiating structure and promoting focus on the task at hand. Successful leaders also emphasize the importance of quality relationships with their group members, which includes concern for the welfare of employees, welcoming dialogue, and encouraging subordinates to share other opinions. Additionally, leaders who focus on getting the job done (often called "task accomplishment") generally have more productive groups as compared to leaders displaying less of a focus on completing tasks. It appears that different situations may account for the success or failure of different leadership strategies. Put simply, what works in one work setting might not work in another. Situational leadership theories suggest that the followers, the task, and existing relationships within a group will all affect what type of leadership is needed. For example, a new employee may require more supervision during onboarding, while a more experienced worker may feel micromanaged with the same level of supervision.

Another important development in leadership research is the increasing understanding that effective leaders have relationships with each individual member of a team, rather than only with the group as a whole, in a phenomenon called leader–member exchange (LMX; Graen & Uhl-Bien, 1995). Leaders high in LMX have a unique relationship with each follower, which helps to bring out the best in individuals. Such a supervisor–employee relationship is characterized by levels of respect, trust, and obligation. Leaders who are high in transformational leadership (i.e., leaders who provide support, motivation, communication, and intellectual stimulation) are more likely to exhibit high-quality relationships with their employees (Wang, Law, Hackett, Wang, & Chen, 2005), which is a key to improved health and well-being of employees.

## The Role of Supervisors and Leadership in Supporting Veterans

We believe the first step in changing the workplace culture to be more prepared to leverage the resilience and skill sets of our transitioning service members, and in turn increase workplace retention, is in training the supervisors and managers in the civilian workplace. Supervisors and managers are often the linchpins in organizations for employees due to the support they provide employees (Hammer, Kossek, Zimmerman, & Daniels, 2007). We argue that changing the workplace culture through managerial/leadership training, such as the project we describe below, can lead to improving the health of workers and their families; more specifically, supervisor supportive training can improve the workplace outcomes such as performance and retention and the health and well-being of veterans, veteran families, and the workplace itself. Prior research has demonstrated that when we train managers and supervisors to be more supportive of workers (e.g., supportive of work–family integration), subordinates report improved physical health, job satisfaction, and decreased intentions to leave the workplace (Hammer, Kossek, Anger, Bodner, & Zimmerman, 2011; Hammer et al., 2015), as well as increased performance (Odle-Dusseau, Hammer, Crain, & Bodner, 2016).

While training civilian supervisors about the military culture and what to expect from former service members in terms of the skills they bring into the workplace is critical, we also argue that training such supervisors on how to create a supportive workplace culture for veterans is important to more generally support our service members in their transition. Programs that focus on modifying the organization of work (e.g., implementation of formal supervisory training on military culture and on veteran-supportive supervisor behaviors that includes allowing subordinates more control over work) in order to help integrate veterans into the civilian workplace improve their work experiences, increase their employment retention, and have the most promise for enduring positive effects. Thus, it has been argued that organizational interventions are needed that include training managers and supervisors on how to provide support and resources to these transitioning veterans who are reintegrating into the civilian workforce (Vinokur, Pierce, Lewandowski-Romps, Hobfoll, & Galea, 2011).

All workers face a number of stressors on the job that affect their performance at work, their relationships at home, and their physical and mental health (e.g., Hammer & Zimmerman, 2011). For those veterans continuing to address physical and/or psychological challenges related to their time serving, these stressors are potentially heightened and must be recognized by managers and leaders. Research demonstrates that organizational support for balancing work and family can be achieved by training managers to be more supportive at work for work–life integration since this can result in the improved health and well-being of workers and their spouses (Hammer et al., 2011; Hammer et al., 2007). Social support in the form of supervisor support for work and family has direct effects on stress reduction and subsequent workplace retention and can specifically be trained with a focus on supporting veterans. While supporting veterans in the workplace is important, it should also be recognized that veterans are valued members of an organization who bring unique leadership skills and attributes to improve organizational functioning.

## Leadership Skills Veterans Bring to the Civilian Workplace

Military service and leadership go hand in hand to such extent that the U.S. Army's official vision statement reads, "The Army is committed to build leaders of character who are technically and tactically proficient, adaptive, innovative, and agile" (U.S. Army, 2016, p. 7). Military service is often viewed as a prerequisite for the utmost leadership positions, notably among government officials and even presidents (58 percent of presidents and 19 percent of the 115th Congress were veterans; Petersen, 2015; Manning, 2017).

Hardison and Shanley (2016) described how military personnel are taught skills that have direct translation into civilian jobs and form a solid foundation for leadership skills. Key military courses and competencies/skills learned are reviewed in the RAND Toolkit (Hardison et al., 2015) for private sector employers that shows direct translation of military skills to civilian jobs. For example, skills learned in Army Basic Combat Training include teaching service members how to participate in dangerous and demanding exercises; this, in turn, helps increase their resilience to work stress. They are taught to work effectively in teams, which enhances their reliability and dependability and contributes to team cohesion in the civilian workplace. Service members are also taught to work collaboratively with a diverse group of people, leading to improved interpersonal skills that translate to any workplace. Furthermore, there are specific "soft" skills learned in military leadership training that can have beneficial impacts on civilian leadership positions. These "soft" skills are the following:

- Decision-making/decisiveness
- Critical thinking
- Leading, motivating, and inspiring others to accomplish organizational goals
- Managing/supervising the work of others
- Project planning
- Continuous learning
- Training others
- Teamwork and team building
- Interpersonal skills
- Oral communication
- Written communication
- Being dependable and reliable
- Conscientiousness and attention to detail
- Situational awareness
- Adaptability
- Handling work stress
- Persistence
- Behaving ethically
- Operating safely

The military places significant emphasis on the importance of leadership. As such, there are many avenues for service members to pursue leadership opportunities through their military assignments, formal education, and self-development opportunities. According to Wong, Bliese, and McGurk (2003), U.S. Army officers can expect to spend 3 years of a 20-year career in Army schools and institutional settings developing leader competencies and skills (a pattern similar in the other branches of the military). In fact, as the military relies exclusively on an internal promotion system in which service men and women ascend the rank structure of the military and leadership roles over the course of their careers in a stepwise fashion, leaders can only be developed from within the organization. Lateral transfers (i.e., hiring a senior-level executive from another company to join a new company in a leadership role) are not possible in the military. Therefore, service members at all levels are groomed within a context of leadership building.

Veterans come from a military culture that not only encourages leadership, but also (some would say) requires it. Service members are placed into leadership positions within weeks of joining the military. These leadership roles may entail leading other soldiers, mission components, or training sessions (see Harrell & Berglass, 2012). As such, understanding what makes leaders effective (including the experiences that build leadership and the skill set many veterans gain while serving in the military) helps to enable employers to understand and leverage the value and capabilities of those who have served in a culture of high-stakes and high-impact leadership. What follows is a discussion of many of the experiences and characteristics of leadership that military members gain through their time serving, while referencing research supporting why these characteristics are worth seeking in employees and leadership for a civilian organization (as originally outlined in U.S. Army Operations Manual; U.S. Army, 2001, 2015; U.S. Army Field Manual FM 6-22 Leader Development).

## Charismatic Leadership and Ambient Behaviors

A particularly important element of military leadership is its ability to extend beyond face-to-face interactions. Research shows that military members are high in charismatic leadership (Shamir, Zakay, Breinin, & Popper, 1998), which includes those leadership characteristics not directed at individual followers. Rather, these leadership traits are "ambient behaviors" that are directed at the unit as a whole, to the collective good of the team (e.g., focusing on collective identity of the group) or to no one in particular (e.g., leader self-sacrifice).

## Critical Thinking

Research demonstrated that military leaders are well trained across all levels of the organization (Wisecarver, Schneider, Foldes, Cullen, & Zbylut, 2011), from sergeant to general. Military training heavily emphasizes critical thinking at strategic, operational, and tactical levels (U.S. Army, 2001), a strategy that many organizations also espouse and would certainly benefit from. Military service members are trained to think critically and calmly in sometimes volatile, complicated, and often ambiguous situations. Military leaders also interface across cultures in their environment, as well as collaborating and coordinating with other military teams (who may also have slightly different cultures and objectives). In fact, system-level military leaders (the definition of which varies between branches, but generally refers to managing units rather than individuals) often have over 30 years' experience and are responsible for people, logistics, and resources at notably large levels with significant impact. For example, a 27-year-old officer may be assigned a leadership position in which he or she commands upward of 250 servicemen and servicewomen along with millions of dollars' worth of equipment.

## Communicating and Interfacing With External Environments and Stakeholders

Service members are also exceptionally well trained in interfacing with external environments, a skill coveted in civilian workplaces as well. Since the period of mandatory military service ended in 1973, there has been an increased effort to maintain connectedness between the military and American society at large. As a result, military leaders are trained to interact with the media, be sensitive to geopolitical situations, and attend to external stakeholders in order to provide visibility of the military's actions and accountability to taxpayers funding the military's operations. Similarly, just as most systems-level leaders in large organizations explore outsourcing to cut costs, the military utilizes private contractors to execute specific tasks and duties. Senior leaders, as in civilian organizations, must grapple with accountability, logistics, security, and control of contractors.

## Coordination and Skills Integration

By and large, military leaders are well trained in both face-to-face interactions and ambient, unit-level leadership. Their skills are useful not only for the management of individuals, but also for managing the morale and climate within a team setting and larger group, through both direct leadership and modeled behavior. The military emphasizes resource and task management for service members, and they are well skilled to implement calm critical thinking in a multitude of circumstances, often including stressful, high-stakes, or ambiguous circumstances. Similarly, service members are well trained to coordinate with others, both outside stakeholders and contractors and other teams working toward a shared goal. Despite such demanding and ambitious goals, service members accomplish their jobs while also meeting high expectations of public representation of the organization; in short, service members are expected to make the military look good.

## Transformational Leadership

Military veterans are in an advantaged position to translate their leadership training to the civilian workplace as organizations who hire and support veteran employees will benefit from their skill set. The dominant model of leadership skills in the military is based broadly in transformational leadership theories (Chemers, 2000). Notably, a study by a group of leadership scholars found that military leaders who were taught transformational leadership strategies (i.e., providing charismatic leadership, focusing on individual relationships, and keeping followers intellectually engaged) saw better outcomes compared to a group of leaders who were not taught these strategies (Dvir, Eden, Avolio, & Shamir, 2002). Results from this study also demonstrated that the subordinates of those leaders who received transformational leadership training were more developed leaders themselves. Additionally, these subordinates also performed better, indicating a causal link between transformational leadership and performance of subordinates.

Other research has demonstrated that transformational leadership in stable conditions predicts better unit performance in stressful conditions (Bass, Avolio, Jung, & Berson, 2003).

## Adaptability

Finally, military service members are skilled in adaptability. The military expects clear and seamless transitions between day-to-day duties, changing assignments and duty stations, training environments, and deployment. Adaptability is conceptualized by scholars as including the ability to handle crisis and stress, the ability to solve problems creatively, the ability to deal with unpredictability and learn new skills, as well as display cultural, physical, and interpersonal adaptability. Military service members are generally high in adaptability, and such skills are related to leadership effectiveness.

## Programs and Resources That Support Hiring and Retaining Veterans

While veteran employment has increased steadily over the past 5 years, some industries more readily recognize the skills and attributes veterans bring to the workforce and are more likely to hire them. For instance, the business and finance industries account for 17.4 percent of veteran employment, and the service industries account for 14.1 percent according to a recent Society for Human Resource Management (SHRM) report (Wilkie, 2016).

To assist with the transition to civilian employment following military service, there are a host of resources available that highlight the nontechnical skills obtained through formal military training that veterans bring to the workplace, including toolkits (e.g., the Hardison et al., 2015, toolkit mentioned above), as well as research documenting characteristics of veterans and ways that supervisor support can improve veteran outcomes at work (e.g., Hammer, Wan, Brockwood, Mohr, & Carlson, 2017). Similarly, there are various professional society– and government-sponsored tools such as the SHRM-sponsored resources for engaging and integrating transitioning veterans (located at https://www.shrm.org/foundation/ourwork/initiatives/engaging-and-integrating-military-veterans/pages/default.aspx). Additionally, programs such as Hire Our Heroes (https://www.

hireourheroes.org), Hire Heroes USA (https://www.hireheroesUSA.org), and Recruit Military (https://www.recruitmilitary.com) aid in the hiring and recruiting of veterans.

The Department of Veterans Affairs offers a free online toolkit (https://www.va.gov/vetsinworkplace/) for employers hiring veterans. Finally, many civilian-to-military occupational translator tools presently exist. One example of a translator for civilian-to-military terminology can be found at https://www.careeronestop.org/BusinessCenter/Toolkit/civilian-to-military-translator.aspx. Most of the resources mentioned here offer career counseling, résumé help, and similar resources for veterans in search of civilian work, in addition to the employer benefits such as leadership training on how to create a military-supportive culture. These resources also make information available about the importance of hiring veterans, as well as the benefits veteran workers can provide to a company. However, there are few resources available for organizations and supervisors that provide training on how to support and retain veterans once they are hired as employees.

Programs that help companies support and retain veteran employees, more generally, are emerging. One such program is PsychArmor (https://psycharmor.org), which is a nonprofit organization that offers cultural awareness training and advice on creating veteran hiring programs and a military-friendly culture within the workplace. PsychArmor bills itself as a resource to "bridge the civilian–military divide" by providing training and resources for nonmilitary individuals to support and understand members of the military and veterans. PsychArmor serves multiple target audiences, including healthcare providers, educators, and employers. PsychArmor's program is largely based on a collection of best practices and policies that are utilized by companies partnering with the nonprofit to ensure the trainings are built from valuable and relevant business experiences. To our knowledge, however, none of the above-mentioned programs have been scientifically evaluated using randomized controlled trials (the gold standard for program evaluation) to establish evidence-based best practices that are directly related to the actual behaviors supervisors should engage in to provide direct support needed to veterans in the civilian workplace. Despite this shortage of scientific evidence regarding the various programs' effectiveness, the various programs and tools available to both veterans and employees are useful as they provide needed guidance and insight. We next touch on a program that is based in science and has been evaluated via the gold standard for program evaluation. The first part of this chapter focused on the leadership skills and experiences of veterans; the remainder of this chapter focuses on (a) how a veteran working as a civilian might be supported by their civilian managers and leaders and (2) providing an example of how scientific methods are used to evaluate the effectiveness of workplace programs through a randomized controlled trial.

## Veteran Supportive Supervisor Training: The Study for Employment Retention of Veterans

Through a project called the Study for Employment Retention of Veterans (SERVe), we have identified a variety of best practices with regard to the evaluation and implementation of training and how to effectively establish a veteran-supportive organizational culture. This next section on SERVe highlights ongoing efforts to establish evidence-based training for supervisors with veteran employees, known as Veteran Supportive Supervisor Training (VSST). SERVe was funded by the Department of Defense to develop and evaluate (via a randomized controlled trial) a supervisor training program aimed at improving knowledge about the military culture and understanding how to provide supportive behaviors to our veterans in the workplace. The VSST draws on the prior work on Family Supportive Supervisor Behavior (FSSB) training principals outlined by Hammer, Kossek, Yragui, Bodner, and Hanson (2009). FSSBs are based on four types of supervisor support: instrumental, emotional, role modeling, and creative work–life management support. When supervisors are rated high on FSSBs by their employees, employees report improved engagement, job satisfaction, reduced turnover intentions, and also are rated as having higher job performance than those employees whose supervisors are rated low on FSSB (e.g., Kossek & Hammer, 2008).

The FSSBs are defined as follows:

- *Emotional*: Behaviors demonstrating a worker is being cared for and their feelings are being considered, for example, by increasing face-to-face contact with employees, asking how employees are doing, or communicating genuine concern about employees' work/life challenges.
- *Instrumental*: Behaviors helping workers manage schedules and working with employees to solve schedule conflicts, for example, helping an employee who will be absent find a replacement.

- *Role Modeling*: Behaviors that show how a supervisor is taking care of her or his own work/life challenges, for example, discussing taking time out to attend a child's school activities and talking about one's own family, leaving work at reasonable hours, or showing that managers value involvement in nonwork life.
- *Creative Work–Family Management/Win–Win Management*: Behaviors aimed at redesigning work to support the conflicting employee work–life demands in a manner that is win–win for both employees and employers, for example, promoting cross-training and the ability for shift trades to jointly enable employee scheduling flexibility needs and work coverage.

The FSSB training intervention developed by Hammer and colleagues (2011) is an example of a domain-specific behavioral health leadership approach. Domain-specific leadership is consistent with a situational model of leadership, as discussed previously in this chapter, in which leaders adjust their leadership approach depending on the needs of the subordinate and situation (Adler, Saboe, Anderson, Sipos, & Thomas, 2014). Other types of domain-specific health leadership behaviors studied in military contexts include the concept of behavioral health leadership (Adler et al., 2014). This domain-specific approach to leadership is used as the basis for the development of the VSST intervention described below.

While available resources exist to enable a civilian workplace to develop a military-supportive culture, to our knowledge no programs directly address the specific behaviors civilian supervisors should engage in. A veteran-supportive workplace training program that relies on evidence-based research and practices is overdue. To address this oversight, we conducted a large-scale randomized controlled study to develop, implement, and empirically test the VSST (i.e., SERVe).

For the SERVe project, we recruited 42 organizations in the northwestern United States to participate in the study and pilot the VSST; ultimately, 35 organizations were included in the final sample, seven being excluded because there were either no participating veterans or supervisors at the organization. The participating organizations represented a fairly even split of public and private companies, as well as a variety of sizes, from about 50 employees up to 17,000, with a median size of approximately 600. Once an organization agreed to participate in SERVe, we recruited veteran employees to complete surveys before and twice after the training. Ultimately, we expected the training to improve the veteran employees' health and work outcomes, so collecting data directly from them was essential to the evaluation. We also sought diversity in our sample of organizations to ensure our results were representative of a variety of employment settings.

We sent secure online surveys to veterans in these companies who had served during the conflicts with Iraq and Afghanistan. Surveys were sent before the training was provided to the veterans' supervisor, at 3 months, and at 9 months after the training. Surveys included questions about how they felt about work, what was going on with their family life, as well as their physical and mental health. We also asked about their military service, especially if and where they were deployed, to better understand our veterans' experiences. Veterans participating received a gift card for each survey they completed. In addition, we also sent surveys to spouses and partners of the veterans if they wanted to participate (they were also compensated for their time). Family members were surveyed because understanding the family context is extremely important (Hammer, Cullen, Neal, Sinclair, & Shafiro, 2005) due to the far-reaching impacts it has on employees across work contexts. The mutual influence of the work and family spheres on one another has long been acknowledged and demonstrated (e.g., Netemeyer, Boles, & McMurrian, 1996). Collecting information from veterans over time (longitudinally) and from other sources such as spouses and partners of the veterans allows for more robust and informative data to draw stronger evidence-based conclusions from.

To deliver the supervisor training, we sent personalized emails to each supervisor with a link to our secure website where the online training was housed. Training was computer based, self-paced, and included integrated quiz questions throughout to keep participants engaged and as a means to evaluate their learning. In addition, to the four dimensions of the FSSB that were modified for the VSST, we also included the dimension of performance support (Kossek, Hammer, Kelly, & Moen, 2014), which encompasses supportive supervisor behaviors that directly affect the work domain. These included measurement and direction, feedback and coaching, providing resources, and health protection. Definitions of each type of support and examples of behaviors, both general and those specifically for veteran employees, can be found in Table 10.1.

**Table 10.1** Overview of Supportive Supervisor Behaviors and Importance to Veterans

*Family Support*: Family support behaviors are designed to help employees meet their family and personal demands and enable them to have fulfilling lives both at work and outside of work.

|  | *Emotional Support & Effective Communication* | *Instrumental Support* | *Win–Win Management* | *Role Modeling* |
|---|---|---|---|---|
| *Explanation* | What you do to help employees and veterans feel listened to and to show that you know and understand their family and personal demands. | Making practical arrangements so employees and veterans can meet both ongoing and unexpected family and personal demands. | Designing work and policies so employees and veterans can meet *both* family and work demands, including preparing for short- or long-term leave. | Demonstrating by example that you care about family and personal priorities and arranging your work so you can meet family and personal priorities. |
| *Why is this important to veterans?* | Understanding military ethos and communication styles are important to maintain the unparalleled relationship between service members and supervisors. | Schedules, while created in advance, frequently change along with personal, family and medical needs. Military training in self-reliance and time management may make service members good candidates for alternative schedules. | Designing work and policies so employees feel support during periods of absence and transitions. Essential for respect, support, and ongoing connections for all employees. | A powerful way to demonstrate value to employee and veterans is to model healthy work–life behaviors yourself. Acknowledging work–life priorities and gaps in experience. |

**Table 10.1** *Continued*

*Performance Support*: Performance support behaviors are the things you do that help employees accomplish their work results and have a fulfilling work life.

| | *Measurement & Direction* | *Feedback & Coaching* | *Providing Resources* | *Health Protection* |
|---|---|---|---|---|
| *Explanation* | Things you do that let employees and veterans know *what* is expected of them, such as setting goals and measuring results. | Guiding communication that ensures employees and veterans know *how* to produce work results, and that they know when they have done well. | Providing equipment or materials that employees and veterans need to produce work results and removing obstacles to productivity. | What you do to protect employee health and well-being, including removing or reducing physical injury hazards and psychological stressors in the workplace. |
| *Why is this important to veterans?* | Coming from the clear and organized military model, the lack of structure in the civilian workplace can frustrate veterans in civilian organizations, causing them to disengage. These are things you do that let employees know what is expected of them, such as setting goals and measuring results. | The military relies heavily on training through on-the-job experiences by allowing service members to observe, engage, and receive feedback immediately. They do not always see the lack of prior experience or differing experiences as a barrier. | Supervisors can play a key role in connecting employees and veteran with social resources that enhance their professional network and work results. Sometimes this type of support involves removing red tape or barriers to productivity. | Employers are responsible for providing a safe work environment, protecting from exposure to known safety and health hazards. Service members may be exposed to highly stressful and dangerous conditions and must place great trust in their leaders. |

The overall structure of the VSST comprised three parts:

1. *Military Culture and Background*: Particularly for supervisors with no prior military experience, the first section provided contextual information about the military, including culture, the aforementioned positive qualities that veterans bring to the workforce, and potential issues, such as post-traumatic stress or traumatic brain injury that veterans may encounter.

2. *Supportive Behaviors*: The next section provided specific supportive behaviors for supervisors to practice with their employees (see Table 10.1). These were presented first generically for all employees and based on previous work by Hammer and colleagues (2011), then specific examples were provided why these were important to and how they might look for veterans. For example, expressing appreciation for a veteran's military service, particularly in the presence of other employees, can be both emotional support *and* role-modeling behaviors. For instrumental support, a specific type of behavior would be to ensure coverage for an employee who is in the National Guard or Reserves and is at training or is being deployed. Finally, an example of win–win management might be to develop new employee onboarding that takes into consideration some issues specific to veterans, such as how military experience might be applied toward retirement given their present employer's policies.

3. *Behavior Tracking*: The final section lasts beyond the actual traditional training and assists with transferring training, like a homework assignment. We asked supervisors to complete a behavior-tracking exercise, where supervisors took the supportive behaviors they learned and put them into action with their employees. For 2 weeks, supervisors logged into the secure SERVe website and tracked the number and type of supportive behaviors they engaged in with their employees—both veterans and nonveterans. As a first step, supervisors would set a goal for the number of supportive behaviors they hoped to log (e.g., the number of their employees, times two, as a guide) and the website tracked their progress toward that goal.

We also assessed how well the supervisors learned the training content with pre- and posttest questions about the training's content and asked questions regarding how well supervisors liked the training and how much they felt they learned. The latter information was paired with the responses to the behavior tracking on the website, such as the number of behaviors in specific areas, and allowed the research team to further assess training effectiveness.

Finally, in addition to the core training provided to supervisors, "above-and-beyond" activities were available to motivated supervisors. This included three additional small training modules on military leave, communication with veterans, and translating military job skills to the civilian milieu. Supervisors also had the opportunity to post questions or comments to an online forum that allowed them to interact with other participating supervisors. Based on our analysis of the pretest and posttest data, as well as these qualitative testimonials of the training, we concluded that the training was effective in changing supervisor behaviors.

The initial baseline survey data are from 493 veterans employed in 35 organizations. These organizations employed post-9/11 service members occupying the following three categories: (a) separated active duty service members ($n$ = 235), (b) separated National Guard/Reservists ($n$ = 171), and (c) actively drilling National Guard/Reservists ($n$ = 87). Most of the service members (86–90 percent) were deployed domestically or internationally at least once. The most frequent civilian occupations that service members reported working in were government (39.1 percent), education/health (14.1 percent), manufacturing (12.9 percent), professional/business occupations (12.1 percent), information (7.0 percent), trade/transport/utilities (5.5 percent), and construction (3.9 percent).

We found that the training was most beneficial for those veterans whose supervisor and coworker support was higher at baseline (Hammer, Wan, Brockwood, Bodner, & Mohr, 2019). Other analyses looking at the supervisors revealed that substantial learning occurred for the 928 supervisors completing the training ($d$ = 3.31), demonstrating that they significantly improved their pre- to posttest knowledge. In addition, the training positively impacted views of the military for supervisors with no prior military service. The posts from supervisors following the training were 92 percent positive, meaning supervisors reported a positive view of the training.

Our goal, which we encourage others developing evidence-based products serving the veteran context to also do, is to make the training available to workplaces to help change the culture and improve the support for our veteran military service members who have transitioned into the civilian workforce. If you are interested in following the results or obtaining the training, please check our study website (https://www.servestudy.org).

## Evaluating Workplace Programs for Veterans and Beyond—Practical Advice

While we used a rigorous randomized controlled trial design for SERVe, this is likely not practical in most workplace settings. It is costly, time consuming, and sometimes logistically impossible. However, below we present a list of "best practices" and things to consider to evaluate a workplace program, particularly for veterans.

1. *Collect data about what you expect to change.* Think about the outcomes that you realistically think could change, like job satisfaction or supervisor support (general or specific to veterans/military). See Chapter 2 in this book for issues and suggestions about measuring the impact and collecting data on the impact of veteran employment programs.
2. *Collect data before and after your intervention.* Being able to measure change over time is extremely important.
3. *If possible, have a control group, preferably randomly assigned.* This may not always be possible given your workplace structure. Also be aware that the treatment group could be seen as having preferential treatment in some way.
4. *Think about your target group.* If you focus exclusively on veterans, they could feel stigmatized in some way, or other employees could feel resentful. Crafting the message about the program requires careful consideration.
5. *Collect data from multiple sources.* In SERVe, we were able to collect and link data from some, but not all, participating veterans and their supervisors. Being able to get multiple perspectives will greatly aid in your understanding of the work context and your results.

## Summary and Conclusions

In summary, this chapter provides a brief overview of military leadership skills that are transferable to the civilian workplace, as well as identification of training programs that prepare the civilian supervisor and manager for better supporting military veterans in civilian companies. Workplace retention of our service members is of utmost importance, and the VSST, as a science-based training for supervisors and as an example, offers a template for training civilian supervisors about military culture and how to better support our returning military veterans in the workplace. We all can make a difference in improving workplace retention, satisfaction, and health—showing support and understanding is one significant way to do so.

# Acknowledgments

Portions of this chapter were supported by the National Institute for Occupational Safety and Health (NIOSH) training grant T03OH008435 awarded to Portland State University and by the Office of the Assistant Secretary of Defense for Health Affairs, through the U.S. Army Medical Research and Development Command Broad Agency Announcement Award No. W81XWH-13-2-0020. The U.S. Army Medical Research Acquisition Activity, 820 Chandler Street, Fort Detrick, Maryland, 21702-5014 is the awarding and administering acquisition office. Opinions, interpretations, conclusions, and recommendations are those of the author and are not necessarily endorsed by the Department of Defense or by NIOSH. Leslie Hammer is principal investigator on both awards.

# References

Adler, A. B., Saboe, K. N., Anderson, J., Sipos, M. L., & Thomas, J. L. (2014). Behavioral health leadership: New directions in occupational mental health. *Current Psychiatry Reports, 16*(10), 1–7.

Adler, A. B., Zamorski, M., & Britt, T. W. (2011). The psychology of transition: Adapting to home after deployment. In A. B. Adler, P. D. Bliese, & C. A. Castro (Eds.), *Deployment psychology* (pp. 153–174). Washington, DC: American Psychological Association.

Bass, B. M., Avolio, B. J., Jung, D. I., & Berson, Y. (2003). Predicting unit performance by assessing transformational and transactional leadership. *Journal of Applied Psychology, 88*(2), 207.

Chemers, M. M. (2000). Leadership research and theory: A functional integration. *Group Dynamics: Theory, Research, and Practice, 4*(1), 27.

Duffy, T. (2006). *Military experience & CEOs: Is there a link?* Korn/Ferry International. https://www.kornferry.com/insights/articles/190-military-experience-and-ceos-is-there-a-link

Dvir, T., Eden, D., Avolio, B. J., & Shamir, B. (2002). Impact of transformational leadership on follower development and performance: A field experiment. *Academy of Management Journal, 45*(4), 735–744.

Graen, G. B., & Uhl-Bien, M. (1995). Relationship-based approach to leadership: Development of leader-member exchange (LMX) theory of leadership over 25 years: Applying a multi-level multi-domain perspective. *Leadership Quarterly, 6,* 219–247. doi:10.1016/1048-9843(95)90036-5

Hammer, L. B., Cullen, J. C., Marchand, G. C., & Dezsofi, J. A. (2005). Reducing the negative impact of work-family conflict on military personnel: Individual coping strategies and multilevel interventions. In C. A. Castro, A. B. Adler, & T. W. Britt (Eds.), *Military life: The psychology of serving in peace and combat: The military family* (Vol. 3, pp. 220–242). Westport, CT: Praeger Security International.

Hammer, L. B., Cullen, J. C., Neal, M. B., Sinclair, R. R., & Shafiro, M. (2005). The longitudinal effects of work-family conflict and positive spillover on depressive symptoms among dual-earner couples. *Journal of Occupational Health Psychology, 10*, 138–154.

Hammer, L. B., Kossek, E. E., Anger, W. K., Bodner, T., & Zimmerman, K. (2011). Clarifying work-family intervention processes: The roles of work-family conflict and family supportive supervisor behaviors. *Journal of Applied Psychology, 96*(1), 134–150.

Hammer, L. B., Kossek, E. E., Yragui, N., Bodner, T., & Hanson, G. (2009). Development and validation of a multidimensional measure of family supportive supervisor behaviors (FSSB). *Journal of Management, 35*(4), 837–856.

Hammer, L. B., Kossek, E. E., Zimmerman, K., & Daniels, R. (2007). Clarifying the construct of family-supportive supervisory behaviors (FSSB): A multilevel perspective. In P. L. Perrewe & D. C. Ganster (Eds.), *Exploring the work and non-work interface* (pp. 165–204). Bingley, UK: Emerald Group.

Hammer, L. B., Truxillo, D. M., Bodner, T., Rineer, J., Pytlovany, A. C., & Richman, A. (2015). Effects of a workplace intervention targeting psychosocial risk factors on safety and health outcomes. *BioMed Research International, 2015*, 836967.

Hammer, L. B., Wan, W. H., Brockwood, K. J., Bodner, T., & Mohr, C. D. (2019). Supervisor support training effects on veteran health and work outcomes in the civilian workplace. *Journal of Applied Psychology, 104*, 52–69.

Hammer, L. B., Wan, W. H., Brockwood, K. J., Mohr, C. D., & Carlson, K. F. (2017). Military, work, and health characteristics of separated and active service members from the Study for Employment Retention of Veterans (SERVe). *Military Psychology, 29*(6), 491.

Hammer, L. B., & Zimmerman, K. L. (2011). Quality of work life. In S. Zedeck (Ed.), *APA handbook of industrial and organizational psychology, volume 3: Maintaining, expanding, and contracting the organization* (pp. 399–431). Washington, DC: American Psychological Association.

Hardison, C. M., & Shanley, M. G. (2016). *Essential skills veterans gain during professional military training: A resource for veterans and transitioning service members.* Santa Monica, CA: RAND. https://www.rand.org/pubs/tools/TL160z3-1.html

Hardison, C. M., Shanley, M. G., Saavedra, A. R., Crowley, J. C., Wong, J. P., & Steinberg, P. S. (2015). *Translating veterans' training into civilian job skills.* Santa Monica, CA: RAND. https://www.rand.org/pubs/infographics/IG124.html

Harrell, M. C., & Berglass, N. (2012). *Employing America's veterans: Perspectives from businesses.* Washington, DC: Center for a New American Security. https://www.cnas.org/publications/reports/employing-americas-veterans-perspectives-from-businesses

Kossek, E. E., & Hammer, L. B. (2008). Supervisor work/life training gets results. *Harvard Business Review, 2008*, 36.

Kossek, E. E., Hammer, L. B., Kelly, E. L., & Moen, P. (2014). Designing work, family, and health organizational change initiatives. *Organizational Dynamics, 43*(1), 53–63.

Lord, R. G., Day, D. V., Zaccaro, S. J., Avolio, B. J., & Eagly, A. H. (2017). Leadership in applied psychology: Three waves of theory and research. *Journal of Applied Psychology, 102*(3), 434–451.

Manning, J. E. (2017). *Membership of the 115th Congress: A profile* (CRS Report R44762). Washington, DC: Congressional Research Service.

Netemeyer, R. G., Boles, J. S., & McMurrian, R. (1996). Development and validation of work–family conflict and family–work conflict scales. *Journal of Applied Psychology, 81*(4), 400.

Odle-Dusseau, H. N., Hammer, L. B., Crain, T. L., & Bodner, T. (2016). The influence of family-supportive supervisors on job performance: An organizational work-family initiative. *Journal of Occupational Health Psychology, 21*, 296–308. doi:10.1037/a0039961

Petersen, H. (2015, February 16). *List of presidents who were veterans*. https://www.va.gov/HEALTH/NewsFeatures/2015/February/List-Of-Presidents-Who-Were-Veterans.asp

Pielstick, C. D. (2000). Formal vs. informal leading: A comparative analysis. *Journal of Leadership Studies, 7*(3), 99–114.

PsychArmor. Home page. http://www.PsychArmor.org

RecruitMilitary. Home page. http://www.recruitmilitary.com

Shamir, B., Zakay, E., Breinin, E., & Popper, M. (1998). Correlates of charismatic leader behavior in military units: Subordinates' attitudes, unit characteristics, and superiors' appraisals of leader performance. *Academy of Management Journal, 41*(4), 387–409.

U.S. Army. (2001). *Field Manual 3, operations*. Washington, DC: U.S. Government Printing Office.

U.S. Army. (2015). *Field Manual 6-22 leader development*. U.S. Army report. Washington, D.C. https://armypubs.army.mil/epubs/DR_pubs/DR_a/pdf/web/fm6_22.pdf

U.S. Army. (2016). War Department, Department of Defense. *The United States Army posture statement*. [Washington, D.C.]. https://www.army.mil/e2/downloads/rv7/aps/aps_2016.pdf

Vinokur, A. D., Pierce, P. F., Lewandowski-Romps, L., Hobfoll, S. E., & Galea, S. (2011). Effects of war exposure on air force personnel's mental health, job burnout and other organizational related outcomes. *Journal of Occupational Health Psychology, 16*(1), 3.

Wang, H., Law, K. S., Hackett, R. D., Wang, D., & Chen, Z. X. (2005). Leader-member exchange as a mediator of the relationship between transformational leadership and followers' performance and organizational citizenship behavior. *Academy of Management Journal, 48*(3), 420–432.

Wilkie, D. (2016, March 16). *HR manager among best jobs for military veterans*. https://www.shrm.org/resourcesandtools/hr-topics/employee-relations/pages/veterans-in-hr.aspx

Wisecarver, M., Schneider, R., Foldes, H., Cullen, M., & Zbylut, M. R. (2011). *Knowledge, skills, and abilities for military leader influence*. Arlington, VA: Personnel Decisions Research Institute.

Wong, L., Bliese, P., & McGurk, D. (2003). Military leadership: A context specific review. *Leadership Quarterly, 14*(6), 657–692.

# 11

# The Employment Situation of Military Spouses

## How Companies Can Source, Assess, Hire, and Retain Service Members' and Veterans' Spouses

*Deborah A. Bradbard*

There are just over one million military spouses of service members currently serving, more than 15 million veterans' spouses, and an estimated 5.8 million surviving spouses of veterans in the United States (U.S. Department of Defense, Defense Manpower Data Center, 2015; Westat, 2010). Because of their numbers, high motivation to work, education, qualifications, and dispersal throughout the United States and abroad, there is a compelling business case to hire military spouses (Bradbard, Maury, & Armstrong, 2016a). But despite these reasons, military spouses are largely overlooked as human capital resources. Military spouses often encounter barriers to maintaining their employment while prioritizing their service members' career. Many spouses experience periods of either unemployment or underemployment as a result of employment barriers related to a need to prioritize their service member spouse (Meadows, Griffin, Karney, & Pollak, 2016). A 2008 study, for example, found that nearly two thirds of military spouses reported that the military had a negative impact on their employment (U.S. Department of Defense, 2015). Approximately 66 percent of military spouses reported they were either working or looking for work (U.S. Department of Defense, 2017), and more than 55 percent of military spouses reported they had difficulty finding their job (Maury & Stone, 2014).

The challenges of maximizing military spouse talent are real. Hiring managers may discount military spouse job applications, résumés, and work histories because they may not conform to industry norms or expectations. Résumés may include gaps in work history, disparate or unrelated positions of short duration, or volunteer instead of paid work. Instead of attributing

Deborah A. Bradbard, *The Employment Situation of Military Spouses* In: *Military Veteran Employment.* Edited by: Nathan D. Ainspan and Kristin N. Saboe, Oxford University Press. © Oxford University Press 2021. DOI: 10.1093/oso/9780190642983.003.0012 discrepancies to the military lifestyle (e.g., frequent relocations) or focusing on the work-related attributes that develop as a result of those challenges, hiring managers may instead conclude that military spouse applicants, who rarely self-identify as military spouses, are unqualified, poor fits, or otherwise deficient for the job at hand. Even when a good fit is apparent, hiring managers may have concerns about retention, given the possibility of a military relocation or other doubts due to the military's lifestyle demands on the family (e.g., deployments that often create additional child care and caregiving needs for the spouse at home). Still, the majority of military spouses want to work—and some need to work—despite the employment challenges or financial hardship they face. Their educational attainment, pursuit of employment, volunteerism, and engagement in related professional development activities further support the will and desire that military spouses can bring to the workforce. Additionally, there is no evidence to suggest that military affiliation negatively impacts success or ability to perform in the workplace. Yet, the unemployment rate among military spouses has remained high compared to the rate among their civilian peers (Bradbard, Maury, & Armstrong, 2016a).

Unemployment is defined by the U.S. Bureau of Labor Statistics as people who do not have a job, have actively looked for work in the past 4 weeks, and are currently available for work (U.S. Bureau of Labor Statistics, 2017). In 2012, the unemployment rate for active duty military spouses between 18 and 24 years of age was 30 percent, compared to just 11 percent for their civilian population equivalent (Maury & Stone, 2014). In that same time frame, the unemployment rate for active duty military spouses between 25 and 44 years of age was 15 percent, whereas the equivalent civilian unemployment rate was 6 percent (Maury & Stone, 2014). This trend was consistent from 2000 to 2012, resulting in military spouses with unemployment rates being as much as three times higher than their civilian peers (Bradbard, Maury, & Armstrong, 2016a). More recent data continue to show a high unemployment rate among military spouses. For example, the Department of Defense's 2017 survey of active duty military spouses indicated that active duty military spouses had an unemployment rate of 24 percent, suggesting the situation for military spouses has room for improvement.

These negative variations in unemployment status for military spouses are largely unknown to most employers. According to Chalabi (2015), only a small portion (7.7 percent) of the general population has served in the military during their lifetime. Thus, employers interested in hiring military spouses may not intuitively understand the barriers and challenges a military spouse may face when applying for a job or maintaining a career. But these challenges are often reflected on an applicants' résumé, and when résumés are used as a primary assessment and hiring tool they can eliminate military spouse candidates from employment consideration before they have a chance to compete. In short, employers may not accurately assess a military spouse's qualifications if a résumé is used as the primary assessment tool (U.S. Department of Veterans Affairs, 2015). Further, employers interested in hiring military spouses may not have developed or even considered the business case reasons that support the hiring of them. For strategic reasons, we believe having a business case for hiring military spouses (in addition to a solid understanding of military culture) provides the essential background and rationale needed to ensure that military spouse hiring initiatives succeed by emphasizing the precise skills that make a military spouse an asset to a given employer (Bradbard et al., 2016b).

The purpose of this chapter is to provide a high-level overview of some of the issues that impact the employment situation of military spouses. This overview is critical because some of the challenges faced by military spouses may, without further examination, seem at odds with the needs of those in charge of hiring and retaining employees. That said, we believe some of the very things that may initially seem like liabilities are in actuality assets for the employer. As such, the information in this chapter is intended to help avoid stigma among hiring managers, human resource professionals, and hiring managers who may have misconceptions about military spouses (e.g., they move frequently and may not be long-term employees).

Military spouse résumés often differ in important ways from those of their civilian peers (and from veterans), and those in charge of hiring decisions may need to use alternative strategies to appropriately assess military spouse candidates for open positions. This chapter also highlights some of the unique characteristics and demographics that impact military spouses and how these factors influence them when they apply for employment. Based on those characteristics, we present a generic business case that can be adapted and customized by companies to clarify how hiring military spouses with targeted skills can benefit their company specifically. In addition, we address some of the collaborative efforts that focus on hiring military spouse job candidates and how employers can access these existing networks, relationships, and resources to improve, build, or expand existing hiring initiatives focused on military spouses. This is important because there is no need to reinvent what already exists when these existing efforts can be leveraged. We conclude by providing specific recommendations for employers interested in hiring military spouses.

## The Employment Situation of Military Spouses

It is hard to make a direct comparison between military spouse unemployment and civilians as the unemployment rates vary by age, gender, and education as well as other demographic factors. As noted previously, the rates for military spouses are generally higher than the unemployment rate for civilian peers. Due to the labor market (e.g., remote locations or overseas), disparities in licensure requirements, the need to take over parenting responsibilities while a spouse is deployed, or unpredictable military schedules, military spouses frequently find themselves working in positions for which they are overqualified by virtue of their educational background or work experience. A 2014 survey found that 33 percent of respondents reported they were overqualified for their current or most recent position based on their educational background (Maury & Stone, 2014). Additional research has found that military spouses have higher rates of underemployment than unemployment, meaning they possess more education or experience needed for the job they hold (Meadows et al., 2016). This may suggest that military spouses sacrifice experience and education to avoid unemployment.

As a group, military spouses are well educated compared to most civilians and often are qualified for a range of careers. Military families, like their civilian counterparts, often require two incomes to meet family expenses. However, military spouses are 9 percent less likely to work than comparable civilians, 10 percent less likely to work full time, and 14 percent less likely to work 33 weeks or more out of the year (Meadows et al., 2016). Erratic and unpredictable spouse schedules (i.e., the service member's demanding military work and training schedule), lack of and cost of child care near military installations, and the responsibilities of single parenting while the spouse is away are other common challenges for military families (Meadows et al., 2016).

Regardless of the reason, when military spouses desire but are unable to obtain fulfilling or consistent employment, quality of life for the spouse individually or for the family as a whole may be compromised (U.S. Department of Defense, 2015). For example, the inability to earn a second income also may put military families at a financial disadvantage when compared to their civilian peers (U.S. Department of Labor, Bureau of Labor Statistics, 2016b). Family finances may impact the readiness of the military force while a service member is on active duty status. Limited employment opportunities for military spouses can also have an effect on national military readiness to the extent that this impacts the desire or willingness of service members to pursue a longer military career. Specifically, military families may weigh the cost–benefit ratio of continued service, comparing financial and employment opportunities to those in the civilian world (U.S. Department of Defense, Defense Manpower Data Center, 2015).

Military spouse employment has not only obvious benefits to the individual but also benefits the entire family, including the service member or transitioning veteran (U.S. Department of Veterans Affairs, National Center for Veterans Analysis and Statistics, 2007). Employing military spouses also can directly and indirectly augment existing corporate diversity and veterans hiring efforts and initiatives. Roughly 200,000 service members are transitioning from the military each year (U.S. Department of Veterans Affairs, 2007), thus nearly one million service members have transitioned over the 5 years. Service members with a working spouse have a financial advantage when they are transitioning from the military if their military spouse faces a substantial period of unemployment. For example, an employed spouse can enable a service member or veteran to attend school, complete industry-recognized certifications, and exercise choices when examining job offers to find the right job fit. Finally, there are individual, emotional, and financial benefits to a spouse having meaningful employment, which include the ability to contribute to family finances, pay off student loan debt, establish credit, accrue savings, establish financial independence, and earn long-term benefits such as retirement. In addition, employment may have intrinsic psychological and social benefits, including increased self-efficacy, sense of purpose, and increased social connection.

## Military Spouse Demographics Impacting Employment

Military spouses tend to share several demographic characteristics that may impact their employment.

## Gender

Active duty military spouses are predominantly female (92 percent), though it is important to also note that 8 percent of military spouses are males who may experience some of the same challenges as their female counterparts (U.S. Department of Defense, 2015). However, there is a gender disparity in employment rates (i.e., males tend to be employed at higher rates than females regardless of whether they are a military spouse or a civilian) (Maury & Stone, 2014). That is, females experience decreased rates of employment in the civilian population; the likelihood of unemployment is compounded further for female military spouses as compared to males. However, given that there are relatively fewer male military spouses overall, little is known about their employment rates as few studies have examined them directly.

## Parenting, Child Care, and Caregiving

Active duty military spouses are more likely to have children (18 and under) at home compared to their civilian counterparts (70 vs. 53 percent) (U.S. Census Bureau, 2015). Research on military families has shown that having young children in the family (especially when a service member is deployed) necessitates the need for child care and is associated with decreased earnings and a higher likelihood of unemployment for the service member's spouse (Hosek & Wadsworth, 2013). The compounded demands of having young children at home, often while being the single caregiver, may influence their desire or ability to seek employment and potentially may decrease satisfaction with employment or the desire to seek employment, particularly if an active duty spouse is deployed or frequently absent. Military spouse job seekers may be more likely to apply for or accept employment when they have opportunities to maintain work–life balance through flexible work schedules, opportunities for remote work, or access to child care resources.

## Military Caregiving

Currently, there are 5.5 million military caregivers in the United States, and nearly 20 percent are caring for someone who served in the post-9/11 military. Here, we use the term *military caregiver* to refer to individuals such as family members (often a military spouse), friends, or others who devote their time to assist wounded, injured, or disabled veterans in their recovery, rehabilitation, or reintegration following an injury, illness, or wound. Caregiving often involves a significant time commitment and may impact the ability to work. Yet, the number of programs and services that help caregivers compensate for income losses are limited (two federal resources include the Department of Defense's Special Compensation Assistance for Activities of Daily Living and the Veterans Administration's Program of Comprehensive Assistance for Family Caregivers). Post-9/11 caregivers also are less likely to have health insurance compared to caregivers of pre-9/11 care recipients; employment may serve as a means to earn income as well as essential healthcare benefits for this population (Ramchand et al., 2014).

## Mobility

On average, active duty families stay 3 to 4 years at each location the military service member is assigned (U.S. Government Accountability Office [GAO], 2015). Although direct comparisons are difficult due to differences in age, occupation, and gender, the average time that female civilian workers stay in the same job is roughly 4 years (U.S. Department of Labor, Bureau of Labor Statistics, 2016a). There is an inaccurate perception that military spouses will not remain in their jobs as long as their civilian colleagues, but these time frames suggest that the spouses' job durations could equal or exceed those of the average civilian's tenure in a job. Anecdotally, spouses may be more likely to remain in one position for the duration of the time in their location precisely because they anticipate a move and are motivated to minimize gaps in their résumés or to prevent unnecessary job changes. The employment challenges military spouses face may, in fact, engender loyalty to the employer and may encourage them to remain with a company especially if a job transfer or remote employment is allowed.

## Outlining a Business Case for Hiring Military Spouses

The business case for hiring veterans was defined by Haynie (2012) as 10 empirically supported propositions. While there may be some similarities between veterans and military spouses, they are not directly comparable, though military hiring initiatives may target both groups simultaneously. Arguably, military spouses have unique employment and educational challenges as a result of the military lifestyle, and while there is some overlap with veterans, many of their strengths and challenges are independent and unique. A specific business case for hiring military spouses separate from veterans is difficult partially because there is limited research that identifies their heterogeneous needs, challenges, and capabilities that result from the military lifestyle itself. The business case for hiring a military spouse, originally outlined in 2016 (Bradbard, Maury, & Armstrong, 2016a), is presented below. This business case proposes that in general, most military spouses are the following:

- *Resilient*: Military spouses face challenges, including family separations, frequent relocation, separation from friends and family, and difficulty finding employment or finishing their education. Yet, despite juggling multiple responsibilities, they report better coping skills than the average civilian (U.S. Department of Defense, Defense Manpower Data Center, 2012).
- *Adaptable*: Military families live with consistent uncertainty. Spousal deployments often occur without warning; families may be asked to move unexpectedly; benefits and allowances frequently change unexpectedly. Despite these challenges, 68 percent of active duty spouses say they are satisfied with the military way of life (Blue Star Families, 2015).
- *Diverse*: The active duty military spouse community has a larger proportion of ethnic and racial minorities as compared to the broader civilian population (U.S. Department of Defense, 2015). In addition, because military families often spend at least one of their military tours overseas, many have had exposure to different cultures and foreign languages.
- *Educated*: Of active duty military spouses, 84 percent have some college education, 25 percent have a bachelor's degree, and 10 percent have an advanced degree (U.S. Department of Defense, Defense Manpower Data Center, 2015).
- *Resourceful Problem-Solvers*: Military spouses often learn to use the resources they have available to them, and they create unique and innovative solutions to problems despite obstacles or challenges.
- *Team Oriented*: Military support infrastructure largely depends on at-home spouses relying on one another through social activities, helping

with child care, and providing overall social support to each other. They have learned to provide support to each other and draw on the support of others.

- *Entrepreneurial*: Of military spouse respondents, 28 percent have either been self-employed or operated their own business, and 34 percent indicated they had an interest in online or work-from-home opportunities (Maury & Stone, 2014).
- *Multitaskers*: In a study of over 6,200 military spouses, 75 percent reported feeling confident in their ability to handle problems despite the fact that they regularly were juggling multiple responsibilities (Blue Star Families, 2015).
- *Civically Engaged*: In their 2014 survey of military families, the Blue Star Families organization found that 68 percent of their respondents reported that they had either formally or informally volunteered in the past year—significantly higher than the 21.8 percent of the general public who formally volunteered with an organization in 2015, as reported by the Department of Labor (U.S. Department of Labor, Bureau of Labor Statistics, 2015).
- *Socially Aware*: Military spouses often interact with a variety of people of different cultures, backgrounds, ages, and ethnicities. The military exposes spouses to social situations, including interaction with VIPs and press and cross-cultural experiences.
- *Operations Security and Operational Safety*: As a result of exposure via their service member's career, military spouses often learn policies, norms, and procedures around operations security and operational safety. To the extent that spouses have been exposed to these norms and have applied them, their experience may be directly applicable to the work environment, increasing an employer's confidence and trust in the employee or potential hire.

## Collaborative Efforts to Impact Spouse Employment

Understanding the challenges military spouses face is important, but an employer cannot base its hiring goals on this understanding alone. A business case encourages a business to consider which military spouse characteristics the company can seek among its prospective job candidates to meet its unique goals and objectives (perhaps with certain positions in mind).

A business case also helps key stakeholders involved with hiring understand and align their employment goals.

As companies develop their business case, it is also important for leadership and those involved with hiring decisions to share their successes and learn from peers and colleagues who are involved with efforts aimed at hiring veterans and military spouses. Several successful road maps and collaborative efforts have recently organized for this purpose. One such roadmap is *Strengthening Our Military Families: Meeting America's Commitment* (Presidential Directive Number Nine, 2011). This document (a) highlighted the importance of a proactive and coordinated federal government approach to help develop career and educational opportunities for veterans and military spouses; (b) provided the impetus for the Joining Forces initiative initiated by former First Lady Michelle Obama; (c) encouraged creative and innovative cross-sector partnerships, improved policy and legislation; and (d) broadened the discussion, initially focused around veteran employment (as well as education and wellness) to include military spouses.

Since 2011, organizations have increasingly worked collaboratively across the government, nonprofit, and corporate sectors and have made noteworthy strides in improving the employment situation of military spouses. Organizations have worked to improve the unemployment rate; introduced legislation that has in many cases worked to improve state licensing procedures (e.g., expedited licensing and reciprocity across state lines), which can impact military spouses who earn a credential in one state but then must go through the credentialing process when they move to a different state; and have enabled access to expanded educational and credentialing opportunities specific to military spouses. While there is an increased awareness of the employment issues that military spouses face, the unemployment rate of military spouses remains consistently high compared to their civilian peers despite an education gap in favor of the military spouses. Likewise, many companies are unaware of the challenges military spouses face related to employment, may not know how to reach out to this population, or do not understand the business case or strategic advantage that hiring both military spouses and veterans might bring (U.S. Department of Veterans Affairs, 2015).

As noted previously, hiring strategies focused on military spouses have mimicked many of the strategies focused on hiring transitioning service members and veterans, and many of the efforts have adopted similar strategies and resources. For example, the aforementioned Joining Forces initiative enlisted the collective support of public, private, and nonprofit partners on behalf of the military. This effort led to a proactive, coordinated, and sustained approach to hiring service members and veterans, and an unprecedented (but secondary) effort to hire military spouses by galvanizing around a growing and shared awareness that the transition from military service presented certain challenges. Chief among these challenges is finding employment. Such efforts have proved successful with regard to veterans. For example, at the height of the recession in 2011, unemployment rates for veterans peaked. An improved economy combined with targeted collaborative efforts over time has led to improved employment prospects for veterans overall and for many veteran subgroups (e.g., rural veterans, female veterans). Unemployment rates for veterans overall are now lower than comparable civilian rates.

A number of collaborative efforts focusing on the employment of military spouses have evolved over time to address the issues with regard to their employment. Within the military itself, there is a growing recognition that the demographics of the military family are changing over time. For example, increasingly service members are married the longer they remain in service (Hosek & Wadsworth, 2013). In the general population, as well as within the military, it is also more common for families to have a spouse who either prefers to work outside the home or works for economic and financial reason (e.g., because two incomes are needed to meet household expenses). The previous models that assumed that military spouses would be "at-home" spouses no longer applies to many modern military families.

As such, addressing spouse employment issues has increasingly become a priority for the Department of Defense as it is seen as being tied to military readiness. For these reasons, the Department of Defense has led a number of spouse employment initiatives and has pursued ongoing partnerships with the corporate and nonprofit sectors to supplement those efforts. Generally, these efforts have focused on three primary areas: (a) cross-sector partnerships; (b) policy, legislation, and research; and (c) targeted human resource efforts by individual employers.

In addition to developing a strong cultural understanding of the military population and developing a business case, it is recommended that companies connect to existing efforts focused on military spouse hiring to develop best practices; identify strategies to source, recruit, and retain candidates; and identify methods to remove barriers to employing military spouses. These partnerships also can connect employers to larger efforts to support military spouse employment, including networking, mentoring, and training programs that support military spouses on the path to employment. We outline some successful partnerships below.

## Cross-Sector Partnerships

Multiple cross-sector partnerships have developed since 2010. They have focused on not only hiring military spouses but also bringing employers together with other stakeholders in the government and nonprofit sectors as well as with military spouses themselves in order to better understand the issues related to spouse employment and to find solutions to address them. Several of these initiatives are listed here next.

## The Military Spouse Employment Partnership

The Military Spouse Employment Partnership (MSEP) is overseen by the Department of Defense. The department has enlisted the support of companies that have committed to hiring military spouse employers. MSEP is part of the Department of Defense's broader Spouse Education and Career Opportunities initiative, which seeks to strengthen the education and career opportunities for military spouses by providing (a) career exploration opportunities to help them understand their skills, interests, and goals; (b) education and training to help them identify academic, licensing, or credentialing requirements; (c) employment readiness assistance to optimize self-marketing skills; and (d) employment connections that help them find and maintain a rewarding career (MSEP, 2017).

## The Chamber of Commerce Foundation Hiring Our Heroes Initiative

The Chamber of Commerce Foundation Hiring Our Heroes Initiative has partnered with hundreds of Fortune 500 companies interested in hiring military spouses. They sponsored hiring fairs across the country, many of which focus on employers interested in military spouse hiring. Hiring fairs feature military spouse–specific workshops, interview assistance, help with developing a succinct "elevator pitch," and access to hundreds of employers that have made a commitment to hiring spouses. In addition, they have developed an online résumé translation tool, *Career Spark*, which enables military spouses to translate relevant volunteer experience into marketable bullet points for a career-ready résumé (U.S. Chamber of Commerce Foundation Hiring Our Heroes, 2020).

## eMentor

eMentor is an online mentoring program for military personnel, veterans, and military spouses. eMentor connects mentors and protégés to help them advance in their professional lives. The military spouse eMentor community includes mentors and protégés who are spouses or widow or widowers of military members and veterans. Representatives of military spouse–friendly firms serve as corporate mentors to assist protégés seeking employment or with other career issues. The eMentor online community connects military spouses with more experienced spouses and corporate and career mentors for guidance and support with challenges of all kinds and for assistance with finding long-term meaningful employment and upward mobility (eMentor, 2020).

## Society for Human Resource Management

Many human resource professionals may be affiliated with the Society for Human Resource Management (SHRM) but are unaware of their resources specifically related to military spouse and veteran hiring efforts. These resources inlcude: (1) information on effective workplace practices to support hiring managers and leaders who wish to incorporate military-family-friendly practices into their organizations across the human resources lifecycle and (2) tools, training materials, and targeted resources including the federal government in order to help HR professionals identify and hire military spouse (SHRM, 2011). More recently, SHRM conducted a meeting including partners from business, nonprofits, and government to identify some of the important issues related to employment following military service. One salient issue focused on the need to train human resource professionals on military cultural competence in order to increase their understanding of military-affiliated job seekers. Arguably such training should include specific information about military spouses, particularly for employers who seek to recruit and hire military spouse candidates as well as veterans.

## Suggestions for Human Resource Professionals, Recruiters, and Hiring Managers

A talent strategy for sourcing, hiring, recruiting, and retaining military spouses may be desirable for many companies for business, philanthropic, or patriotic reasons. Many businesses view themselves as integral parts of their community, and hiring military spouses can be a useful strategy to support their "brand" image and garner customers who also support the military. Likewise, companies that focus on hiring military spouses find that the military spouse often shares the companies' values, such as teamwork and adaptability. Companies are more likely to succeed in sourcing, hiring, and retaining military spouse employees if they have a clear understanding of the challenges they face, how to engage with military spouses in their community, and how they can communicate effectively with one another so that each hire is mutually beneficial for the military spouse and for the company. Toward this end, we offer specific suggestions for employers in the paragraphs that follow.

### Military Spouse Résumés

Approximately 56 percent of military spouses report they are working in their area of education or training (U.S. Department of Defense, Defense Manpower Data Center, 2016). However, many spouses, by necessity, work in areas inconsistent with their education or training because of the job market where they reside. At first glance, these seemingly disparate experiences might appear disconnected on their résumés as compared to more traditional applicants. However, these diverse experiences also may make their résumés stand out and demonstrate how they may be capable of performing a wider variety of available job functions, activities, and responsibilities compared to other applicants.

Military spouses may experience periods of unemployment or underemployment because they only live in one location for a limited time or because of supply and demand in the labor market where they reside. Employers should not automatically misperceive résumé gaps to be skill or experience deficiencies, when spouses may actually be actively seeking additional training, credentialing, certifications, or volunteer work experience that enhances their skills during times of underemployment or unemployment.

A strong résumé clearly conveys a work history that aligns with a particular job description and level of experience. A résumé often is the difference between a candidate being in the "yes" or "no" pile of applicants. But, military spouses may have trouble demonstrating that they are a good fit through their résumé alone. Military spouses' résumés often have many short-term positions listed instead of fewer long-term positions, which may—to an undiscerning eye—suggest that the individual lacks commitment or direction. For military spouses, the latter often is far from the truth. Human resource professionals should remember the context within which they are hiring a military spouse to account for the differences present in their résumés. Some spouses may have gaps in their employment histories, volunteer experiences in lieu of paid positions, or positions that appear disconnected (Bradbard et al., 2016b).

Below are a few common features of military spouse résumés:

- Functional versus chronological résumés (i.e., military spouses often prefer a functional format that avoids highlighting lapses in their employment history which are salient in a chronological format).
- Gaps in education or employment.
- A history of employment with disparate or unrelated jobs (geographic relocation may necessitate employment that is inconsistent with education or prior employment background).
- Employment that is unrelated to educational background or level of education.
- Volunteer experience.
- Short-duration jobs due to frequent military moves.
- Underemployment.
- Part time jobs versus full-time jobs or temporary work.
- Incomplete education or prolonged time in school, attendance at multiple schools, or multiple degrees.
- Certifications in lieu of college or university-based education (i.e., spouses may opt for a certification rather than an academic degree in order to complete the requirements before relocating or because of cost).

- Long-term unemployment.
- Unclear demonstration of advancement or increasing responsibilities over time.

## Recommendations for Human Resource Professionals, Hiring Managers, and Corporate Executives

Companies that wish to hire military spouses may have to use multiple strategies to assess whether a candidate is a good fit in order to reconcile the résumé with the job-specific qualifications. Résumés may not accurately reflect the breadth of experiences that a military spouse brings to the workplace. It also may not reflect the nontechnical skills or "soft skills" that could be observed in an interview, speaking with references, or simply by asking candidates to talk about the experiences that qualify them for a job; these may not appear on their résumé. Enabling spouses to self-identify as a military spouse may provide an opportunity to have an open dialogue about any concerns that the employer or prospective employee may have. However, keep in mind candidates may be reluctant to self-identify due to concerns about potential misconceptions (Bradbard et al., 2016b).

## Recommendations for Employers

The recommendations that follow are related to hiring military spouses and more broadly supporting their employment goals.

### Train to Avoid Stigma and Identify Opportunities

- Coordinate with networking groups, on social media, on LinkedIn, with nonprofit groups, and with military spouse employees to determine how to source military spouse candidates.
- Consider providing training to your human resource professionals, hiring managers, and leadership team to help them understand how to review military spouse résumés, how they may appear different from other résumés, and how to evaluate military spouses.

- Do not assume that spouses will be unable to continue in a job for only a short period of time. National Guard, Reserve, and veteran family members as well as many active duty spouses may remain in the same locations for extended periods or just as long as some civilians.
- Consider telework, remote, or transferable opportunities where appropriate and for appropriate employees.

## Leverage Existing Options and Benefits Rather Than Creating New Ones

- Consider 1099 (self-employed individuals) employment options as well as traditional employment.
- Examine position openings to determine if they can be offered as remote or flex-time positions to incentivize hiring military spouse candidates.
- Consider using existing benefits to enable flexibility for military spouse employees (e.g., pooling unused sick leave hours to be used by the spouse when a service member deploys).
- Establish a resource list to connect military spouse employees with local child care providers to enable seamless work starts.
- Consider military spouses for positions requiring security clearances given possible exposure to operational security policies and procedures and to potentially minimize costs (for spouses with existing clearances).
- Institute a military affinity group to provide networking opportunities for spouses within your organization.
- Provide mentorship opportunities for spouses returning to the workplace.
- Identify and assess for gaps where training could be provided to ensure a smooth transition to the workplace.
- Do not assume that someone is or is not appropriate for a particular job due to their age or prior experience (e.g., that they are applying for a job for which they are overqualified).
- Identify specific steps new employees can take to develop skills or proficiencies.

- Consider offering flexible benefits packages that reflect the needs of military spouse employees (e.g., child care credits in lieu of paying health-care expenses).
- Do not assume that a military spouse job candidate will be moving immediately: Veteran spouses and National Guard spouses often stay in the same location for the same amount of time as those families who are not in the military.
- Avoid assumptions about nonlinear career paths. Military spouses' careers may diverge from expected career paths or may have progressive advancements over time in their careers.
- Efforts to assist military spouses with employment do not need to be limited to hiring them. Companies can support military spouses in a variety of ways, including supporting the efforts of nonprofits, joining coalitions focused on military spouse hiring, helping to support research that supports military families, developing training materials or shared collateral materials to inform your employees or other organizations, participating on panels to provide information to spouses about the needs of employers, and sponsoring networking events. Also look to include military spouse–owned companies in your supply chain or look into how you can use military spouses as vendors or contractors to your company.

## Communicate

- Treat military spouse hiring efforts separately from veteran hiring efforts (though there may be overlap), using unique outreach, assessment, and retention methods.
- Consider the business case for hiring military spouses that is unique to your organization and determine why it makes sense to hire spouses, which spouses, and where they can belong in your organization.
- Spouses vary concerning whether they prefer to self-identify as military spouses. Employers can encourage self-identification by developing materials that promote their interest in hiring military spouses. This sends the message that spouses will not be penalized for self-identifying during the hiring process, which can increase the chances that employers and prospective employees can communicate with one another about their mutual expectations.

# Conclusion

Research shows that military spouses' employment rates are often impacted because military spouses serve in tandem with their service member, who may be required to move repeatedly, work long and unpredictable hours, or deploy for extended periods of time. While performing an important and sometimes unacknowledged role by maintaining family functioning at home and enabling service members to perform their military-specific duties, spouses often simultaneously suffer negative and, in many cases, long-term employment-related consequences. When their partner's military service itself prevents their spouses from working on their own career, military service becomes a less viable and perhaps less desirable option for families who may require two incomes or for a spouse who simply prefers to be employed. This in turn can impact the readiness of our nation's military to protect us. Employers can be a necessary and essential bridge in helping these talented, resourceful, and educated individuals enter and stay in the workforce alongside their spouses.

Using the strategies in this chapter, employers can maximize the benefits gained from hiring military spouses by gaining motivated, loyal, and dedicated employees who align with their own unique business case. This chapter addresses simple strategies employers can use to assess, recruit, hire, and retain military spouse candidates. The chapter also demonstrates the mutually beneficial role that employers can play not only by hiring military spouses, but also through other efforts such as training, mentoring, or participating in collaborative efforts (e.g., sharing best practices with like-minded employers; supporting nonprofit partners focused on spouse employment efforts). The opportunity for employers is that, through awareness of military-specific challenges, they can simultaneously (a) gain talented, motivated, loyal, diverse, and well-educated employees and (b) help mitigate some of the negative impacts of the military lifestyle and thus reduce challenges military spouses face while seeking employment.

# References

Bradbard, D. A., Maury, R., & Armstrong, N. A. (2016a, July). *The force behind the force: A business case for leveraging military spouse talent* (Employing Military Spouses, paper no. 1). Syracuse, NY: Institute for Veterans and Military Families, Syracuse University.

https://ivmf.syracuse.edu/wp-content/uploads/2016/07/Prudential_Report_7.21.16_REVISED_digital.pdf

Bradbard, D. A., Maury, R., & Armstrong, N. A. (2016b, November). *The force behind the force: Case profiles of successful military spouses balancing employment, service, and family* (Employing Military Spouses, paper no. 2). Syracuse, NY: Institute for Veterans and Military Families, Syracuse University. https://ivmf.syracuse.edu/article/the-force-behind-the-force-case-profiles-of-successful-military-spouses-balancing-employment-service-and-family/

Blue Star Families. (2015). *2014 Blue Star Families' annual military family lifestyle survey.* Washington, DC: Author. https://bluestarfam.org/wp-content/uploads/2016/04/2014_bsf_annual_report.pdf

Chalabi, M. (2015, March 15). What percentage of Americans have served in the military? *Five-Thirty-Eight Blog.* https://fivethirtyeight.com/datalab/what-percentage-of-americans-have-served-in-the-military/

eMentor. (2020). *Join the eMentor program.* https://www.ementorprogram.org/militaryspouse-ementor/

Haynie, J. M. (2012). *The business case for hiring a veteran: Beyond the clichés.* Syracuse, NY: Institute for Veterans and Military Families, Syracuse University. https://ivmf.syracuse.edu/article/the-business-case-for-hiring-a-veteran-beyond-the-cliches/

Hosek, J., & Wadsworth, S. M. (2013). Economic conditions in military families. *Future of Children, 23,* 41–59.

Maury, R., & Stone, B. (2014). *Military spouse employment report.* Syracuse, NY: Institute for Veterans and Military Families, Syracuse University. https://ivmf.syracuse.edu/article/military-spouse-employment-survey/

Meadows, S. O., Griffin, B. A., Karney, B. R., & Pollak, J. (2016). Employment gaps between military spouses and matched civilians. *Armed Forces and Society, 42*(3). doi:10:1177/0095327XI5607810

Ramchand, R., Tanielian, T., Fisher, M. P., Vaughan, C. A., Trail, T. E., Batka, B., . . . Dastidar, M. G. (2014). *Hidden heroes: America's military caregivers.* Santa Monica, CA: RAND. http://www.rand.org/pubs/research_reports/RR499.html

Presidential Directive Number Nine. (2011, January). *Strengthening our military families: Meeting America's commitment.* http://www.defense.gov/home/features/2011/0111_initiative/strengthening_our_military_january_2011.pdf

Society for Human Resource Management (SHRM). (2011, April 12). Press release: *SHRM joins White House in supporting military spouses, families.* https://www.shrm.org/about-shrm/press-room/press-releases/pages/joiningforces.aspx

U.S. Bureau of Labor Statistics. (2017, October). *Labor force statistics from the current population survey.* Washington, DC: U.S. Bureau of Labor Statistics https://data.bls.gov/timeseries/LNS14000000

U.S. Census Bureau. (2015). *American Community Survey (ACS): Public Use Microdata Sample (PUMS)* [Data file and codebook]. Washington, DC: Author. https://www.census.gov/programs-surveys/acs/technical-documentation/pums.html

U.S. Census Bureau. (2015). *American Community Survey (ACS): Public Use Microdata Sample (PUMS)* [Data file and codebook]. Washington, DC: Author. https://www.census.gov/programs-surveys/acs/technical-documentation/pums.html

U.S. Chamber of Commerce Foundation Hiring Our Heroes. (2020). *Hiring our heroes.* Washington, DC: Author. https://www.hiringourheroes.org

U.S. Department of Defense, Defense Manpower Data Center. (2015). *Military family life project: Active duty spouse survey.* Washington, DC: Author. http://download. militaryonesource.mil/12038/MOS/Reports/MFLP-Longitudinal-Analyses-Report. pdf

U.S. Department of Defense, Military Spouse Employment Partnership (MSEP). (2017). *Military spouse employment partnership partner portal.* Washington, DC: Author. https://msepjobs.militaryonesource.mil/msep/

U.S. Department of Defense Office of the Deputy Assistant Secretary of Defense (Military and Community Policy). *2015 profile of the military community.* Washington, DC: Author. http://download.militaryonesource.mil/12038/MOS/Reports/2015-Demographics-Report.pdf

U.S. Department of Defense, Office of People Analytics. (2012). *2012 Survey of active duty spouses.* Washington, DC: Author. https://download.militaryonesource.mil/12038/MOS/Surveys/ADSS1201-Briefing-Support-Deployment-Reintegration-PCS-WellBeing-Education-Employment.pdf

U.S. Department of Defense, Office of People Analytics. (2017). *2017 Survey of active duty spouses.* Washington, DC: Author. https://download.militaryonesource.mil/12038/MOS/Surveys/Survey-Active-Duty-Spouses-2017-Overview-Briefing-MSO.pdf

U.S. Department of Labor, Bureau of Labor Statistics. (2015). *Economic news release: Volunteering in the United States.* Washington, DC: Author. http://www.bls.gov/news.release/volun.nr0.htm

U.S. Department of Labor, Bureau of Labor Statistics. (2016a). *Economic news release, Employee tenure summary.* Washington, DC: Author. https://www.bls.gov/news.release/tenure.nr0.htm

U.S. Department of Labor, Bureau of Labor Statistics. (2016b). *News release: Employment characteristics of families summary.* Washington, DC: Author. http://www.bls.gov/news.release/famee.nr0.htm

U.S. Department of Veterans Affairs. (2015). *2015 veterans economic opportunity report.* Washington, DC: Author. U.S. Department of Veterans Affairs, National Center for Veterans Analysis and Statistics. http://www.benefits.va.gov/benefits/docs/veteraneco nomicopportunityreport2015.pdf

U.S. Department of Veterans Affairs, National Center for Veterans Analysis and Statistics. *VetPop 2007 data, table 2s: Separations by state, period, age group, gender 2000-2036. Estimated years 2016–2020.* Veteran Population Projections Model (VetPop 2007), Table 2S. Office of the Actuary. Washington, DC: Author. https://www.va.gov/vetdata/Veteran_Population.asp

U.S. Government Accountability Office (GAO). (2015, September). *Military compensation: DoD needs more complete and consistent data to assess the costs and policies of relocating personnel.* Washington, DC: Author. https://www.gao.gov/products/gao-15-713

Westat. (2010). *National survey of veterans, active duty service members, demobilized national guard and reserve members, and surviving spouses.* GS-23F-8144H. Washington, DC. Prepared for Department of Veterans Affairs. https://www.va.gov/SURVIVORS/docs/NVSSurveyFinalWeightedReport.pdf

# 12

# Supporting the National Guard and Reservists as Civilian Employees

*Michael Kirchner and Ann M. Herd*

The U.S. military's Reserve component comprises the National Guard and Reserves, and with its approximately 800,000 part-time service members it makes up roughly 40 percent of the U.S. military (Congressional Research Service, 2021). For simplicity throughout this chapter, we refer to of both National Guards members and Reservist members as Reservists. Reservists often maintain nonmilitary employment beyond their monthly trainings, and their military service is frequently unknown to the nonmilitary organization where they are employed. The majority of Reservists perform their military service on weekends and during a 2-week period of focused annual training. Some Reservists have a specific job that requires them to report during the standard Monday through Friday work week, but these roles are not as common as the traditional Reservists' duty schedule, which requires weekend military service and annual training. Some Reservists may be called up to active duty service for months or even a year when the military deems that Reservists' role is mission critical. Military service obligations interfering with civilian employment responsibilities are a frequently-cited concern of employers when hiring veterans, which may lead Reservists to avoid disclosing their military role to civilian employers.

Numerous transition issues and military-friendly best practices have already been discussed in preceding chapters. A majority of these topics and suggestions can be similarly applied to Reservists. However, organizations employing Reservists have numerous obligations that may be misunderstood or entirely overlooked. These obligations can cause a great deal of frustration for all involved civilian stakeholders (e.g., organization leaders, coworkers, veteran employee, and their families), particularly when Reservists and their civilian employers are unaware of the voluntary as well as legal aspects pertaining to service member employment. In addition, civilian employers

Michael Kirchner and Ann M. Herd, *Supporting the National Guard and Reservists as Civilian Employees* In: *Military Veteran Employment*. Edited by: Nathan D. Ainspan and Kristin N. Saboe, Oxford University Press. © Oxford University Press 2021. DOI: 10.1093/oso/9780190642983.003.0013 are often unaware of the unique benefits derived from this source of talent, including but not limited to active security clearances, nontechnical and technical skills, and other employer-desired personal attributes that the employees gain through their military experiences and training.

This chapter addresses several aspects related to Reservists and how to hire and retain them as employees in civilian organizations, beginning with a discussion about service obligations, training schedule, and potential transition issues experienced by Reservists. Additionally, we address employers' obligations toward supporting Reservists and offer guidance to help organizations alleviate periodic challenges that both the employer and Reservist may encounter. Similarly, both Reservists and employers are afforded rights and have obligations to consider. These legalities are discussed, and corresponding resources are outlined further in the chapter. In addition, we present strategies for organizations to successfully help acclimate an activated Reservist's return to civilian employment after a time period when they were activated into military duty. This chapter provides a better understanding of the expectations and support programs available that are related to employees who are also service members in a Reserve component.

## Service Requirement Distinctions

Active duty service members share numerous similarities with Reservist service members, such as fulfilling minimal enlistment requirements, completing the same basic training, learning identical job specialties, and maintaining a high level of physical fitness. However, several distinctions can be identified that are necessary for employers to consider. These differences may impact service members' work attendance, as well as present an entirely new set of challenges for employers that have yet to be discussed. Table 12.1 provides a consolidated overview of some of the distinctions between service members in active and reserve status.

Each branch of the armed forces has a Reserve component, whose purpose is to maintain availability and readiness for active duty service if needed to support the active services. The Reserve components are federally funded and controlled by the military service under which they fall. In addition, the Army and Air Force have National Guard components, which, while also federally funded, are primarily controlled by the state where their units reside (National Guard, n.d.). Reserve components of the Armed Forces learn

**Table 12.1**  Distinctions Between Active Duty Members and Reservists

| Distinction Type | Active Duty | Reserve/National Guard Status |
| --- | --- | --- |
| Commitment to the military | Full time | Usually part time but may be activated into full time |
| Traditional work schedule[a] | Variable (primarily Monday–Friday though nights and weekends common) | One weekend per month, two additional weeks per year |
| Employment options outside the military | Restricted to military service obligations | Unrestricted; service member may seek nonmilitary employment |
| Purpose | Serve the people and defend the nation | Maintain trained units available for active duty when needed (Reserve); protect local communities and support active duty military forces (National Guard) |
| Enlistment requirement | At least 2-year service obligation | At least 6-year service obligation |
| Duty station | Can be stationed anywhere domestic or abroad, depending on mission requirements | Most often local/nearby |
| Retirement[b] | Eligible to receive full retirement benefits after 20 years OR participate in blended retirement system | Eligible to receive modified retirement benefits after 20 years of service and once 60 years of age or older |

[a]Work schedules can be highly variable for military given the wide array of occupations and jobs fulfilled by service members. Some active duty have atypical schedules; some Reservists serve according to specialized schedules depending on their career specialty and type of Reserve commitment.

[b]Active duty service members may now be eligible to receive some retirement benefits without completing 20 years of service.

jobs identical to those who serve on active duty but learn and train in part-time status after completion of basic training and military occupation specialty schools. Reservists may be called to active duty for deployment when needed. The deployment—stateside or abroad—can range in length from only a few days to over a year. In fact, the conflicts since the 9/11 attacks have led to the largest and most frequent mobilization of reserve units since World War II, with approximately 10 percent of Reservists having served previously on active duty (South, 2018). On completing a deployment, the service member returns to reserve status unless called on again for subsequent redeployment. Their reserve status remains until their enlistment is complete.

## Reserve Component Training Requirements

Training in the Guard or Reserve components generally occurs one weekend per month (referred to as "drill"), with an additional 2 weeks over the year. These training obligations often impact Reservists and the organizations employing them. While the one weekend a month claim is accurate, the training period might begin before Saturday. In some instances, Reservists may choose or be asked to support preparations for drill weekend by reporting a day or two early. If the training starts on a Friday, the Reservist, assuming a traditional civilian Monday through Friday workweek, would have competing work obligations. Although Reserve unit commanders are generally willing to work with Reservist service members who are maintaining nonmilitary employment, there are instances where training requires time away from civilian employment. More explicitly, military training in the National Guard or Reserve is a requirement of service. Service members are obligated to complete prescheduled training each month. These instances can blur the lines between civilian employer and Reservist responsibilities. In any case, if the Reservist has orders documenting their reporting requirements, they should be cleared of their civilian work responsibilities.

While on drill, service members should not be expected to complete nonmilitary work. Work hours during drill weekends can extend far beyond the traditional 8-hour workday. The trainings may also require the service members' attention throughout the weekend and severely inhibit their ability to complete outside activities. Further, depending on training location, cell phone or Internet service may not even be available. The service obligation can create tension between civilian employers and Reservists if civilian supervisors are not aware of their responsibilities. Awareness of the time requirements related to drill and annual training will reduce the likelihood of future issues.

## Legal Rights and Responsibilities

### Legal Rights of Reservists and Employers

Despite an overwhelming majority of organizations expressing support for military veterans, issues can arise when Reservists are being called to serve.

Although members of the National Guard and Reserve are afforded many rights that protect their job, they are not without responsibilities to their civilian employers. Whether prior to training, during a deployment, or after returning from duty, Reservists have obligations to their employer. Many of the legal requirements are straightforward and generally aspects of being a good employee or employer, but some of the requirements have a bit of a gray area that can be confusing for all parties.

## Legal Rights of Reservists

Most U.S.-based organizations try to work with Reservists (e.g., accommodating their training schedule), but there are additional legal rights to consider. These rights have been established through the Uniformed Services Employment and Reemployment Rights Act (USERRA) of 1994. USERRA, a federal statute, protects service members' and veterans' civilian employment rights, such as protections from discrimination and reappointment at work (Department of Justice, 2015). The rights of Reservists are protected from initial employment throughout their tenure with the organization. The statute generally protects Reservists' nonmilitary employment rights while they concurrently serve in the Armed Forces. Under USERRA, the following are legal requirements that employers cannot deny a Reservist (Department of Justice, 2015):

- Initial employment
- Reemployment
- Retention in employment
- Promotion
- Any other benefit of employment

Additionally, Reservists have the right to

- Military leaves of absence
- Prompt job reinstatement after service duty
- Accumulation of seniority benefits (as if they never left)
- Immediate reinstatement of health insurance (when they return)
- Maintenance of pension benefits
- Training/retraining of skills provided to non-Reservist employees

**Table 12.2** Service Time Requirement for Reservists Completing Service

| |
|---|
| 1–30 Days → Report next scheduled workday after service, safe transportation, and 8 hours rest |
| 31–180 Days → Reapply to employer within 14 days |
| 181+ Days → Reapply to employer within 90 days |

These protections are not always clearcut. For instance, although Reservists are entitled to prompt job reinstatement after a service obligation is complete, that does not necessarily mean they are entitled to return to the same job they held prior to leaving. Employers may instead offer a position of comparable status, seniority, and pay to fit the organization's requirements. Similarly, if the Reservist was injured while deployed and that would impede their ability to perform their former job, an organization must make reasonable efforts to accommodate the disability, whether through revising the current position or finding an appropriate alternative. Concurrently, employers are required to maintain reemployment opportunities for a period of 5 years for any Reservist who is activated to serve on full-time active duty for a temporary period of time. On returning home, the Reservist has requirements for how quickly they are to report back to work. Depending on the length of the service obligation, the Reservist may have the right to take time away from nonmilitary employment prior to returning. The window between deployment and returning to the workplace is important as it allows the Reservist time to reacclimate, resolve issues that may have arisen while gone, and begin closing a potentially difficult chapter of their lives. Table 12.2 outlines the time requirements that Reservists must report or reapply to their jobs after being activated, depending on the length of deployment.

## Legal Rights of Employers

Employers are afforded their own rights and protections as soon as they hire a member of the National Guard or Reserve. As noted, service members have training obligations that can impede their civilian work schedule. These training schedules are often known months in advance, and Reservists have a responsibility to provide sufficient notice to their civilian employers about all service obligations. Service members have paperwork (called "orders") that clearly defines when their drill or training occurs. This paperwork can be provided by their unit commander and is a common request of employers. Service members are responsible for providing the paperwork on request. Advanced notice requirements are fairly loose and can cause issues, but the Reservist should always be able to produce written documentation from their unit leadership that details the dates of training or deployment that may conflict with work. Civilian employers can ask Reservists for documentation, and the Reservists are expected to provide it to their employer on request.

While Reservists are deployed, organizations are afforded additional protections that allow for some flexibility. For example, organizations are not required to hold jobs for as long as the service member chooses to or is away for service. Instead, a temporary replacement can be hired to fill in for the activated Reservist to help for the duration of the deployment. Once the Reservist returns to work, the temporary employee may be retained, released, or transferred to a different position. Organizations are also not required to maintain employee health benefits or pay the Reservist their salary. The military covers the Reservists' health insurance costs and compensates the service member for their time; however, as noted in the next section, some organizations choose to maintain some benefits for their Reservist employees as part of being a military-friendly employer.

## The Business Case for Reserve Component Talent Management

Talent management is often seen as consisting of three prongs of human capital management: (a) assessment, (b) development, and (c) retention. The term also connotes a recognition that an organization's talent (i.e., employees at all levels) provides a foundational strength for meeting an organization's strategic objectives. Reservist talent management may be particularly critical as well as challenging for employers. Reservist employees represent a significant source of talent for organizations, including employees, individual contributors, managers, and executives at all levels and in all professions. Compared to a civilian employee in a related job and with similar years of experience, a Reservist often brings to the table a wealth of additional broadening experiences and team, project management, self-management, cross-cultural, and leadership competencies. For example, when comparing two junior-level financial analysts—one a civilian and one a Reservist—each with a bachelor of science degree in finance and with 2 years of work experience in the same healthcare organization, the Reservist may already have had significantly greater responsibilities than his or her civilian counterpart. Often, the Reservist has already led a 20- to 40-person platoon in complex field training exercises requiring strategic and tactical planning equivalent to that required of civilian midlevel managers. These additional Reservist employee competencies should to be acknowledged and leveraged by the civilian employer's talent management practices.

Along with a wealth of additional competencies, Reservist talent represents potentially significant challenges for employers in all three prongs of the talent management equation. On the selection and assessment prong of talent management, employers as well as Reservists report uncertainty in civilian/military cross translation of competencies gained in military and civilian jobs and organizational experiences (e.g., some military occupations that are directly related to combat arms positions do not have directly comparable civilian occupations). Even in the majority of cases where civilian and military occupations are comparable (e.g., truck driver), the Reservist often has gained additional competencies as part of their military service. Employers' typical assessment and selection processes often neglect to measure the additional competencies fostered by military service. In addition, research suggests that employers are prone to stereotyping and other biases about military service (e.g., the perception that service members suffer from post-traumatic stress disorder or are not skilled in collaborative or participative leadership) that may attenuate the validity of their judgments during selection and assessment processes (Stone & Stone, 2015).

Lack of knowledge about the service member's military duties also may hamper an employer's ability to provide appropriate talent development initiatives for Reservist employees. For example, the Reservist may already be skilled in areas where their civilian employer assumes additional training is required. Reservists participate in a great deal of training, such as in leadership and problem-solving, and much of this training can be valuable across organization types. On the other hand, Reservist employees may have additional and unique talent development needs that their civilian counterparts may not have, including the need to be able to manage the constant transitions between their civilian and military jobs and navigate across organizational cultures.

Retaining Reservist talent can also pose a challenge for employers. For many Reservists, there may be a disconnect between their military and civilian pay. Senior Reserve leaders can often make a significantly higher salary in their civilian jobs than in their military jobs, causing them to question the feasibility of maintaining their military service as they move up the ladder in their civilian career. On the other hand, some Reservists receive a higher compensation package from the military than from their civilian work, thus causing potential retention issues for the civilian employer. In both cases, it is incumbent on the civilian employer to have valid assessment and performance management processes in place to identify and retain high-potential and high-performing Reservist employees, and recognizing the additional competencies that Reservist talent often brings to the table, in order to meet their strategic talent needs.

By far the biggest Reservist talent management challenges reported by employers have to do with the frequent and often unpredictable absences required by Reservist military service. As noted, the traditional perception that Reserve service entails only one weekend a month plus 2 weeks during the summer is erroneous and underrepresented. The military service time commitment, particularly for noncommissioned officers and officers, is often much greater. Scheduling around these absences poses significant challenges for civilian employers, particularly those in smaller organizations. Whereas large enterprises can often delegate duties and responsibilities that are a normal part of the Reservist's civilian job, small organizations have fewer employees who are more likely to be responsible for filling multiple roles and job descriptions. When Reservist employees are activated for a long-term duty assignment, their employing organizations may struggle to reassign the workload without missing a beat. As a result, morale among coworkers who must bear additional duties to support their Reservist colleagues during their absences can also suffer. Managing and communicating expectations around Reservist service absences is key for effective talent management across the workforce in both large and medium-small enterprises.

## Challenges Faced by Reserve Component Talent

To effectively manage Reservist employees, an understanding of the individual challenges faced by Reservist employees is imperative. These challenges primarily stem from the continuous and ongoing transitions that Reservists face as they navigate two jobs and two organizational cultures. Inherent within these ongoing transitions are potential role conflict, identity conflict, work–life balance, and career management challenges, discussed below.

## Continuous and Ongoing Transition

Military-to-civilian career transitions are often thought of as a one-time occurrence that occurs for active duty service members transitioning out of the military; however, Reservists go through a major military–civilian job transition at least twice per month (from civilian to service member for monthly service commitments and back to civilian life) as they serve their monthly commitments. As previously noted in this chapter and the other chapters in this book, military organizational culture is quite distinct from that of many civilian organizational cultures. The Armed Forces operate under a disciplined, hierarchical structure, whereas nonmilitary organizations are generally less rigid and structured. From long work hours to uniform and training obligations, Reservists who are also working in a nonmilitary job are required to repeatedly adapt their behaviors depending on the work environment they are currently in. The bimonthly transition can be stressful as the Reservist is forced to make adaptations that may be significantly different from their nonmilitary employer. Table 12.3 offers a simplified visual comparison between military and more traditional workplace cultures. Although the table offers insight, it should not be broadly applied across all organizations and workplace cultures as every organization is different.

Table 12.3 Comparison of (Typical) Military Versus Nonmilitary Workplace Cultures

| Military Culture | Corporate Culture |
| --- | --- |
| Hierarchy/vertical structure | Matrix structure |
| Clearly defined roles and structure | Ambiguity in roles and structure |
| Clearly defined career progression with fixed terms of enlistment | Less-defined or undefined career progression without terms of enlistment |
| Organization-defined values and beliefs (protect citizens of the nation) | Corporate culture-defined values and beliefs (grow the organization) |
| Collectivist, mission oriented | Individualistic, individual focused |
| Pay determined by rank and service time | Pay determined by market value |
| Rules of conduct enforced by law | Rules of conduct enforced by employer |

## Role Conflict

With a variety of cultural differences and expectations associated with each of their employment roles, Reservist employees may experience challenges relating to several types of role conflict. Interrole conflict can occur when the behaviors expected for one job conflict with the expectations in the other job. Potential examples of interrole conflict can occur with any of the numerous examples of cultural differences between the Reservist employee's military and civilian organizational cultural role expectations. As an example, cultural differences in how leadership is expected to be enacted can cause interrole conflict. Reservist employees may be expected to take charge and explicitly tell subordinates what to do during certain military exercises, whereas in their civilian jobs a more collaborative or facilitative leadership approach may be expected. The reverse may also be true—where employees are expected to take charge and show more initiative in their civilian role than in their military role—depending on the requisite military and civilian job role requirements. In another example, organizational cultural differences in norms and values related to taking initiative and selfless service can lead to interrole conflict. In a military culture, there may be an expectation that members—regardless of their formal position or role—step up and show initiative to address a gap that is evident in order to accomplish a task. This same behavior in a civilian organizational context may be seen as undesirable and could be seen as competitively "showing off" in order to make one's coworkers look like slackers. The strong cultural military value and norms around the core military organizational value of "selfless service" may lead Reservist employees to volunteer for undesirable task assignments in their civilian job, thinking that the volunteering will be recognized and rewarded during performance appraisal time when in fact the behavior is seen as a lack of savvy in career management competencies. Thus, organizational cultural differences provide different lenses through which an employee's behavior is perceived and interpreted. Reservist employees face the challenge of learning and understanding these cultural differences in order to understand how their behavior in the military job role may be evaluated differently in their civilian job role.

Role ambiguity is another role challenge that Reservist employees may experience. When navigating a variety of role expectations, nailing down the exact specifics of the behavioral norms that are expected in the civilian versus the military jobs and understanding how these norms change over time as the job and organizational environments and concomitant demands change can be challenging. As one example, a Reservist employee with whom we spoke regarding his experience related (with humor) how he immediately stood when his civilian chief executive officer entered a meeting, only to quickly realize and remember that this was not an expected norm for managers in his position in his civilian organization.

Another role challenge that a Reservist employee may experience is intraperson role conflict. This type of role conflict can occur when Reservist employees feel that they are being asked or required to do things that go against their values. For example, a person who likes to give their all to every job may experience intraperson role conflict when they realize that they must spread themselves out across their military, civilian, and nonwork roles and it is not possible to stay completely immersed in any one role. In this example, employers may offer time management classes and/or coaching opportunities in support of Reservist employees' managing of numerous roles and responsibilities.

Related to this example, role overload is perhaps the greatest role challenge for Reservist employees. Role overload occurs when the expectations associated with their civilian, military, and nonwork roles do not align; that is, it is not possible to accomplish all the behavioral and performance expectations associated with all of the roles. The Reservist employees with whom we spoke mentioned role overload as an issue most frequently, noting that performance of their Reservist military service roles often entailed many additional unacknowledged hours and days involved in traveling to and from their duty station, conducting preparations for their duty time, and after-action reviews of their military assignments. Likewise, as they progressed in their civilian jobs, the expectations for additional time devoted to professional development and performance excellence increased, so that even with the best personal discipline and time management competencies, perpetual trade-off and triaging decisions were required to navigate the role overload challenges between the military and civilian employment roles. Role overload, along with the other role challenges discussed here, can lead to stress, burnout, and reduced productivity in all roles. It is incumbent on employers to understand and address these challenges faced by their Reservist employees.

## Work–Life Balance

With role responsibilities in both their military and civilian jobs, balancing the additional responsibilities of family and other nonwork roles can be particularly challenging for Reservist employees. Research suggested that individuals vary in their preferred styles for balancing work and nonwork commitments (Cohen, Duberley, & Musson, 2009). These styles or strategies for balancing work and nonwork responsibilities include a *segmenting approach* (the individual keeps work and nonwork activities and identities separate); an *integrating approach* (individuals freely blend and integrate both work and nonwork activities throughout the day); and/or a *cycling approach* (individuals focus primarily on work or nonwork roles in cycles). For example, an individual who uses a segmenting approach may be careful about performing only work-related tasks while in the workplace and only performing home-related tasks while at home. An individual using an integrative approach, on the other hand, may be likely to perform work tasks while at home and vice versa, with few boundaries between their work and nonwork roles. An individual using a cyclist approach may gear up and focus all their energy on one role (e.g., their Reserve deployment) for an extended time period, to the neglect of their other roles, and then switch and focus on their other roles (e.g., civilian and/or personal) exclusively for a time. These work–life balance strategies are used by both civilian and military employees; the difference is that Reservist employees have an entire additional set of responsibilities to balance with their military service.

Keys to success in the use of any work–life balance strategy include the amount of control the individual has over their work and nonwork boundaries and their perceptions of how supportive their employer is of the pursuit of work–life balance (Allen, 2001; Lapierre et al., 2008). Because of the increased workload demanded by their military responsibilities with little flexibility, many Reservist employees experience low control over their work and nonwork boundaries; they must accomplish their military work during the designated weekend and duty times. Their employer's policies and supervisor's and organizational support of work–life balance thus become quite salient in the ways that Reservist employees are able to address work–life balance challenges. Employer best practices for acknowledging and assisting the Reservist with work–life balance strategies include explicit coaching conversations about how available the Reservist employee may or may not be (during each weekend rotation or deployment) to address their civilian work emails, client calls, or other responsibilities, and proactively planning for ways to fill the gaps when the Reservist employee is not available. In addition, a flex-time schedule and flex-place work arrangements can assist the Reservist employee with navigating the boundaries between their roles. Research suggests that flexible work arrangements work best when there are agreed-on work deliverables and opportunities for open communication among all coworkers so that role responsibilities are clear, transparent, and acknowledged.

## Career Identity

Related to role conflict and overload, Reservist employees may experience identity conflict in terms of their intersecting career and nonwork identities. Similar to interrole conflict, identity conflict can occur when one's values and behaviors associated with one identity are perceived as being different from, or conflicting with, the values and behaviors associated with another identity. Studies suggest that one's career identities are often a central component of their overall identity and sense of self-worth. For example, when introducing themselves, one of the first components of an introduction is one's job or career. The military as an organization is known for having strong and consistent structures that emphasize the organization's mission, values, and cultural norms in order to promote a strong personal military career identity. From wearing a military uniform to taking part in such recognized and automatic norms as saluting or farewell and promotion ceremonies, the socialization practices in the military provide for easy identification with one's military career. Likewise, many civilian careers also foster a strong sense of career identity, including workplace uniforms or dress codes for appropriate attire and shared values across the profession.

To handle their intersecting and potentially conflicting military and civilian career identities, several Reservists we interviewed said that they had to deliberately and mindfully don a new identity and mindset as they changed from their military clothing to their civilian clothing. Reservists we interviewed also reported using transition time—such as when commuting—to put themselves into the concomitant framework needed for their upcoming job role. For example, a Reservist employee may have an exceptional level of autonomy in their nonmilitary job, while having very little autonomy in their military role. Alternatively, a Reservist in the military may have attained a leadership position and be responsible for overseeing any number of service members during a drill weekend; however, they may be new in their nonmilitary job and be relegated to completing mundane tasks. Regardless of role, Reservists frequently need to adapt their behaviors to fit with corresponding job responsibilities and the organization's culture.

## Career Management

Managing careers in two different organizations can be challenging for Reservist employees. Military versus civilian organizational cultural differences related to career management are one source of this challenge. Career management in the military is considered both an individual and a leadership responsibility, with every effort made throughout the organization's talent management practices to reduce the ambiguity of suggested steps, performance metrics, and timelines for promotion. Emphasis is on developing the whole person, with continuous learning a bedrock of military talent and career management. Service members are scheduled and required by their military leaders to attend various trainings and military schools as an expected prerequisite for promotion to the next rank. In addition, for each Military Occupational Specialty, there are known positions and job experiences that are desirable for increased chances of promotion. The military performance management system is tied to career management processes, so that service members understand that they have a greater probability of landing positions and "stretch" assignments desirable for promotion when they have received favorable performance reviews. The military performance management system combines a graphic rating scale approach (with ratings on performance of military core values, e.g., selfless service); detailed text, a management-by-objectives approach (with written comments providing behavioral evidence and evaluative comments regarding how well the service member performed job-related duties and goals); and a forced-distribution rating system (with senior raters being expected/allowed to provide a constrained percentage of "top-block" or highest category ratings). At nearly every rank, a service member is rated on their own performance and how well they develop their subordinates. Career management thus is seen in the military as a responsibility for the entire organization and leaders at all levels, as well as an individual employee's responsibility.

In contrast to general career management processes in the military, civilian career management processes generally place greater locus of control on the individual. Unlike previous notions of careers being a linear progression in a single organization, modern conceptualizations of a career include the "protean" and "boundaryless" careers. A protean career is one in which the individual takes complete responsibility for their own career by continually scanning the job market, keeping their skills and competencies updated, and seizing opportunities for career growth or personal balance goals, even if this means job-hopping among a variety of organizations and job types. Likewise, a boundaryless career is one that is not limited by organizational structures and may include a patchwork of part-time and entrepreneurial roles among various organizations.

These current career models, most relevant to today's workforce, connote a heavy emphasis on self-directed behavior and career adaptability to manage one's own career in a dynamic work environment. The employee is seen as having primary responsibility for learning the ropes and gaining an understanding of the implicit norms regarding what behaviors and job experiences are rewarded. In addition, the onus is on the employee to proactively seek promotion-worthy job experiences while avoiding less-desirable assignments and to develop their own mentoring and politically positive networks. The individual employee is seen as the primary "architect" and "self-agent" of their own career in civilian sectors (Briscoe, Hall, & DeMuth, 2006). The idea of one's employer providing formal guidance and mechanisms for advancing in the company and into new roles, which is standard in the military, would be foreign in many civilian companies, where individuals are more commonly expected to take control of their career development and advancement.

## Employer Best Practices in Supporting Reservists

Many of the employer-led best practices already discussed in other chapters, such as employee resource groups and mentoring programs, are also applicable for Reservist employees. Other frequently cited programs include veteran hiring initiatives, support for local veteran service organizations, volunteerism, and tailored job training for veterans. Additional opportunities intended to support Reservist employees are also available, which should be considered when establishing military-friendly programming. An appropriate starting point may be to connect with the local Employer Support of the Guard and Reserve (ESGR) representative in your area to schedule more in-depth training on employer responsibilities and related support services. You can contact ESGR via their Customer Service Center at (800) 336–4590, Option 1, or by email at OSD.USERRA@mail.mil. ESGR state contacts can be located online (https://www.esgr.mil/About-ESGR/Contact/Local-State-Pages).

Established in 1972, ESGR is a Department of Defense program designed to promote the cooperation and understanding between service members and their civilian employers (ESGR, n.d.). ESGR representatives are available in every state, are well versed on legal rights of Reservists and organizations, and can serve as a liaison between Reservist service members and their employers. Periodic consulting with an ESGR ombudsman regarding service member employment obligations and issues is a highly valuable but underutilized resource for civilian employers. ESGR ombudsmen provide education and remain neutral through the process, with the intent on best meeting the needs of both the Reservists and the organization employing them. These resources can serve as a bridge between the employer and Reservist when work disputes occur. The ombuds (as they are called) are a free service provided by ESGR and can answer questions or address concerns that arise, providing an effective strategy for resolving disputes outside of the courtroom at no cost.

Additionally, ESGR annually recognizes employers who fulfill their legal responsibilities and those that go above and beyond in their support of their Reservist employees. Employees and others can nominate their employer or their boss for awards. (Information about the ESGR awards is available at https://www.esgr.mil/Employer-Awards/ESGR-Awards-Programs.) There are now seven ESGR-sponsored awards that recognize employers for their overall support of Reservists and their spouses, with awards generally offered in progressive forma (i.e., an initial award must be won prior to being eligible for the next tier). Organizations are generally nominated by one of their Reservist employees. Information about the different types of awards can be found on the ESGR website. The process is competitive, and the number of organizations recognized for some certificates or awards is limited. However, once selected, the corresponding certificates or awards are proudly displayed in many organizations today and are a symbol of recognition regarding how organizations meet the needs of their Reservist employees.

As noted previously in the chapter, Reservists are required to participate in military training monthly. The trainings occur at a unit or base generally near the service member's home; however, travel to training locations may require an extensive trip. Reservists working full time may then have a short turnaround between jobs. Although service members have a legal right to 8 hours off between military duty and reporting back to work, that time does not necessarily include travel time or sleep. For Reservists required to travel 2 hours or more to their duty station, organizations can consider offering an early release from work or a later start time on returning.

Military-friendly organizations integrate numerous recommendations that have already been shared in this book and also apply to helping recruit, support, and retain Reservist service members. Other additional services can be offered to support Reservist employees in addition to the ones offered in the other chapters of this book. For one, providing full pay (i.e., paying the Reservist their full civilian salary regardless of their military salary) or differential pay (i.e., paying the difference between the military and civilian salary) to employees who are activated for service is a common approach for employers supporting Reservist employees. Active duty pay is often below what the Reservists are paid in their civilian job, and, as such, activation for deployment can cause financial hardship. Differential pay can help overcome new or ongoing financial expenses that are incurred during the Reservists' deployment. Organizations who choose to include differential pay as an employment benefit should consider how they implement their policy. The most frequent offering of differential pay occurs for Reservists being deployed overseas; however, employers interested in fully supporting Reservist employees activated for service are encouraged to consider extending the benefit for all military duty requirements. Additionally, organizations should clearly communicate their differential pay policies during the onboarding process to avoid unintentionally surprising their Reservist employees. Once activated, Reservists may also become ineligible to receive employer-sponsored health benefits, which could place undue burden on Reservists' families. Offering and maintaining health insurance for family members is a similar extended benefit provided by military-friendly employers that are effective with this population.

Perhaps most important, periodic discussions with employees who are also serving part time in the military can be beneficial. Established schedules to discuss service obligations, potential upcoming training or deployment conflicts, and any other concerns improves communication and transparency between both parties. Organizations can gain clarity in how the Reservist's time may be occupied in the upcoming months and be proactive in addressing potential issues. The allocated time promotes inclusivity on behalf of the organization to ensure the Reservist understands their dual responsibility is valued and supported.

## Keep in Mind the Business Case for Reservist Talent Management

The recommendations that follow summarize best practices for employers' talent management practices for their Reservist employees.

### Assessing, Developing, and Retention Policies

Valid assessment, development, and retention of high-potential/high-performing talent is a critical task for all organizations, and these talent management activities are especially important for managing Reservist talent. Reservist employees bring with them a wealth of skills and competencies that they develop during their military service duties, including leadership, teamwork, time management, self-discipline, resilience, and project management competencies. At the same time, Reservist employees are human, with inherent individual differences in their performance and potential in their civilian jobs. Valid, job-related talent management practices for assessing their performance and potential are critical to your company, so find ways to develop and address their competency gaps and manage their needs to retain these employees.

### Include Reserve Service Experience in Your Human Resource Information System

An important but often-neglected tool for talent management is the organization's human resource information system. In order to leverage the additional competencies offered by Reservist talent, it is important to document the competencies that are continuously developed by their military service in Reservist employees. Outside of your organization, Reservists participate in a variety of intense and extensive training and development courses and field or deployment experiences throughout their military service, including language courses, college-level and degree-earning programs, and courses related to their military occupational specialty. In addition, Reservist employees frequently develop skills related to diversity and inclusion, adaptability, and cross-cultural navigation during their military exercises and deployments. Ensure that you measure and capture these competencies during your performance management and talent identification assessment and selection activities.

## Avoid Assumptions and Stereotypes With Valid Performance Management Systems

As much as possible, question the evaluative assumptions and interpretations made about a service member's behavior as being caused by their military identity and service. Studies suggest that service members are frequently labeled as "heroes, victims, or violent aggressors" in the way their behavior is interpreted and reported by various media outlets, including movies and television shows (Eisler, 2013). Rarely, if ever, can any individual's behavior or performance be explained by one evaluative label, as exemplified by research on evaluative biases such as the halo effect, contrast errors, and stereotyping shows. For example, a Reservist who stands at attention when their civilian supervisor enters a room may be perceived as overly bureaucratic or hierarchical in their approach to authority, when in fact the Reservist may simply be momentarily mixing up their two different organizational cultures. Likewise, Reservist employees who raise their voice may be perceived as verging on aggression, while civilian coworkers exhibiting the same behavior may be perceived as appropriately assertive.

The best employer strategies for avoiding these types of errors lies with using valid assessment and performance management systems that measure performance behaviors and job-related results and outcomes rather than relying primarily on subjective judgments of raters. For example, employers should make note of specific behavioral examples and provide immediate feedback to the Reservist employee about positive and negative performance situations. These behavioral examples and coaching conversations will help ensure there are fewer biases involved in how the supervisor interprets a Reservist's performance behavior and will also allow Reservist employees to understand how their actions are perceived.

## Become Familiar With Military Culture and Values

The military–civilian knowledge gap exists between those who have served in the military and those who have not and thus may never fully understand the military. But, organizations that make an effort to better understand who their Reservist employees are, the training they have received, and how the military has potentially influenced their development will benefit from these efforts. As repeatedly noted, the military is similar to all other organizations, where a culture is developed, reinforced, and instilled into its members. Despite taking off their uniform after each training or deployment, Reservist employees maintain aspects of a military identity, while also receiving exposure from their personal lives, family, friends, and broader environmental surroundings. The merging and sometimes contradicting cultures help shape Reservist employees' work beliefs and core values—each of which can be leveraged or addressed by organizations that seek to understand military operations. Leveraging military employee resource groups and sponsoring organization-wide military culture activities are two examples of ways to increase awareness among all employees of their colleagues who are also members of the military.

## Acknowledge Intersecting Identities and Role Expectations of Reservist Talent

Research suggests that effective strategies to handle role conflict issues include the following: (a) *reactive role behavior,* or trying to do it all, and meet the expectations of all roles; (b) *personal role redefinition,* or personally prioritizing which role expectations are most aligned with one's own goals and values; and (c) *structural role redefinition,* or proactively communicating with role senders to negotiate different role expectations and priorities (Hall, 1972). Some employees may often start with a strategy of reactive role behavior and try to keep up with all the expectations from their role senders, including their military and civilian supervisors and coworkers, as well as fulfill the expectations in their personal roles. When this strategy fails to be effective, these individuals may prioritize various tasks in their own minds (or personal role redefinition) to alleviate some of the stress of not completing (perceived) lower priority tasks. Structural role redefinition requires proactive effort to directly communicate with role senders (e.g., supervisors, coworkers, family members) to gain agreement on scheduling rearrangements, task priorities, and taking some tasks off the plate. While each of these role-handling strategies is appropriate and effective in different situations, research suggests that proactive communication strategies may offer the greatest opportunities for success and lead to lower rates of burnout. Thus, it will help employers to keep the lines of communication open and regularly discuss the strategic, tactical, and day-to-day role expectations of Reservist employees. Open communication about upcoming military assignments as well as civilian job responsibilities and top priorities will help both the Reservist employee and employer to navigate the sometimes-conflicting role demands as well as acknowledge the importance of both sets of identities. Regular one-on-one meetings and coaching sessions are a best practice for all leaders and are particularly efficacious for keeping the lines of communication open regarding Reservist employees' intersecting identities and roles.

## Provide Flexibility for the Fluid Workload of Reservist Employee Talent

We discussed the strain an activated Reservist employee can have on coworkers who become responsible for filling their colleague's void while Reservist employees are away from their civilian job serving the country. Large enterprises often have the flexibility to hire a replacement or delegate a Reservist's job responsibilities to several remaining employees. Alternatively, small organizations are frequently left with a much larger gap to fill and can benefit from intentional management and preparation for activation of Reservist employees.

Prior to a Reservist's activation, organizations can begin cross-training all team members. The cross-training should consist of ensuring each position and employee in the department or unit can be performed by two or more employees. Cross-training has been widely used in organizations as part of succession planning, but rarely considered as a strategy for addressing Reservist activations. Through prolonged cross-training, employees should begin by teaching at least one colleague about their role and job responsibilities and demonstrate successful performance. On training completion, colleagues should fill the role of their trainer until they become proficient in each area of responsibility. The process should be repeated until every employee has learned at least one other position in the department.

If the decision is made to hire a short-term replacement for the activated Reservist employee, a current and accurate job description is required.

However, outdated and incomplete job descriptions often cause recruitment, training, and employee performance issues that can persist for extended periods. Particularly for smaller organizations, frequent reviews of existing job descriptions for accuracy and completeness can alleviate challenges experienced when Reservist employees are activated. Expanding annual examinations of job knowledge, skills, position requirements, and criteria for successful performance is recommended. These examinations can be completed any number of ways, including observation of employees' day-to-day tasks; employee, supervisor, and direct report interviews; and reviews of similar job titles across related organizations. Although committing to updating a job description can be time consuming, the payoff will be readily seen when a new hire is needed.

One final suggestion for addressing Reservists' activations is to be as proactive as possible in preparing for possible deployments. Although employers are well aware of the possibility, organizations rarely plan ahead of time, instead leaving to chance that their Reservist employee will not be activated. The lack of preparation in and of itself contributes to the challenges faced by smaller organizations. Even before notification of deployment, organizations can develop plans for delegating job responsibilities, communicating process or procedural changes, and adapting to a reduced workforce. The plans should be well thought out, documented, and involve participation from all stakeholders during the development process. Similar to succession planning, being proactive about how the organization would address a Reservist employee's potential deployment can reduce the overall frustration and negative impact felt by leaders and coworkers.

## Provide Structures to Assist With Continuous Transitions

The transition back into the nonmilitary workplace can be especially challenging for a Reservist deployed for an extended period. Just as life continues to move forward at home for a Reservists' family, organizations continue to grow, develop, and change. Reservists, however, are often unaware of all that has transpired since their last day at work. The return back to their nonmilitary job leads to potentially new stressors as organization structures, reporting lines, priorities, and challenges in the organization all have evolved. These changes are generally communicated to employees as they happen, but Reservist employees do not receive the same communications. Thus,

Reservist employees need to be brought up to speed about everything that has happened since deploying.

A consolidated onboarding program can be used to help reintegrate Reservist employees after deployment. Whereas onboarding programs traditionally consist of paperwork, job training, and a tour of the facilities, a consolidated program would address only the identified needs of the returning employee. The onboarding should begin on the first day back to work and be a requirement before returning to perform the actual job. Consolidated onboarding programs for Reservists should be well designed and include feedback from Reservists, supervisors, and incumbents during the development stage. Similar to traditional onboarding programs, paperwork for reinstatement is likely necessary. Beyond paperwork addressing benefits, responsibilities, and expectations, a one-size-fits-all approach would likely not be appropriate; however, some common characteristics to properly onboard a returning Reservist employee include the following:

- Training on new systems, software, or equipment.
- Updated organization structure/chain of command.
- Scheduled introductory meetings with employees who have started since the Reservist left and who the Reservist may directly or indirectly engage.
- Meeting with direct supervisor or senior executive to share updates on organization priorities, goals, and overall strategic plan.
- Formalized reintegration training to reflect existing culture and employee expectations.
- Presentation of the internal, local, and national resources available to assist returning veterans.

Organizations may also consider identifying a "buddy" colleague to assist with the onboarding process. Buddies may be military-affiliated employees or anyone with background knowledge about both the organization and veteran transitions. While returning Reservist employees have more knowledge and insight into the organization than a brand-new employee, procedures, personnel, strategy, and performance expectations may have changed. These changes often go unannounced or overlooked for a returning Reservist employee and may cause frustrations for both Reservist employees and their employer. A buddy can thus be assigned to the Reservist to help bring that employee back up to speed over an extended period of time. Buddies can begin connecting with Reservist employees even before the service member returns to their job or on their return date. Most important, the buddy and Reservist need to define relationship expectations, communication strategies, and frequency for discussing challenges of the reintegration process. Similar to new employees, it takes time to fully acclimate to a new culture and organization, and a buddy can serve as an important go-to resource for Reservist employees.

Each of the outlined strategies already exist to some extent in organizations today. USERRA regulations represent the floor or lowest level for supporting veterans, with many truly veteran-friendly companies implementing additional programming and services. As each organization is unique in their demographics (i.e., industry, size, function, and veteran/Reservist employees) the strategies may or may not be appropriate. Organizations should closely examine available strategies with current and future workplace needs. Once developed and implemented, continuous assessment and reevaluation of needs can ensure military-friendly programming is relevant and advantageous for all.

## Conclusion

Despite roughly 40 percent of the armed services being comprised of Reservists, support for military veterans who are transitioning from active duty is often at the forefront of employers' military-friendly programming. Members of Reserve components—which include both Reserves and National Guard service members—acquire similar skill sets to their active duty counterparts and are likely to seek employment in organizations near their duty station. Organizations interested in hiring and retaining Reservist employees can benefit from this chapter by implementing many of the practices discussed and furthering their own knowledge regarding military support and transition issues. Though sometimes difficult to see or support, the knowledge and skills retained by Reservist service members are desirable and transferable into nonmilitary organizations. By improving efforts to be military friendly to all who serve, organizations can make themselves even more appealing to prospective Reservist employees, in turn providing a competitive advantage to a well-trained and disciplined talent pool.

# References

Allen, T. D. (2001). Family-supportive work environments: The role of organizational perceptions. *Journal of Vocational Behavior, 58*(3), 414–435.

Briscoe, J. P., Hall, D. T., & DeMuth, R. L. F. (2006). Protean and boundaryless careers: An empirical exploration. *Journal of Vocational Behavior, 69*(1), 30–47.

Cohen, L., Duberley, J., & Musson, G. (2009). Work–life balance? An autoethnographic exploration of everyday home–work dynamics. *Journal of Management Inquiry, 18*(3), 229–241.

Congressional Research Service. (2021, January 28). Defense primer: Reserve forces. fas.org/sgp/crs/natsec/IF10540.pdf

Department of Justice. (2015). Uniformed services employment and reemployment rights act of 1994. Retrieved March 15, 2021, from https://www.justice.gov/crt-military/uniformed-services-employment-and-reemployment-rights-act-1994

Eisler, D. (2013, August 5). The dangers of a sensationalist portrayal of veterans. *New York Times.* https://atwar.blogs.nytimes.com/2013/08/05/the-dangers-of-a-sensationalist-portrayal-of-veterans/

ESGR. (n.d.). Who is ESGR. Retrieved March 15, 2021, from esgr.mil/About-ESGR/Who-is-ESGR

Hall, D. T. (1972). A model of coping with role conflict: The role behavior of college educated women. *Administrative Science Quarterly, 17*(4), 471–486.

Lapierre, L. M., Spector, P. E., Allen, T. D., Poelmans, S., Cooper, C. L., O'Driscoll, M. P., & Kinnunen, U. (2008). Family-supportive organization perceptions, multiple dimensions of work–family conflict, and employee satisfaction: A test of model across five samples. *Journal of Vocational Behavior, 73*(1), 92–106.

National Guard. (n.d.). Federal mission. Retrieved March 15, 2021, from https://www.nationalguard.mil/About-the-Guard/Army-National-Guard/About-Us/Federal-Mission/#:~:text=That%20mission%20is%20to%20maintain,fulfilling%20the%20country's%20military%20needs

South, T. (2018, November 2). Active-duty retention success hurts reserve and guard recruiting. *Military Times.* https://www.militarytimes.com/news/your-military/2018/11/02/active-duty-retention-success-hurts-reserve-and-guard-recruiting/

Stone, C., & Stone, D. L. (2015). Factors affecting hiring decisions about veterans. *Human Resource Management Review, 25*, 68–79.

# 13

# Retention of Veteran Employees

*Mark Goulart*

Since 2011, significant progress has been made as a result of both public and private veteran hiring initiatives, collaborative partnerships, and coalitions with the ultimate goal of battling the systemic issue of veteran unemployment. Reverberations from the prioritization and increased focus surrounding the hiring of veterans is demonstrative evidence of the impact both employers and veterans are having on our workforce. Employers today view the hiring of veterans not only as a singular component of their larger hiring goals and strategies but also as a necessity to maintaining a diverse corporate culture that is rich with individuals who bring skills that are unique and not readily available in today's labor force. Governmental and industry veteran hiring and retention initiatives are indicative of a stable demand signal and emphasize that veteran hiring will remain an employer's strategic priority. While organizations have improved in their veteran hiring retention indicators, attrition data and research have shown that organizations still struggle with retaining veterans (Maury, Stone, & Roseman, 2014). This can be attributed to a number of varying factors, but it remains an emergent issue that must be further addressed for any sizable impacts to be realized and addressed.

Initial reports indicated organizations have started to allocate considerable resources and attention to veteran attrition and retention-related issues. The U.S. Chamber of Commerce (Hiring Our Heroes, 2016) identified challenges across the veteran employee life cycle and encouraged employers to focus on

- Assessing veteran "fit" prior to hiring,
- Implementation and/or expansion of veteran onboarding and retention practices, and
- Identifying opportunities to customize transition programs for greater success.

Mark Goulart, *Retention of Veteran Employees* In: *Military Veteran Employment*. Edited by: Nathan D. Ainspan and Kristin N. Saboe, Oxford University Press. © Oxford University Press 2021. DOI: 10.1093/oso/9780190642983.003.0014

To further address veteran retention and attrition issues, the Chamber of Commerce also suggested that additional progress must be made to more widely communicate and advocate for the adoption and integration of retention practices, including added resourcing and attention at each stage of the veteran employee life cycle.

## The Veteran Attrition Dilemma

In recent years, public, private, and nonprofit organizations have placed a major focus on veteran employment. Programs like the White House's Joining Forces Initiative, the Chamber of Commerce's Hiring Our Heroes initiative, the USO's Transition Workshops, and many others helped propel veteran employment issues into the national spotlight. Major companies report that veterans are consistently a top recruiting target, and veteran-specific training opportunities and business resource groups are becoming more common. These efforts have achieved unprecedented and positive results. By 2018, the veteran monthly unemployment rate was consistently below 3 percent, the lowest rate since 2000 (U.S. Department of Labor, 2020) (see Department of Labor's monthly unemployment rates for current metrics, https://www.dol. gov/agencies/vets/latest-numbers). This is even more impressive as virtually every month the veterans' unemployment rate overall has remained below the national average in recent years; the national average (before the Covid19 pandemic) has hovered around 4 percent unemployment. While this success is certainly worth celebrating, it is critical to look at other factors that tell the full story of veteran employment.

Instead of viewing employment as simply the state of having a job, we must think more holistically about the employment life cycle, which includes recruiting, hiring/onboarding, and retention. As unemployment numbers remain low, the primary question shifts form whether or not veterans have a job to whether they have the *right* job. In many cases, we are finding the answer does not paint as great a picture as the unemployment rate alone might suggest. As *The Wall Street Journal* (Fuhrmans, 2017) recently pointed out, "After a collective push to hire more than a million U.S. military veterans in recent years, business is wrestling with a new challenge: holding on to them." There are many reasons why this might be the case. Deloitte research helped think through some of these issues when first exploring ways to enhance veteran transition and retention. In 2013, Deloitte found in an internal research project that veterans were leaving their practice more often than their civilian counterparts, leading to the all-important question—why?

## Detailing the Dilemma

Before diving into the potential causes and solutions related to veteran at-trition, let us first set the stage for what the landscape actually looks like across the United States. In 2016 a report produced by the U.S. Chamber of Commerce's Hiring Our Heroes program cited findings that out of 1,000 veterans surveys, 44 percent left their first postmilitary jobs within a year. If you were told that your company would hire 1,000 people in 2018, and before 2019, nearly half (440) of them would leave, you would likely not be very happy with those results and you should not be. A Center for a New American Security (Schafer, Swick, Kidder, & Carter, 2016) study found that retention is not just a surface issue—it negatively impacts company financial performance. The 2016 report by the U.S. Chamber of Commerce (Hiring Our Heroes, 2016) found that the average cost of hiring an employee is more than $4,000, and that it takes an average of 42 days to fill an empty position. Moreover, less quantifiable costs include the potential impact on the morale of other employees and the lost time and productivity it takes for new team members to effectively learn the business. Furthermore, a study cosponsored by ZipRecruiter and the Call of Duty Endowment found that, of the compa-nies surveyed, the majority reported that veterans performed "better than" or "much better than" nonveterans in the workplace (Barrera & Carter, 2016). Given this, losing veteran employees to attrition may be even more conse-quential than concerning nonveterans.

In summary, retention of veterans is an issue that employers are begin-ning to notice and explore ways to address. As an interesting caveat to these numbers, ZipRecruiter found that while veterans may leave their first ci-vilian job faster than nonveterans, veteran turnover over longer periods of time were lower throughout a veteran's entire career. Therefore, there appears to be a gap between the desire that companies have for the skills veterans pro-vide, attempts to retain newly hired veterans (veterans with longer company tenure tend to stay longer than their nonveteran peers), and veterans finding a job and company that best fits them. This leads to some key questions that we explore throughout the rest of this chapter:

- Why do veterans leave jobs?
- What is the difference between positive and negative veteran attrition?
- What is underemployment?
- What are some best practices for retaining veterans?

## Possible Causes of the Dilemma

As discussed above and throughout this book, there is evidence that in some cases veterans are leaving their first job postmilitary service at rates much higher than nonveteran employees. This should be alarming to companies with dedicated strategies in place to recruit and hire veterans. Increased and sustained levels of attrition among any employee pools, not just veterans, negatively impacts companies. It has an effect on organizational resource expenditures and time allocation to support the hiring, training, and retention processes. Therefore, it is important not only for the sake of understanding the veteran's experience but also for the company's bottom line to are leaving jobs. Underemployment, or employment below an individual's objective skill level, has emerged as a leading indicator of veteran retention issues. While difficult to measure, some studies have identified a link between veteran attrition issues and underemployment. For example, some research has suggested that many veterans report their experience and skills are greater than what is required for their current job, potentially indicating that veterans are not being effectively matched with jobs that use their applicable skills.

According to a study from the Institute for Veterans and Military Families, 9 of 10 respondents identified the opportunity to use their skills and abilities as the most important aspect of civilian employment (Maury et al., 2014). This disconnect between the desire by veterans to fully utilize their skill sets and experience and the perception by the majority of veteran employees that they are "underemployed" may identify a potential cause of veteran retention.

This also leads to a larger point related to the civilian–military divide that has been well documented in the United States as a consequence of an all-volunteer force. Less than 1 percent of the population is actively serving in the military, and less than 10 percent of the entire U.S. population are veterans (e.g., have previously served in the military). The lack of interaction and population representation between those that have served in the military and those that have not is referred to as the civilian–military divide. The divide means hiring managers potentially lack sufficient knowledge of military careers, skill sets, and/or have misperceptions related to a veteran's military service and experiences. This knowledge gap may lead to veterans being placed in positions that are not fully in line with their skills, experience, and/or expectations.

In order to effectively address the veteran retention dilemma, organizations should first recognize and expect that attrition will occur, and that this will remain a constant variable in striving to sustain employee tenure. Hence, in certain circumstances, attrition should not be negatively viewed—for neither the veteran nor the organization. In some instances, attrition has positive effects for a veteran, such as when an employee leaves a company because they move to a job that is a better fit, located in a more desirable location, offers a higher salary, or provides increased responsibility. However, attrition can be negative if the veteran leaves a position because of issues directly related to the environment of the organization, opportunity, or reasons related to a lost sense of purpose or mission. This negative attrition might occur because a veteran is not being provided sufficient experiences or adequate amounts of responsibility to develop professionally, if a cultural misalignment exists between the veterans and the organization, if the organization fails to clearly communicate its purpose, or if there is a lack of veteran/employee support structures. These ideas, as well as how to tailor retention strategies to the specific challenges faced, are examined in greater detail in the next section.

To address the topic of retention, Deloitte conducted an internal study to begin looking at veteran retention within our firm. The study found that when challenges were reported by veterans employed at Deloitte, they typically faced challenges across three main areas when starting a new position: (a) interacting, (b) performing, and (c) connecting. To successfully transition from the military to a civilian occupation, especially in professional services, veterans in the Deloitte study discussed challenges they faced as they adapted to their new organizational culture and learned to interact and communicate effectively with their new colleagues. Additionally, Deloitte's study found veterans sometimes struggled to clearly understand expectations for their performance and how to successfully navigate their career path. Finally, some veterans expressed difficulty finding both meaning and appropriate balance in their new role. This internal research led to some key insights and recommendations that Deloitte is looking to implement. This example of the research conducted by Deloitte highlights the importance of talking directly to employees about their experiences and needs, conducting research using sound research methodology, and being open to the insights gained in order to find solutions enacted by organizations to fill gaps and address challenges experienced by employees.

## Searching for Solutions

Having established that veteran attrition is an issue for many organizations and developed a working understanding of possible causes of attrition, we can begin to turn toward possible solutions to implement across the full employment life cycle of recruiting, hiring/onboarding, and retention. This section further discusses potential attrition issues and lays out best practices some companies have implemented to increase retention across their veteran employees.

## Examination of Attrition Issues

As mentioned in the previous section, attrition is not always a bad thing, and many of the positives outweigh the negatives, particularly as veterans working in professional settings ascend to more senior, desired, or specialized roles in the workforce. These individuals have life and professional experiences that are markedly different from many of their nonveteran counterparts, translating into a competitive advantage for employers due to highly valuable and transferable hard and soft skills desired. Additionally, veterans bring unique diversity to the workplace due to the breadth and depth of experience military service entails. They also enter the civilian workforce later in their careers and with that bring maturity, a professional approach to relationship building, and resilient and tested mindsets. This maturity and diverse experience can be leveraged through internal mentoring programs (which aid retention; mentoring is discussed in detail in Chapter 9) in addition to matching employees with projects that play to their strengths and experience. It should also not be forgotten that in some markets, such as in defense contracting companies or aerospace companies that work in close collaborations with militaries and government institutions or in organizational settings that value "service before self," merely identifying as a veteran brings clout and respect that other employees may not receive without some period of "proving themselves." In short, the professional veteran employee is highly sought after, as employees that possess competitive skills and experiences that attract employers across numerous sectors in the global marketplace.

Even when veterans leave one employer for another opportunity, many are appreciative of their employment experience and their employer relationship. Components of this positive experience include feeling engaged with a company, organization's mission, and existing employee community; encountering new professional challenges; and feeling a sense of purpose and fulfillment in their work. At Deloitte, recruiting managers attempt to proactively identify veteran hires and provide them with resources and the opportunity to participate in a year-long acclimation program designed to reinforce the positive experiences of transitioning into civilian life and to better prepare veterans for civilian employment by arming them with the necessary tools and knowledge for success in a new job role. Initial hiring experiences may make veterans feel susceptible and vulnerable to outside employers looking for professionals with their unique skill sets and military background. Follow-up hiring offers to supplement the original offer often come with add-on elements that are intended to enrich the offer and make it more enticing: more money, more time at home, greater schedule flexibility, more leadership potential, and/or better location, to name a few. The process of recruiting, negotiating, and onboarding a new veteran employee can be positive for both the veteran and the employer. Transitioning veterans, either from military or postservice educational opportunities, have gained valuable experiences that help prepare them for employment. Veterans leverage their individual experiences to find follow-on opportunities that encourage continued growth, propelling them further into their professional development and career pathway.

By capitalizing on a new employment role, veterans have the potential to locate better opportunities that meet their desired employment criteria, further propelling them toward career success, increased responsibility, and improved compensation. This may also fill an undisclosed and personal gap that they perceived was missing in their previous job. It is apparent that the gaining employer acquires a motivated and better adjusted new hire, but even the losing employer garners some positive effects from the attrition. First and foremost, employers have the opportunity to identify and validate employee candidate archetypes and desired employee experiences that helped or hurt the veteran's ability to thrive in their organization. Knowledge of current and newly departed veteran employees will enable employers to adjust their practices to ensure future veteran hiring efforts are more effective, more focused, and potentially less complex. Second, current veteran employees succeeding in their role and that are a good fit provide the company an opportunity to highlight successful veteran recruiting efforts and demonstrate the company's ability to provide growth and desired opportunities for those with a background in the military.

Alternatively, consistent with what many associate with attrition as a topic, it can also be a negative scenario for both employer and veteran employee. In this scenario, the attractiveness in the market for veteran talent is actually the escape hatch that the veteran uses to leave a situation where the culture fit is misaligned for one or both parties, the work lacks fulfillment, or there is not a community with which a veteran feels a part of or is supported within their company. Unfortunately, many companies have experienced firsthand veterans "jumping ship" and quickly moving to a different company. This can happen for a number of reasons, both avoidable (feeling underemployed, undervalued, disconnected from the company culture) and unavoidable (misalignment with company culture, better growth opportunity or salary elsewhere, or improved work–life balance). More often than not, the root cause of this negative attrition scenario is a result of a misalignment of expectations on the part of both the veteran and the company. This often manifests in the veteran expecting but not finding a sense of purpose in their work and a community to join after integrating into the company. Even if the veteran's goals (industry, location, compensation) align with the company, much of the veteran's background includes fundamentals like a well-understood mission, specific daily routines, clearly defined measures of success, and an unmistakable and easily recognizable hierarchy. If the veteran cannot find these in the employer's organization or support functions to help them adjust to a different context and workplace culture, then mismatch may occur.

Since the military is essentially organized into a series of missions, tasks, and purposes, with some integrated across services and others specific to subordinate elements, each member clearly understands where they fit and finds themselves immediately surrounded by a ready-made team mindset that will teach, train, and mentor them. This provides a feeling of mutual support, as well as a transfer of institutional knowledge and a mentality of shared successes. The absence of many of these common elements in a new employer can prompt veteran employees to look elsewhere or feel unfulfilled. They may find themselves unsure of their purpose within the company, possibly working in isolation, in a role that they are either over- or underqualified for or in a team with a substantially different background or outlook than them. When a veteran employee has spent the majority of a military career surrounded by camaraderie and shared experiences, being exposed to a flat or matrixed organization where their paths for guidance and direction are ambiguous or unclear can leave them feeling puzzled and overwhelmed.

While employers may often believe they have met veteran employee expectations, they unfortunately may not even recognize some of the missing elements and fail to proactively monitor the veteran employees' performances and development to ensure that they are receiving the experience they are seeking. In many cases, veterans have left military positions where they were making executive-level decisions with the flexibility and autonomy similar to a senior executive in industry. So, it is important for employers to recognize that many junior and middle management roles that a veteran finds themselves in after first transitioning do not allow for a parallel level of responsibility. The discrepancy between their past level of responsibility in the military and their present responsibility as a civilian employee can leave the veteran feeling stifled and make them more apt to look for an opportunity elsewhere to meet these objectives and enable better perceived fit between expectations and reality. Further aggravating the attrition statistics are veterans in general following the trends of their generational cohorts (i.e., "millennial veterans") and changing jobs more frequently than other generational counterparts. Without investigation and proactive analysis of these trends, a company may fail to learn from this negative attrition scenario, making it more likely many veterans will leave a company for common but preventable reasons.

## Discussion of Retention Activities and Best Practices

In the sections above, we suggest that attrition takes place for both positive and negative reasons. This section aims to provide an overview of the research and initiatives related to veteran retention that exist in the marketplace as well as examples of what Deloitte, as a continued example throughout this chapter, has seen and heard from clients. Fortunately, a series of best practices are beginning to emerge to model how to best address veteran retention within an organization.

## What Do Leading Organizations Do?

This section explores initiatives such as mentorship programs and affinity groups that are examples of established good practices in improving veteran retention. To collect some of these practices, beginning in late 2016, Deloitte held a series of veteran employer summits. The intent of these summits was to bring together leaders from companies nationwide to share best practices, collaborate, and develop new ideas to address key challenges veterans are facing. The end state was a supportive community focused on veteran success as they transition from the military into professional civilian careers.

A highlight from one of these summits in particular included a discussion of how corporations are utilizing data to understand the veteran life cycle and experience. One participant talked about how their organization took a data-driven approach to understanding the business partners that were the most "veteran ready" and where veterans were most successful in the business. This organization spoke to their ability to use data to develop "quadrants" for where veterans are hired and perform well in the business so they can develop even stronger business relationships to place future hires. They leveraged internships as an effective way to open the door for new hires to find a place in a particular business. Finally, the organization understood the importance of incentivizing veteran hiring from the top and working with business partners to create simple, flexible internship arrangements that are designed to put talent where it is needed.

Two of the more common approaches for retaining veterans arising from these summits included creating mentorship programs and affinity groups. (For more on mentoring programs and affinity groups, see Chapter 9 of this book.) During the summit, examples of mentoring programs and affinity groups were presented for PNC Bank and JPMorgan Chase, where they have long-standing formal and informal mechanisms in place to provide a sense of community and purpose for veterans. It should be noted that these efforts are not exclusive to these companies and are considered best practices within organizations looking to support specific populations within their organization. Table 13.1 outlines the programs from these companies.

Additionally, the creation and growth of internal veteran communities empowered to develop programs and initiatives can be a meaningful way for veterans to have a sense of purpose, impact, ownership, and an outlet to give back. Participating in an effort that benefits the veteran community can help veterans feel engaged and valued at the firm, while also contributing to the firm's

Table 13.1 Veteran Mentoring Programs From JPMorgan Chase (JPMC) and PNC Bank

| Organization | Program/Initiative | Description |
|---|---|---|
| JPMC | *Pathfinder Sponsorship Program* | This sponsorship program is based on peer-to- peer relationships between new and experienced veterans. Pairings are made between employees at the same role level and provide opportunities for veterans to talk through key transition themes. |
| JPMC | *MOEDP and MVIP Programs* | These programs seek to hire veterans in cohorts. They create various in-person networking events to facilitate the development of an internal veteran community. There is also a program manager who is selected to advocate for and manage each cohort. |
| PNC | *Military Employee Business Resource Group (MEBRG)* | The MEBRG builds annual operating plans to impact three factors: associates, shareholders, and communities served. The operating plans include programs that offer a sense of mission and purpose, which speaks to the veteran's desire to serve. This also eases one element of transition shock. |
| PNC | *Mentoring* | Mentoring at PNC Bank takes place through a formal matched pairing of self-selected internal mentors and mentees. Mentor and mentee objectives and outcomes are discussed and monitored to ensure progress goals. There is also a separate external partnership with American Corporate Partners (ACP) that provides another avenue for formal mentorship. Informal mentorship is also encouraged via self-initiated one-on-one connections. |

ability to recruit, integrate, and retain veteran talent. The Boeing Company provides a good example of the impact of engaging veterans to improve retention. In 2016, according to a report by CNBC profiling the company, Boeing's veteran hire retention rate was reported to be 92 percent (Hess, 2017). What enabled such high retention rates within polled populations? This was the result of a sense of purpose and community created through their employee resource group for veterans, then termed their Boeing Military and Veterans Engagement Team. As mentioned above in the examples of comments owing to the importance of finding community and belonging, employee resource groups can provide both formal and informal means to help onboard new veterans, a group of friendly colleagues to support a new employee, and opportunities to engage in outreach within and external to a company.

## What Empirically Drives Best Outcomes?

In addition to the examples of established good practices provided above, research exists that casts light on what works when it comes to veteran retention. As highlighted by the Center for New American Security, "Incentivizing employers to value and measure veteran fit and performance rather than focusing on hiring metrics alone could improve retention, requiring a renewed look at how veteran hiring initiatives evaluate success and promoting programs such as mentorship and affinity groups" (Schafer et al., 2016, p. 2). A shift in the types of metrics that are used to measure successful veteran employment practices is a critical step that organizations can take to address attrition issues.

A report by VetAdvisor and Syracuse University's Institute for Veterans and Military Families found that increased benefits, increased opportunity for advancement, and increased opportunities for professional development were the most frequently cited responses for what would have kept veterans at their first civilian job longer (Maury et al., 2014). The report went on to recommend that organizations seeking to increase veteran retention should

- Provide education on translation of military skills to corporate recruiters and human resource professionals,
- Develop veteran-centric employee benefit programs to assist veteran employees in developing a postmilitary career path, and
- Develop streamlined and expedited job search programs for veterans to provide a better match between employers and job seekers.

In the 2014 report, *Veteran Employment: Lessons From the 100,000 Jobs Mission* (Hall, Harrell, Bicksler, Stewart, & Fischer, 2014), the RAND Corporation found two retention initiatives that were identified by many of the participating firms as effective in improving veteran retention results: veteran business resource groups (also known as employee resource groups or affinity groups) and veteran-specific mentoring programs. The value of mentoring and affinity groups is discussed in Chapter 9.

One recent study, "How Your Company Can Better Retain Employees Who Are Veterans" (Watson et al., 2017), provided the following recommendations based on the authors' research of veteran hiring and retention trends:

- Educate managers, recruiters, and leaders about military culture and language,
- Design a specific onboarding and integration program for veterans,
- Help veterans establish and sustain connections within the organization, and
- Find ways to connect everyday responsibilities to overall organizational purpose.

## Summary and Next Steps

Since the advent of the Joining Forces Initiative in 2011, began under the Obama administration through the advocacy of both First Lady Michelle Obama and Second Lady Jill Biden, there has been significant progress, visibility, and an unwavering commitment to hiring veterans across the United States. Deloitte and many other corporations, both large and small, have been successful in retaining veterans by scrupulously fostering cultures of acceptance and commitment to veterans' career success. Businesses that are successful in retaining veterans are anecdotally also those that are successful at driving strong brand recognition externally in the marketplace and are able to further solidify benefits to hiring and retaining bold and talented veteran leaders. Veteran hiring should remain an integral component of any business' hiring and retention strategy and must capitalize on the robust and varied experiences that veterans bring to the workforce.

While Deloitte remains steadfast in its commitment to veteran hiring, there have been critical retention observations that have provided the basis for the development of multidimensional modalities and the execution of a holistic approach to more effectively equip, educate, and assimilate veterans in a more structured and expedient manor. As companies have matured in their understanding of best practices for employing veterans, many have taken the same approach as Deloitte by pursuing enterprise-wide holistic and multifaceted approaches. In Table 13.2 are a few strategies and tools that

**Table 13.2** Deloitte's Recommendations for Retaining Veteran Employees

| Retention Observation | "How Deloitte Does It" |
| --- | --- |
| *Veteran new hires are largely unaware of veteran-specific affinity groups and available resources to assist onboarding and transitions.* | Deloitte developed a retention strategy that outlines critical milestone events that are essential for Deloitte veteran development and integration within the first 12 months of tenure with the firm. The "Veteran's Journey" is focused on formalized programs and events across Deloitte; the basis of the journey is the standardization of those experiences and complimentary programs in order to enhance the retention of veteran practitioners. This strategy centralizes firm resources, human resources, and talent professionals and supporting veteran employees in a cohesive manner at the national level. |
| *No centralized mechanism for identifying veterans for the purpose of delivering support and retention related resources.* | Deloitte deployed a multifunctional management team called the Veteran Program Management Office (VPMO) comprising existing employee veterans, talent, human resources, and strategic leadership, which was charged with performing and managing the back-end administrative functions for the seamless coordination and execution of Deloitte veteran support programs, providing educational, mentoring, and transition support. Additionally, outreach activities and communications play an integral role in alerting veterans of available support resources and programs. |
| *Veterans transitioning directly from the military have increased difficulties assimilating to corporate culture and structure, and some also struggle to find meaning in their new work.* | Deloitte understands that veterans have varying backgrounds, experiences, and aptitudes for successful integration to a new organization after a period of military service, requiring a unique approach to delivering meaningful support resources. To better address the unique needs of veterans who are starting their careers with Deloitte, the VPMO evaluates each veteran's background using a holistic classification methodology. Veterans are placed within one of four distinct program tracks that have been tailored to address perceived levels of preparedness. Support for each track is dependent on historical levels of success specific to similar veteran experiences and identified challenges inherent to each track. |
| *Veteran-specific educational resources are disparate and not available to all incoming new hires.* | Deloitte developed comprehensive procedures to capture hired veterans onboarding with the Firm. Deloitte's veteran identification mechanism identifies all incoming veterans, maintaining crucial sensitivities to new veteran employees. The identification process allows more accurate provision of critical support resources and programs to newly hired veterans on an "opt-in"/"opt-out" basis. |

Deloitte has developed that can be adopted by any organization to address core retention issues identified as core challenges for veteran employees.

## Recommendations

The 2011 Joining Forces Initiative driving added resources for and focus on veteran employment along with its underlying call to action resulted in significant support for veterans from the private sector. Today, the issue is not in hiring a veteran; rather, it is how to retain a veteran past their first year with a company. The current focus for veteran employment stakeholders, particularly industry leaders, is to understand why approximately 43 percent of veterans leave their first postmilitary job within 12 months (Maury et al., 2014).

As referenced as a common case study throughout this chapter, the approaches Deloitte has taken to improve employment experiences for veterans are informed by data resulting from internal research, such as the analyses presented when discussing the retention dilemma. Through the collaborative veteran employment summits with leading veteran employers, additional insight has been gathered into the common experiences of employers, their lessons learned, and best practices. The remainder of this chapter presents the recommendations and common successful practices, identified through these employer summits, for employers, the public sector, and nonprofit organizations to consider when exploring how to optimize veteran retention.

Understand the difference between positive and negative attrition.
*Is all attrition bad?*

- Positive attrition is defined as an employee leaving a company for reasons not directly related to that employer (i.e., a better fit, new location, more money, or more responsibility).
- Negative attrition is defined as leaving a company for reasons directly related to the environment of the organization (i.e., the employee has not been given the opportunity to grow, there is cultural misalignment, the veteran does not perceive a clear purpose, and/or there is lack of a supportive environment).

Focus on the critical touch points, interactions, and educational experiences. *What integration and communication opportunities exist or should be created?*

- Identify critical touch points, interactions, and educational experiences that will support transition to civilian employment and prepare veterans with the necessary skills and guidance to be successful and thrive.
- Prioritize integration and communication between business leaders, internal business divisions, talent, and human resource professionals in order to establish a fully integrated network that can support the hiring, retention, and sustainment of the organization's veteran community.
- Understand the effect that internal networks, mentors, and education have on the success of veteran employees and set out to bolster these focus areas.
- Recognize that increased benefits, increased opportunity for advancement, and increased opportunities for professional development were the most frequently cited responses for what would have kept veterans at their first civilian job longer.

Understand the data.
*What empirically drives better retention outcomes?*

- Understand what company data are available related to veteran and employee retention.
- Work with veteran employment partners to understand how data might be aggregated for trend analysis and shared.
- Contribute to the ongoing discussion in the veteran employment community related to identifying veteran employment metrics and key outcomes.

Share lessons learned and leading practices.
*How can the veteran employment community identify opportunities to share leading practices and lessons learned?*

- Expand and/or create opportunities to share leading veteran employer lessons learned and leading practices with the veteran employment community.
- Identify opportunities to start the job fit discussion with transitioning service members during their job search (i.e., before their first job).
- Partner with federal, state, and local agencies and nonprofit organizations to share industry leading practices and lessons learned and to identify opportunities for continued collaboration.

Viewing employment as simply the state of having a job is a narrow and potentially hazardous point of view; we must think more holistically about the employment life cycle, which includes recruiting, hiring/onboarding, and retention and employment experiences. We are continuing to see low veterans' unemployment statistics, which allows our focus to shift from merely ensuring veterans have a job to that they have the right job. There is no cookie-cutter solution for mitigating these challenging issues; however, a strategy that retools retention and pulls leading practices of industry forward is a sound approach for success. Committing to engagement through the employment life cycle is crucial for developing a meaningful retention strategy, while engraining a culture of value that is measured by veteran fit along with performance is vital to a lasting veteran retention strategy.

# References

Barrera, C., & Carter, P. (2016). *Challenges on the homefront: Underemployment hits veterans hard.* Call of Endowment and ZipRecruiter. https://static.ziprecruiter.com/pdf/ZipCODE_Vet_Report_FINAL.pdf

Fuhrmans, V. (2017, March 28). Hiring veterans is easy: Keeping them is hard. *Wall Street Journal.* https://www.wsj.com/articles/the-battle-to-keep-veterans-from-quitting-corporate-jobs-1490702401

Hall, K., Harrell, M. C., Bicksler, B., Stewart, R., & Fischer, M. P. (2014). *Veteran employment: Lessons from the 100,000 Jobs Mission.* Santa Monica, CA: RAND. https://www.rand.org/pubs/research_reports/RR836.html

Hess, A. (2017, November 10). *The 10 best companies for veterans.* CNBC, make it. https://www.cnbc.com/2017/11/10/the-10-best-companies-for-veterans.html

Hiring Our Heroes. (2016, November). *Veterans in the workplace: Understanding the challenges and creating long-term opportunities for veteran employees.* Washington, D C: Author. https://www.uschamberfoundation.org/sites/default/files/Veterans%20in%20the%20Workplace_0.pdf

Maury, R., Stone, B., & Roseman, M. A. (2014). *Veteran Job Retention Survey: Summary.* Syracuse, NY: Institute for Veterans and Military Families, Syracuse University. https://ivmf.syracuse.edu/wp-content/uploads/2016/10/VetAdvisor-ReportFINAL-Single-pages.pdf

Schafer, A., Swick, A., Kidder, K., & Carter, P. (2016, November). *Onward and upward: Understanding veteran retention and performance in the workforce.* Washington, DC: Center for New American Security. https://s3.amazonaws.com/files.cnas.org/documents/CNAS-Report-Onward&Upward-Finalc.pdf?mtime=20161102114417

U.S. Department of Labor. (2020, March). *Employment situation of veterans summary.* Washington, DC: U.S. Department of Labor.

Watson, K. W., Perry, M., Ripley, B., & Chittum, R. (2017, July 11). How your company can better retain employees who are veterans. *Harvard Business Review.* https://hbr.org/2017/07/how-your-company-can-better-retain-employees-who-are-veterans

# Military Pay Grade and Ranks by Service Branch

These charts list the military ranks for the five services with a general civilian description of the ranks by groups. Use the charts to help understand résumés and translate comments from interviews.

## Warrant Officer Insignia: Enlisted Member Ranks by Military Service Branch

### Entry-Level Ranks

Pay grades E-1 through E-3 typically are service members in a training status (e.g., basic training or a specialized training course that follows basic training) or are in their initial assignment.

| Rank | Army | Marine Corps | Navy | Air Force | Coast Guard |
|------|------|--------------|------|-----------|-------------|
| E-1 | Private | Private | Seaman recruit (SR) | Airman basic | Seaman recruit (SR) |
| E-2 | Private (PV2) | Private first class (PFC) | Seaman apprentice (SA) | Airman (Amn) | Seaman apprentice (SA) |
| E-3 | Private first class (PFC) | Lance corporal (LCpl) | Seaman (SN) | Airman first Class (A1C) | Seaman (SN) |
| E-4 | Specialist (SPC) Corporal (CPL) | Corporal (Cpl) | Petty officer third class (PO3) | Senior airman (SrA) | Petty officer third class (PO3) |

## Midlevel Enlisted Ranks

Midlevel enlisted ranks experience significant increases in leadership and management responsibilities. These ranks are identified formally with the title of these ranks as non-commissioned officer (NCO) and petty officer. NCO ranks begin at E-5 levels for the Army (sergeant) and Air Force (staff sergeant). An E-4 is considered an NCO in the Marine Corps (corporal). The Navy NCO equivalent is a petty officer and is achieved at the level of an E-4.

| E-5 | Sergeant (SGT) | Sergeant (Sgt) | Petty officer second class (PO2) | Staff sergeant (SSgt) | Petty officer second class (PO2) |
|---|---|---|---|---|---|
| E-6 | Staff sergeant (SSG) | Staff sergeant (SSgt) | Petty officer first class (PO1) | Technical sergeant (TSgt) | Petty officer first class (PO1) |
| E-7 | Sergeant first class (SFC) | Gunnery sergeant (GySgt) | Chief petty officer (CPO) | Master sergeant (MSgt) First sergeant | Chief petty officer (CPO) |

## Senior Enlisted Ranks

At the levels of E-8 and E-9, services have different names within pay grades depending on the position someone holds. The different titles signify different roles and responsibilities as they relate to command structures and formal authority.

Service members at the E-8 and E-9 levels have between 15 and 30 years of military job experience. The primary roles and responsibilities at this senior enlisted level include serving as the commanding officers' senior advisers for all enlisted matters.

The most senior enlisted member in each service holds a unique title, as represented by the final row of E-9 ranks.

| E-8 | Master sergeant (MSG) | Master sergeant (MSgt) | Senior chief petty officer (SCPO) | Senior master sergeant (SMSgt) | Senior chief petty officer (SCPO) |
|---|---|---|---|---|---|
| | First sergeant (1SG) | First sergeant | | First sergeant | |
| E-9 | Sergeant major (SGM) | Master gunnery sergeant (MGySgt) | Master chief petty officer (MCPO) | Chief master sergeant (CMSgt) | Master chief petty officer (MCPO) |
| | Command sergeant major (CSM) | Sergeant major (SgtMaj) | Fleet/command master chief petty officer | First sergeant Command chief master sergeant | Fleet/command master chief petty officer |
| E-9 (Senior enlisted leader) | Sergeant major of the Army (SMA) | Sergeant major of the Marine Corps (SgtMajMC) | Master chief petty officer of the Navy (MCPON) | Chief master sergeant of the Air Force (CMSAF) | Master chief petty officer of the Coast Guard (MCPOCG) |

Adapted from https://www.defense.gov/Resources/Insignia

## Warrant Officer Insignia: Warrant Officer Ranks by Military Service Branch

Warrant officers are specialized experts who hold a commission starting at the level of WO-2 but remain specialists. Commissioned officers in the military are given their commissioned authority and are considered direct representatives of the president and the U.S. Constitution. Warrant officers' specialization differentiates them from other military commissioned officers, who are considered generalists.

| Pay Grade | Army | Marine Corps | Navy | Air Force | Coast Guard |
|---|---|---|---|---|---|
| | *Rank (Abbreviation)* | | | | |
| W-1 | Warrant officer 1 (WO1) | Warrant officer 1 (WO1) | USN Warrant Officer 1 (WO1) | N/A | N/A |
| W-2 | Chief warrant officer 2 (CW2) | Chief warrant officer 2 (CWO2) | USN Chief Warrant Officer 2 (CWO2) | N/A | Chief warrant officer 2 (CWO2) |
| W-3 | Chief warrant officer 3 (CW3) | Chief warrant officer 3 (CWO3) | USN chief warrant officer 3 (CWO3) | N/A | Chief warrant officer 3 (CWO3) |
| W-4 | Chief warrant officer 4 (CW4) | Chief warrant officer 4 (CWO4) | USN chief warrant officer 4 (CWO4) | N/A | Chief warrant officer 4 (CWO4) |
| W-5 | Chief warrant officer 5 (CW5) | Chief warrant officer 5 (CWO5) | USN chief warrant officer 5 (CWO5) | N/A | N/A |

Adapted from https://www.defense.gov/Resources/Insignia

## Officer Ranks by Military Service Branch

Commissioned ranks are the highest rank a service member can hold in the military. Officers are commissioned by the president and are confirmed at each rank by the Senate. An officers' primary responsibilities are as the leaders of the military.

| Pay Grade | Army | Marine Corps | Navy | Air Force | Coast Guard |
|---|---|---|---|---|---|
| | *Rank (Abbreviation)* | | | | |

O-1 to O-3 pay grades are considered company-grade officers (Army, Air Force, and Marine Corps) or junior-grade officers (Navy and Coast Guard). These ranks are considered first-line to midlevel managers responsible for leading between 1 and 200 service members, with each rank responsible for an incrementally larger scope and head count.

| Pay Grade | Army | Marine Corps | Navy | Air Force | Coast Guard |
|---|---|---|---|---|---|
| | *Rank (Abbreviation)* | | | | |
| O-1 | Second lieutenant (2LT) | Second lieutenant (2ndLt) | Ensign (ENS) | Second lieutenant (2d Lt) | Ensign (ENS) |
| O-2 | First lieutenant (1LT) | First lieutenant (1stLt) | Lieutenant junior grade (LTJG) | First lieutenant (1st Lt) | Lieutenant junior grade (LTJG) |
| O-3 | Captain (CPT) | Captain (Capt) | Lieutenant (LT) | Captain (Capt) | Lieutenant (LT) |

O-4 to O-6 pay grades are called field-grade officers (Army, Air Force, and Marine Corps) or midgrade officers (Navy and Coast Guard). These ranks are considered midlevel to executive-level managers responsible for up to 5,000 people depending on the role.

| Pay Grade | Army | Marine Corps | Navy | Air Force | Coast Guard |
|---|---|---|---|---|---|
| O-4 | Major (MAJ) | Major (Maj) | Lieutenant commander (LCDR) | Major (Maj) | Lieutenant commander (LCDR) |
| O-5 | Lieutenant colonel (LTC) | Lieutenant colonel (LtCol) | Commander (CDR) | Lieutenant colonel (LtCol) | Commander (CDR) |
| O-6 | Colonel (COL) | Colonel (Col) | Captain (CAPT) | Colonel (Col) | Captain (CAPT) |

O-7 and above pay grades are general officers (Army, Air Force, and Marine Corps) or flag officers (Navy and Coast Guard). These ranks are the senior executives of the military.

| Pay Grade | Army | Marine Corps | Navy | Air Force | Coast Guard |
|---|---|---|---|---|---|
| O-7 one star | Brigadier general (BG) | Brigadier general (BGen) | Rear admiral lower half (RDML) | Brigadier general (Brig Gen) | Rear admiral lower half (RDML) |
| O-8 two star | Major general (MG) | Major general (MajGen) | Rear admiral upper half (RADM) | Major general (Maj Gen) | Rear admiral upper half (RADM) |
| O-9 three star | Lieutenant general (LTG) | Lieutenant general (LtGen) | Vice admiral (VADM) | Lieutenant general (Lt Gen) | Vice admiral (VADM) |
| O-10 four star | General (GEN) | General (Gen) | Admiral (ADM) | General (Gen) | Admiral (ADM) |
| O-10 five star (reserved for wartime only) | General of the Army | N/A | Fleet admiral | General of the Air Force | Fleet admiral |

Adapted from https://www.defense.gov/Resources/Insignia

# Index